Seaforth

WORLDNAVALREVIEW

2011

Seaforth WORLD NAVAL REVIEW

2011

Editor
CONRAD WATERS

Seaforth
PUBLISHING

Frontispiece: The US Navy's new 'Klingon Imperial Cruiser', the littoral combat ship *Independence* (LCS-2), pictured on sea trials in July 2009. Her hull – based on that used for the commercial high-speed trimaran *Benchijigua Express* – provides both speed and stability. *(US Navy)*

The editor welcomes correspondence and suggestions from readers. Please contact him via Seaforth at **info@seaforthpublishing.com**. All correspondence should be marked **FAO: Conrad Waters**.

First published in Great Britain in 2010 by
Seaforth Publishing
An imprint of Pen & Sword Books Ltd.
47 Church Street, Barnsley
S Yorkshire S70 2AS

www.seaforthpublishing.com
Email info@seaforthpublishing.com

British Library Cataloguing in Publication Data
A CIP data record for this book is available from the British Library

ISBN 978-1-84832-075-8

Typeset and designed by Stephen Dent
Printed and bound in China through Printworks International Ltd.

CONTENTS

Note on Tables: Tables are provided to give a broad indication of fleet sizes and other key information but should be regarded only as a general guide. For example, many published sources differ significantly on the principal particulars of ships, whilst even governmental information can be subject to contradiction. In general terms, the data contained in these tables is based on official information updated as of June 2010, supplemented by reference to a wide range of secondary and corporate sources, such as shipbuilder websites.

1 OVERVIEW

INTRODUCTION

'If a man does not know to what port he is sailing, no wind is favourable,' wrote the Roman philosopher Seneca the Younger, one-time tutor to the Emperor Nero, in the first century AD. This opening quotation to the 2011 edition of the *Seaforth World Naval Review* is particularly relevant to the leading Western navies as they grapple with increasing budgetary pressures in the aftermath of the global 'credit crunch'. Both the United States Navy (USN) and British Royal Navy, in particular, face an era of potentially severe austerity as their respective governments face up to the imperative of tackling crippling budget deficits. The way that their leaders and, more importantly, their political masters respond to this challenge could have a significant impact on the *de facto* Anglo-Saxon command of the seas that has been a key force in shaping global history over the past 200-odd years.

Of the two fleets, the USN seems – at first glance – to be more advanced in reshaping its priorities to revised financial realities. The 2010 Quadrennial Defense Review released on 1 February 2010 suggested a largely unchanged naval force structure up until 2015 against an overall re-emphasising of efforts towards winning current wars and being better able to deal with asymmetric threats.[1] Decisions have been taken to cap or cancel construction of high-technology but hugely expensive surface combatants such as the DDG-1000 destroyer and follow-on CG(X) cruiser in favour of extended production of proven and cheaper designs, thereby making the future shipbuilding programme more affordable. Whilst this approach suggests progress has been made towards the goal of maintaining fleet numbers at a time when funding is tight, it may well prove inadequate in the medium term. As shown by Table 1.0.1, US military expenditure still remains far in excess of all other nations under most measurements. This situation seems unsustainable given the stretched state of US finances. Indeed, in a speech at the Navy League Sea-Air-Space Exposition at New Harbour, Maryland, on 3 May 2010, US Defense Secretary Robert Gates questioned the current emphasis on carrier strike groups and high-end amphibious capabilities in an era of increasingly finite resources. It therefore seems that more fundamental changes in USN posture might emerge over the next few years. These are likely to include increased reliance on inter-service co-operation through ideas such as the USAF/USN 'Air-Sea' Battle concept, as well as a further rebalancing of forces towards more cost-effective vessels better able to operate in the littoral.[2]

Meanwhile, the Royal Navy awaits the results of the first UK strategic defence review for thirteen years in an environment where the new governing Conservative-Liberal Democrat coalition also needs to achieve significant reductions in state expenditure. In spite of a significant diversion of effort to support primarily land-based operations firstly in Iraq and then in Afghanistan, the Royal Navy has been making good progress transforming itself away from a focus on Cold War anti-submarine warfare in the North Atlantic to a structure more capable of global power projection. However, this process has been slow and protracted. As such, key elements of the planned new fleet such as the two new *Queen Elizabeth* aircraft carriers have been left vulnerable to curtailment or cancellation. Much will depend on whether the new administration validates the previous emphasis on power projection – also referred to as 'strategic raiding' – or favours a more land-based 'boots on the ground' approach typified by the war in Afghanistan. The results of the defence review are likely to be announced shortly after this volume appears on bookshop shelves and will undoubtedly be covered in some depth in our planned 2012 edition.

Table 1.0.1: COUNTRIES WITH HIGH NATIONAL DEFENCE EXPENDITURES – 2009

RANK	COUNTRY	TOTAL: US$	PER CAPITA: US$	SHARE OF GDP: %
1	United States	661.0bn	2,100	4.3%
2	China	100.0bn	75	2.0%
3	France	63.9bn	1,026	2.3%
4	United Kingdom	58.3bn	946	2.5%
5	Russian Federation	53.3bn	378	3.5%
6	Japan	51.0bn	401	0.9%
7	Germany	45.6bn	555	1.3%
8	Saudi Arabia	41.2bn	1,603	8.2%
9	India	36.3bn	30	2.6%
10	Italy	35.8bn	598	1.7%
	World	1,531.0bn	224	2.7%

Information from the Stockholm International Peace Research Institute (SIPRI) – http://milexdata.sipri.org
The SIPRI Military Expenditure Database contains data on 174 countries over the period 1988–2009.
Notes:
1 Spending figures are at current prices and market exchange rates.
2 Figures for China and the Russian Federation are estimates.
3 Data on military expenditure as a share of GDP (Gross Domestic Product) relates to 2008.

Elsewhere, the aftermath of the global financial crisis continues to be felt quite widely, especially in Europe. The so-called 'Club Mediterranean' countries to the south of the continent have been particularly adversely impacted by the economic downturn, with – for example – both Greece and Spain likely to experience a significant curtailment of previous naval acquisition plans as increased emphasis is placed on reducing government debt. However, more puritanical northern Europe has not entirely escaped the crisis's financial aftershocks. A notable casualty here has been the collapse of the ambitions of Germany's ThyssenKrupp Marine Systems (TKMS) to lead the consolidation of the European shipbuilding sector following the emergence of significant losses at its ThyssenKrupp group parent. A new strategic partnership in the area of surface warships has been formed with the Abu Dhabi MAR group, which is set to take majority stakes in the group's Blohm & Voss and Hellenic Shipyards subsidiaries. The historic Nordseewerke facility in Emden has been sold off and its future will largely be focused on wind farm production. Although the submarine-dominated activities of the other core TKMS subsidiaries, HDW and Kockums, remain in group hands for the time being, they are also reported to be for sale if a suitable buyer can be found.[3] Taken together with the previous acquisition of the largely complex merchant ship construction facilities of Aker Yards (including the huge former Alston shipyard of Chantiers de l'Atlantique in Saint Nazaire) by Korea's STX Corporation, it would seem that the steady eastwards transfer of Western shipbuilding skills

Right: The US Navy's Flight IIA *Arleigh Burke* class destroyer *Jason Dunham* (DDG-109) pictured during pre-commissioning trials on 20 May 2010. The United States has decided to recommence construction of proven units such as the *Arleigh Burke*s to bring the future shipbuilding programme back into balance with available funding. *(General Dynamics via US Navy)*

An impression of the new British aircraft carriers *Queen Elizabeth* and *Prince of Wales* in company. Whether this vision will be realised in practice is contingent on the outcome of the UK's current strategic defence review. *(Aircraft Carrier Alliance)*

FLEET REVIEWS

Estimates of major fleet strengths as of mid-2010 are set out in Table 1.0.2, which also contains the equivalent figures contained in *Seaforth World Naval Review 2010* by way of comparison. Clearly, insufficient time has elapsed to reveal any significant changes but the following observations are, perhaps, pertinent:

- The leading Anglo-Saxon fleets – the USN and Royal Navy – display surprising stability, with the USN actually achieving some increase in major surface vessels as series production of Flight IIA *Arleigh Burke* (DDG-51) class destroyers swells its ranks. However, both navies are likely to experience more pressure on escort numbers going forward as the remaining elderly FFG-7, Type 42 and Type 22 classes are retired.
- France's *Marine Nationale* is experiencing some reduction in numbers of minor war vessels. In addition to the fall in mine-countermeasures vessels shown in the table, the relatively new P-400 patrol vessels used to police France's overseas territories are also being steadily withdrawn.
- India has rejoined the small club of countries capable of operating nuclear-powered submarines with the planned lease of the Russian Project 971 'Akula II' submarine *Nerpa*. She will be joined within the next twelve months by the indigenously-constructed strategic missile submarine *Arihant* that has emerged from the Advanced Technology Vessel (ATV) programme.
- South Korea is continuing to evolve its fleet

referenced in last year's introduction to the *Seaforth World Naval Review* continues apace.

It is certainly the case that the developing nations of Asia have experienced the least fall-out from the economic downturn, with growth in countries such as China and India little reduced from longer-term averages. As such, it is their military – and, therefore, naval – budgets that continue to see most growth, reinforced by ongoing regional tensions evidenced by the apparent sinking of the South Korean light corvette *Cheonan* by a North Korean submarine. There can therefore be little surprise that it is developments in Asia and the Pacific that feature most prominently in the fleet reviews that form the first of the three main sections into which this book is sub-divided.

Table 1.0.2: MAJOR FLEET STRENGTHS 2009-2010

COUNTRY	USA		UK		FRANCE		ITALY		SPAIN		RUSSIA[2]		INDIA		CHINA[2]		JAPAN		S KOREA	
Year[1]	2009	2010	2009	2010	2009	2010	2009	2010	2009	2010	2009	2010	2009	2010	2009	2010	2009	2010	2009	2010
Aircraft Carrier (CVN/CV)	11	11	–	–	1	1	–	–	–	–	1	1	–	–	–	–	–	–	–	–
Support Carrier (CVS/CVH)	–	–	3	3	1	–	2	2	1	1	–	–	1	1	–	–	1	1	–	–
Strategic Missile Sub (SSBN)	14	14	4	4	3	4	–	–	–	–	16	15	–	–	3	3	–	–	–	–
Attack Submarine (SSGN/SSN)	57	57	8	8	6	6	–	–	–	–	20	20	–	1	5	5	–	–	–	–
Patrol Submarine (SSK)	–	–	–	–	–	–	6	6	4	4	20	20	16	16	55	55	16	16	11	12
Battleships/Battlecruisers (BB/BC)	–	–	–	–	–	–	–	–	–	–	2	2	–	–	–	–	–	–	–	–
Fleet Escort (CGN/CG/DDG/FFG)	107	109	24	24	18	18	16	16	10	10	35	30	20	21	45	45	43	41	19	19
Patrol Escort (DD/FFG/FSG/FS)	1	2	–	–	15	15	8	8	–	–	55	55	8	8	30	30	8	6	28	25
Missile Attack Craft (PGG/PTG)	–	–	–	–	–	–	–	–	–	–	50	50	12	12	65	75	6	6	1	1
Mine Countermeasures (MCMV)	14	14	16	15	16	14	12	12	6	6	45	45	10	8	20	20	29	30	9	9
Major Amp (LHD/LPD/LPH/LSD)	31	31	7	7	4	4	3	3	2	3	1	1	1	1	1	1	3	3	1	1

Notes:

1 Data refers to fleet strengths as of mid-year 2009 and 2010.

2 Figures for Russia and China are approximate.

towards a 'blue water' structure. Delivery of the first batch of three Type 214 air-independent propulsion (AIP) equipped submarines is now complete and the second KDX-III Aegis destroyer will follow shortly. In contrast, the number of light frigates more suited for littoral operations is falling – exacerbated by *Cheonan*'s destruction – although the imminent arrival of more PKX fast attack craft should provide some compensation.

As a general caveat, it should be noted that this table and the additional, more detailed tables, set out in the following Fleet Review chapters can only hope to provide an approximation of fleet strengths. Whilst information on changes to the composition of the more established 'Western' navies is generally quite readily accessible, this is much less the case for some of the expanding Asian fleets and a degree of estimation is therefore necessary. The components of China's People's Liberation Army Navy (PLAN) and the Russian fleet are particularly difficult to track, partly due to remnants of Cold War secrecy and partly due to the difficulties inherent in assessing the operational status of large numbers of obsolescent vessels with marginal combat capability.[4]

Another potential limitation in the coverage provided by the Fleet Review chapters is their inevitable focus on the larger fleets. This tends to ignore the rise of the capabilities of mid-tier navies that has been a feature of changes in the balance of global economic prosperity. This year's detailed fleet supplements therefore focus on two of the emergent, mid-ranking fleets by way of balance. The Turkish Navy is rapidly recreating its historic role as a dominant regional power in the Eastern Mediterranean. This is supported by a far-sighted industrial programme aimed at bolstering the country's indigenous maritime defence sector that is described by Devrim Yaylalı. By contrast, Leon Engelbrecht's review of the South African Navy demonstrates some of the challenges that can arise in the absence of a coherent and up-to-date maritime defence strategy.

SIGNIFICANT SHIPS

The second main section examines some of the more significant new warship designs that are now being put into service. Here, the emphasis turns again towards the larger fleets. Scott Truver follows last year's appraisal of the USN's first innovative littoral combat ship, Lockheed Martin's *Freedom* (LCS-1), with an assessment of the competing General

South Africa's German-built Type 209/1400 submarine *Manthatisi*. Although South Africa's navy has benefited from significant capital investment, a lack of both strategic direction and operating funds means that it is failing to meet its potential. *(Thyssen Krupp Marine Systems)*

Independence (LCS-2) is the second of the US Navy's innovative littoral combat ships. The United States will shortly decide whether to put this or the *Freedom* (LCS-1) variant into series production. *(US Navy)*

A *Marine Nationale* Rafale M jet prepares for take off from the French aircraft carrier *Charles de Gaulle*. It is just one of the naval fighter aircraft described in this volume's overview of naval aviation. *(Copyright Alex Paringaux via Dassault Aviation)*

Above: Norway's *Otto Sverdrup* is seen here on exercises with two of her *Fridtjof Nansen* class sisters. They are the smallest ships yet to enter service with the Aegis weapon system. *(Navantia)*

Left: This view of *Farragut*'s (DDG-99) forward superstructure provides a clear view of one of the fixed SPY1-D multifunction radar arrays associated with the Aegis weapon system. The development of multifunction radar has revolutionised warship defences against missile attack. *(US Navy)*

Dynamics trimaran design represented by *Independence* (LCS-2). The United States intends to select one of these for series production in the course of 2010. Across the Atlantic, the Royal Navy is, at last, starting to see the fruits of its previously troubled nuclear-powered attack submarine (SSN) programme with the long-awaited commissioning of *Astute*. The first of a class of up to seven boats being constructed by BAE Systems at Barrow, she is described by Richard Beedall.

India's naval construction projects have also been marked by delays, which are at least partly a consequence of utilising a mixture of Western and Russian technologies. The resulting ships have occasionally been described as somewhat akin to 'Frankenstein's monsters', albeit they also tend to be powerful and imposing vessels. Mrityunjoy Mazumdar focuses on what are arguably the most complex of these designs with his review of the Project 15 *Delhi* class destroyers commissioned during 1997-2001 and the follow-up Project 15A and 15B variants that are now, respectively, under construction and development. An alternative view of international collaboration is provided by the editor's description of Norway's *Fridtjof Nansen* class frigates, which were constructed by Spain's Navantia with significant input from the United States, Norway and other Western defence manufacturers. They are the smallest ships yet in service to incorporate the Aegis weapons system.

TECHNOLOGICAL DEVELOPMENTS

Aegis also features prominently in the book's concluding section, which commences with Norman Friedman's review of multifunction radar systems on current warship capabilities. These appear to have mitigated the threat previously posed by saturation attack from 'pop up' weapons fired by submerged submarines and, most notably, stand-off missiles launched from aircraft beyond the range of air-defence systems, albeit their capabilities have yet to be comprehensively tested in a 'live fire' situation. The other side of this equation is touched upon by David Hobbs, who supplements in his annual review of developments in the world of naval aviation with an overview of current fixed-wing and rotary maritime aircraft, not least the Lockheed Martin F-35 'Lightning II'. This new jet incorporates the latest stealth technologies to gain an edge in its primary strike role, albeit at a potential price that has resulted in questions about its overall cost-effectiveness.

The book concludes with a shorter chapter by the editor examining the last refit of a British Type 42 destroyer, *Edinburgh*, against the context of significant changes in the way UK warship support is being conducted. Whilst potentially a somewhat esoteric subject, it is important to note that operating and maintenance costs typically account for a much larger proportion – possibly up to three-quarters – of 'through-life' expenses for a major warship than the initial acquisition budget.[5] As such, achieving economies in these areas, not only through reduced maintenance expense but also as a result of lower manning or fuel charges, could have a key role to play in squaring the circle of retaining capabilities at a time of budget pressure.

SUMMARY

In summary, the traditional Western maritime powers continue to enjoy the advantages of freedom of trade and manoeuvre that ascendancy over the world's oceans confers but which are all too easily taken for granted. They have generally been taking sensible steps to restructure their naval forces towards a practical and cost-effective configuration for 21st-century operations. However, they have yet to feel the full impact of the recent global credit crunch on stretched government finances. Some of the consequences of the need for retrenchment will doubtless become apparent over the next twelve months.

More fundamentally, the shift in the balance of economic power towards many of the developing countries has been accelerated by the financial crisis, with China and India amongst the clear relative beneficiaries. When considered in combination with the longer term emergence of regional economic powers such as Brazil, Korea, Turkey and South Africa, it is difficult to see how the United States can afford to maintain the current extent of its naval hegemony in the medium term. Although the shift in the naval balance will be slow and, doubtless, mitigated by both historic and emerging alliances, the world's waterways are likely to become more volatile and, potentially, more dangerous in the years ahead.

ACKNOWLEDGEMENTS

As previously, this book has been made possible through the co-operation of many people. I would particularly like to acknowledge publishing editor Rob Gardiner's ongoing support of our aim to provide an authoritative yet affordable annual overview of the world naval scene. This endeavour has benefited greatly from the efforts of a strong group of expert contributors, many of whom have continued their involvement from the inaugural edition. Another key influence has been the expertise of designer Steve Dent (a published naval historian in his own right) in giving these contributions a clear visual form. Equally significant has been the supply of illustrations and information by many defence companies and government ministries, with the help of Kristina Crowe of BAE Systems, Esther Benito Lope of Navantia, Ute Arriens of HDW and of Adrian Rondel and Frank van de Wiel of Thales particularly indispensable. Lastly, I must thank my family for their continued patience, not least my wife Susan for helping again with the initial proof-reading.

The ongoing success of the *Seaforth World Naval Review* will, however, ultimately depend on its readers' support. The comments and criticisms received in respect of the first edition were extremely valuable and have shaped parts of this year's book. We continue to welcome your observations and suggestions of areas for future focus – please feel free to pass these on via the contact address given opposite the contents page.

Conrad Waters, Editor
30 June 2010

Notes

1. Please see *Quadrennial Defense Review Report – February 2010* (Washington DC, US Department of Defense, 2010). This can be found at www.defense.gov/qdr

2. Please refer to Chapter 2.1 for a more detailed overview of USN developments.

3. A good explanation of the rather complicated restructuring impacting ThyssenKrupp Marine Systems (TKMS) can be found on the authoritative Defense Industry Daily website. Please refer to the article 'German Shipbuilding Restructured: UAE's Firm buys Blohm & Voss' posted to www.defenseindustrydaily.com on 11 March 2010.

4. In general terms, the data contained in these tables is based on official information updated as of June 2010, supplemented by reference to a wide range of secondary and corporate sources, such as shipbuilder websites. It is interesting to note how many published sources differ significantly on the principal particulars of ships, whilst even governmental information can be subject to contradiction.

5. Reference should be made to Chapter 2 of P J Gates' *Surface Warships: An Introduction to Design Principles* (London, Brassey's Defence Publishers, 1987) for an overview of cost considerations in modern warship procurement.

2.1 REGIONAL REVIEW

Author:
Conrad Waters

NORTH AND SOUTH AMERICA

The last twelve months have been eventful for the navies of North and South America. Strategic developments, natural and man-made disasters, as well as a significant historical anniversary, have all played a part. As always, events in the United States have dominated the regional maritime scene. February 2010 saw the publication of both the Quadrennial Defence Review and an updated Long-Range Shipbuilding Plan, the latter after a two-year gap. A new operations concept was released shortly afterwards in May. 'Naval Operations Concept 2010' (NOC-2010) follows on from the overall US maritime strategy first set out in October 2007 in 'A Co-operative Strategy for 21st Century Seapower' (CS-21), articulating the way naval forces will be deployed to achieve CS-21's overall objectives.[1] Describing when, where and how US naval forces will contribute to enhancing security, preventing conflict and prevailing in war, NOC-2010 effectively sits midway between strategy and tactical doctrine. Intentionally avoiding any reference to the specific fleet size required to meet strategic objectives, it was criticised by the influential *Navy Times* publication as a document containing few surprises that failed to address how a shrinking navy could sustain ongoing high operational tempos.

Given the challenging financial environment highlighted in the Introduction, it is not surprising that one of the USN's key objectives in recent years has been increasing use of partnerships and alliances to take up the strain. Most attention has focused on efforts to strengthen existing relationships with regional maritime powers such as Australia and Japan, as well as the development of new links with emerging superpowers such as India. However, another dimension to this approach is an emphasis on more effective inter-working between the US's own forces. This is best demonstrated by the developing Air-Sea Battle concept that was referenced in the Quadrennial Defence Review and has resonances with the Cold War Air-Land Battle doctrine of the 1980s. The approach envisages a collaborative response to the development of anti-access capabilities by countries such as China and Iran that threaten America's ability to project power in the Western Pacific and Persian Gulf. For example, USN Aegis-equipped ships would be deployed to supplement the anti-missile defences of forward-deployed United States Air Force (USAF) bases, whilst USAF aircraft would be more actively employed on maritime anti-surface and anti-submarine duties than hitherto.[2] The new concept will face significant inter-service cultural hurdles to overcome if it is to be developed effectively. Additionally, some of the new items of equipment it will require, for example long-range strike aircraft, are expensive. However, with the Pentagon already showing a willingness to demonstrate more flexible thinking, most notably in the September 2009 decision to switch the emphasis on European anti-ballistic missile defence plans from land to sea-based systems, it seems that inter-service co-operation will be a more common feature of USN operations.

Elsewhere in the region, Canada celebrated the 100th anniversary of the formation of the Canadian Navy with a day of commemoration and celebration on 4 May 2010 and centenary fleet reviews on the west and east coasts during June and July. The celebrations were somewhat overshadowed in mid-May by the leaking of a directive from the head of the navy, Vice-Admiral Dean McFadden, to lay up half the fleet of *Kingston* class mine-countermeasures vessels that are used for coastal patrol and reduce the combat effectiveness of several other surface vessels due to lack of operating funds. Whilst the order was quickly rescinded by Chief of the Defence Staff Walter Natynczyk after the resulting political uproar, the underlying position does not look particularly positive given the likely future burden of renewing an increasingly elderly fleet.

Turning southwards, the USN and, particularly, its sister service, the US Coast Guard, have been heavily occupied in combating the environmental fallout from the Deepwater Horizon explosion and oil spill in the Gulf of Mexico. However, arguably greater challenges have been faced by the Chilean Navy, which suffered material damage to its principal submarine base and the neighbouring ASMAR shipyard in Talcahuano as a result of an earthquake and tsunami on 27 February 2010. Although the navy was fortunate to escape substantial harm to most of its major units, dockyard facilities suffered significant damage that will take years to repair. Local press reports suggest that substantial military procurement funding will now be diverted towards earthquake reconstruction work. Initial estimates of the cost of repairs to the shipyard and base alone are around US$450m.

The USN's *Nimitz* class aircraft carrier *Carl Vinson* (CVN-70) pictured in March 2010 whilst on a deployment to Latin America to facilitate operations in a multi-national environment. Strengthening relationships with key regional maritime powers is a major USN objective. *(US Navy)*

Table 2.1.1: FLEET STRENGTHS IN THE AMERICAS – LARGER NAVIES (MID-2010)

COUNTRY	ARGENTINA	BRAZIL	CANADA	CHILE	ECUADOR	PERU	USA	VENEZUELA
Aircraft Carrier (CVN/CV)	–	1	–	–	–	–	11	–
Strategic Missile Submarine (SSBN)	–	–	–	–	–	–	14	–
Attack Submarine (SSN/SSGN)	–	–	–	–	–	–	57	–
Patrol Submarine (SSK)	3	5	4	4	2	6	–	2
Fleet Escort (CG/DDG/FFG)	4	9	15	8	2	9	109	6
Patrol Escort/Corvette (FFG/FSG/FS)	9	5	–	–	6	–	2	–
Missile Armed Attack Craft (PGG/PTG)	2	–	–	7	3	6	–	6
Mine Countermeasures Vessel (MCMV)	–	6	12	–	–	–	14	–
Major Amphibious Units (LHD/LPD/LPH/LSD)	–	2	–	–	–	–	31	–

MAJOR NORTH AMERICAN NAVIES – CANADA

A summary of principal Canadian Forces Maritime Command – the official name for the Canadian Navy – is set out in Table 2.1.2. There have been no material changes in fleet composition over the past twelve months. The backbone of the surface fleet remains the twelve *Halifax* frigates delivered between 1992 and 1996 and which are scheduled to commence eighteen-month mid-life modernisation refits from October 2010 through to July 2015. They are supplemented by the three surviving elderly *Iroquois* class destroyers first commissioned as long ago as 1972. Modernisation of the four *Victoria* (former Royal Navy *Upholder*) class submarines slowly continues, with *Victoria* herself likely to rejoin the sole operational boat, *Corner Brook*, in the active fleet by the end of 2010.

The Canadian government has set out a number of maritime acquisition programmes as part of the 'Canada First' defence strategy implemented from 2006. The most immediate of these are the purchase of up to eight armed Arctic patrol vessels to strengthen the country's presence in and around the North-West Passage and three JSS Joint Support Ships to provide an enhanced capacity for expeditionary warfare and replace ageing replenishment vessels.[3] Both projects have suffered from delays and have now tied up with realisation of a new National Shipbuilding Procurement Strategy (NSPS), announced on 3 June 2010. The strategy has been driven by the need to eradicate the previous boom-to-bust cycle in the shipyards that has significantly eroded the country's shipbuilding industry since the conclusion of the last major construction phase in the mid-1990s.

The NSPS aims to rebuild a stable domestic maritime sector through sub-division of future government workload into three streams, viz. construction of large vessels, construction of smaller vessels and refit and repair, with contracts relating to the first-mentioned being channelled through just two pre-selected yards. One of these facilities will be focused on fabrication of all future combat vessels, initially the Arctic patrol vessels and then a new Canadian surface combatant that will eventually

Canada is looking to build up to eight Arctic patrol vessels to strengthen its presence in and around the North-West Passage. Technical specifications for the ships have been drawn up but orders await realisation of Canada's new National Shipbuilding Procurement Strategy. *(HM The Queen in Right of Canada (2009))*

replace the *Iroquois* and *Halifax* classes. The other yard will be focused on non-combat vessels such as the JSS. Smaller, sub 1,000-ton ships will be sourced by competitive tender from other facilities. The selection of the two principal yards will be made during the 2011-12 timeframe, after which umbrella agreements on future orders will be signed with the companies concerned. Whilst undoubtedly a sensible approach which mirrors recent arrangements in the UK and elsewhere, the time that will be needed to identify and then negotiate with the core shipyards inevitably risks accentuating current delays.[4]

MAJOR NORTH AMERICAN NAVIES – UNITED STATES NAVY

The USN appears to be achieving some success in stabilising front-line fleet numbers at around 280-290 warships following the previous steady decline experienced since the end of the Cold War. The summary of principal fleet units set out in Table 2.1.3 shows only slight changes over the past year. The commissioning of additional Flight IIA *Arleigh Burke* (DDG-51) type destroyers and the second littoral combat ship *Independence* (LCS-2) has modestly increased overall numbers of surface escorts. Other trends are the steady replacement of veteran *Austin* (LPD-4) amphibious transport docks by the new *San Antonio* (LPD-17) type, as well as the similar displacement of *Los Angeles* (SSN-688) nuclear-powered attack submarines in the underwater forces by the much-improved *Virginia* (SSN-774) boats. The proposed FY2011 shipbuilding

Canada celebrated the 100th anniversary of its navy's foundation with fleet reviews on both the east and west coasts. This view shows ships from Australia, Japan, New Zealand and the US alongside those of the host nation off the west coast naval base at Esquimalt on 12 June 2010. France was also represented at the west coast review. *(Canadian Navy)*

Table 2.1.2: CANADIAN NAVY: PRINCIPAL UNITS AS AT MID-2010

TYPE	CLASS	NUMBER	TONNAGE	DIMENSIONS	PROPULSION	CREW	DATE
Principal Surface Escorts							
Destroyer – DDG	**IROQUOIS**	3	5,100 tons	130m x 15m x 5m	COGOG, 29 knots	280	1972
Frigate – FFG	**HALIFAX**	12	4,800 tons	134m x 16m x 5m	CODOG, 29 knots	225	1992
Submarines							
Submarine – SSK	**VICTORIA** (UPHOLDER)	4	2,500 tons	70m x 8m x 6m	Diesel-electric, 20+ knots	50	1990

The backbone of Canada's surface fleet remains the twelve *Halifax* class frigates, represented here by *Calgary*. *(Canadian Navy)*

programme continues a reasonably healthy construction rate, envisaging orders for nine ships – as well as a further allocation of US$2.6bn to the CVN-78 carrier programme – at a total cost of US$13.8bn. The new ships are:

- Two *Virginia* (SSN-774) class nuclear-powered attack submarines.
- Two Flight IIA *Arleigh Burke* (DDG-51) class destroyers.
- Two *Freedom* (LCS-1) or *Independence* (LCS-2) class littoral combat ships.
- One *America* (LHA-6) amphibious assault ship.
- One *Fortitude* (JHSV-1) joint high speed vessel.
- One MLP-1 mobile landing platform.

Future fleet composition and construction projections are detailed in the updated thirty-year Long-Range Shipbuilding Plan for FY2011. This uses the target 313-ship battle-force inventory established as a result of a 2005 force structure analysis as its starting point but sets out a number of changes that suggest a new long-term requirement of around 322-323 vessels.[5] Details of the implied change in force structure are shown in Table 2.1.4 on p.19. Whilst this increase in numbers would appear to be an overwhelmingly positive development at first glance, the adjustment is mainly based on the acquisition of a larger number of cheaper ships such as the small joint high-speed vessel troop transports (JHSVs). When taken with decisions such as the stretching of the carrier procurement 'drumbeat' from four to five years and the resumption of cheaper DDG-51 destroyer construction in place of new designs, a clear shift from quality to quantity is evident.

This view is confirmed by an examination of the budget required to support the thirty-year construction plan. The estimate of total costs has fallen to US$476bn from the US$718bn contained in the previous, FY2009 plan. The decline is a result of a projected fall in the cost of each ship ordered to US$1.7bn from US$2.4bn, as well as a reduction in the total number of ships ordered to 276 from 296 units, mitigated by a decision to extend the service lives of existing ships. Even under this scenario, two further problems present themselves. One is the fact that the shipbuilding programme's likely cost is still somewhat higher than recent funds allocated to naval construction. The other is that the USN's own estimates suggest projected construction will be insufficient to meet the targeted baseline, with a peak of 320 ships in FY2024 falling back to around 300 at the thirty-year mark. In short, it seems that the USN's planners have made some real progress in outlining a sustainable force structure but that further work is still needed.

Around half the ongoing future surface fleet will comprise surface combatants and greater clarity is now emerging as to likely future construction of these key units. The approved FY2010 defence budget confirmed termination of the troubled and costly DDG-1000 destroyer programme at just three ships in favour of renewed construction of the tried and tested Flight IIA *Arleigh Burke*s. One new ship – DDG-113 – was authorised in the FY2010 plan at a total cost of US$2.24bn. The relatively high price

Table 2.1.3: UNITED STATES NAVY: PRINCIPAL UNITS AS AT MID-2010

TYPE	CLASS	NUMBER	TONNAGE	DIMENSIONS	PROPULSION	CREW	DATE
Aircraft Carriers							
Aircraft Carrier – CVN	**NIMITZ** (CVN-68)	10	101,000 tons	340m x 41/78m x 12m	Nuclear, 30+ knots	5,700	1975
Aircraft Carrier – CVN	**ENTERPRISE** (CVN-65)	1	93,000 tons	342m x 41/76m x 12m	Nuclear, 30+ knots	5,900	1961
Principal Surface Escorts							
Cruiser – CG	**TICONDEROGA** (CG-47)	22	9,900 tons	173m x 17m x 7m	COGAG, 30+ knots	365	1983
Destroyer – DDG	**ARLEIGH BURKE** (DDG-51) – Flight IIA	29	9,200 tons	155m x 20m x 7m	COGAG, 30 knots	380	2000
Destroyer – DDG	**ARLEIGH BURKE** (DDG-51) – Flights I/II	28	8,800 tons	154m x 20m x 7m	COGAG, 30+ knots	340	1991
Frigate – FFG	**OLIVER HAZARD PERRY** (FFG-7)	30	4,100 tons	143m x 14m x 5m	COGAG, 30 knots	215	1977
Littoral Combat Ship – FSG	**FREEDOM** (LCS-1)	1	3,100 tons	115m x 17m x 4m	CODAG, 45+ knots	<50[1]	2008
Littoral Combat Ship – FSG	**INDEPENDENCE** (LCS-2)	1	2,800 tons	127m x 32m x 5m	CODAG, 45+ knots	<50[1]	2010
Submarines							
Submarine – SSBN	**OHIO** (SSBN-726)	14	18,800 tons	171m x 13m x 12m	Nuclear, 20+ knots	155	1981
Submarine – SSGN	**OHIO** (SSGN-726)	4	18,800 tons	171m x 13m x 12m	Nuclear, 20+ knots	160	1981
Submarine – SSN	**VIRGINIA** (SSN-774)	6	8,000 tons	115m x 10m x 9m	Nuclear, 25+ knots	135	2004
Submarine – SSN	**SEAWOLF** (SSN-21)	3[2]	9,000 tons	108m x 12m x 11m	Nuclear, 25+ knots	140	1997
Submarine SSN	**LOS ANGELES** (SSN-688)	44	7,000 tons	110m x 10m x 9m	Nuclear, 25+ knots	145	1976
Major Amphibious Units							
Amph. Assault Ship – LHD	**WASP** (LHD-1)	8[3]	41,000 tons	253m x 32/42m x 9m	Steam, 20+ knots	1,100	1989
Amph Assault Ship – LHD	**TARAWA** (LHA-1)	2	40,000 tons	250m x 32/38m x 8m	Steam, 24 knots	975	1976
Landing Platform Dock – LPD	**SAN ANTONIO** (LPD-17)	5	25,000 tons	209m x 32m x 7m	Diesel, 22+ knots	360	2005
Landing Platform Dock – LPD	**AUSTIN** (LPD-4)	4	17,000 tons	171m x 25m x 7m	Steam, 21 knots	420	1965
Landing Ship Dock – LSD	**WHIDBEY ISLAND** (LSD-41)	12[4]	16,000 tons	186m x 26m x 6m	Diesel, 20 knots	420	1985

Notes:

1 Plus mission-related crew.   2 Third of class, SSN-23 is longer and heavier.   3 LHD-8 has many differences.   4 Includes four LSD-49 HARPERS FERRY variants.

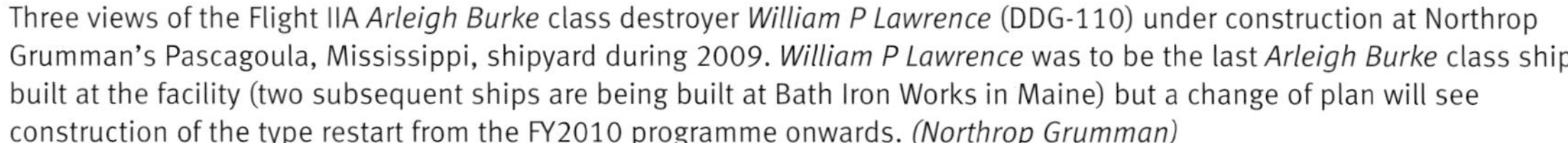

Three views of the Flight IIA *Arleigh Burke* class destroyer *William P Lawrence* (DDG-110) under construction at Northrop Grumman's Pascagoula, Mississippi, shipyard during 2009. *William P Lawrence* was to be the last *Arleigh Burke* class ship built at the facility (two subsequent ships are being built at Bath Iron Works in Maine) but a change of plan will see construction of the type restart from the FY2010 programme onwards. *(Northrop Grumman)*

The *Virginia* class submarine *New Mexico* (SSN-779) pictured on sea trials off the Virginia coast in December 2009. Construction of the type will accelerate to two per year from the FY2011 shipbuilding programme. *(Northrop Grumman)*

reflected the expense of restarting production of a design that was last ordered under the FY2005 programme. A further two *Burke*s will be procured under the FY2011 budget at a cost of around US$1.75bn each, with a further six following at a rate of one or two per year up until FY2015. Production will then shift to a modified Flight III variant focused on ballistic-missile defence, replacing orders for the planned CG(X) cruiser that the FY2011 budget formally abandons. The revised plan avoids the higher building costs and technological risks associated with DDG-1000 and, particularly, CG(X) construction. However, it also channels future production of major surface combatants towards a hull design that first originated in the late 1970s and that might have limited capacity for future growth. It is also debatable whether the DDG-51 design can be adapted to benefit from the lower through-life manning and support costs available with modern warship designs; it is instructive to note that a Flight IIA *Arleigh Burke* requires a crew of over 350 compared with less than 200 in a broadly comparable British Type 45 destroyer.

The other strand of future USN surface construction will be based on the often-criticised littoral combat ship (LCS) programme. The first of this new type – Lockheed Martin's *Freedom* (LCS-1) – was fully described in *Seaforth World Naval Review 2010* and has now completed an accelerated maiden operational deployment. The prototype for the alternative General Dynamics/Austal USA *Independence* (LCS-2) design was commissioned on 18 January 2010 and is subject to a full review by Scott Truver in Chapter 3.4. The USN will decide during the summer of 2010 which of the two designs will be selected for series production to meet a targeted fleet of fifty-five vessels. At an estimated future cost of around US$600m per ship the littoral combat ship is significantly cheaper than the DDG programme but still relatively expensive compared with overseas designs.

Beneath the waves, the FY2011 budget has confirmed previous plans to accelerate construction of *Virginia* (SSN-774) boats to two per year to counterbalance ongoing withdrawal of the Cold War *Los Angeles* (SSN-688) class. The programme – a collaboration between General Dynamics Electric Boat facility at Groton, Connecticut, and Northrop Grumman's Newport News shipyard in Virginia – stands out as a major success in US shipbuilding's otherwise recent chequered track record. The sixth class member, *New Mexico* (SSN-779), was commissioned on 27 March 2010 after a record building time. The seventh boat, *Missouri* (SSN-780), is likely to follow her into service at the end of July. The class is benefiting from the USN's process of spiral design improvements, with construction now underway on the Flight III variant. Featuring a redesigned bow with a revised sonar arrangement and simplified weapons launchers to increase effectiveness whilst reducing cost, the Flight III configuration has been adapted for all boats from *North Dakota* (SSN-784) onwards. Further, more cosmetic changes might be required as a result of a policy change first announced in February 2010 allowing women to serve on US submarines for the first time.

Aircraft carriers remain at the heart of USN power projection capabilities. Another stage in the transition from the *Nimitz* (CVN-68) class design that currently constitutes ten of the eleven-strong carrier fleet was marked in November 2009, when the keel of the first of the new *Gerald R Ford* (CVN-78) class was laid at Newport News. Advance construction work on the ship, which features enhancements such as a new, more efficient nuclear power plant, revised flight deck and island arrangements and innovative electro-magnetic aircraft launch systems (EMALS) in place of traditional catapults, commenced in 2005 but it will be 2015 before she is delivered. She will

Table 2.1.4: USN FLEET LONG-RANGE FORCE PROJECTIONS

UNIT TYPE	2010 FLEET	313-SHIP FLEET PLAN	REVISED FLEET PLAN[1]	2040 ESTIMATE
Aircraft Carrier (CVN)	11	11	10-11	11
Strategic Missile Submarine (SSBN)	14	14	12	12
Attack Submarines (SSN/SSGN)	57	52	48	45
Fleet Escorts (CG/DDG)	79	88	88	76
Fleet Escorts – Frigates (FFG)	30	–	–	–
Littoral Combat Ships (LCS)	2	55	55	55
Amphibious (LHD/LPD/LSD/LCC)	33[2]	31	33	30
Other	60	62	76	72
Total	286	313	322-323	301

Notes:

1 Numbers in the Revised Fleet Plan are derived from Congressional Budget Office (CBO) estimates of the USN requirements, themselves based on language contained in the FY2011 Long-Range Shipbuilding Plan and the contents of related briefings.

2 Figure includes two amphibious command ships.

replace the long-serving *Enterprise* (CVN-65), which has now returned to operational service following completion of her final refit in April 2010. She will be retired during 2013, reducing the active carrier fleet to a new low of just ten ships until *Gerald R Ford* is delivered.

The USN continues to operate at a high tempo across the world's oceans. Whilst the emergence of anti-access threats from the likes of China and Iran seemingly have the greatest impact on strategic thinking, it is possibly lower-profile activities such as the interdiction of drugs and arms trafficking in the Caribbean and the more newsworthy anti-piracy operations in the Indian Ocean that have most immediate significance. Operations in both areas appear to be achieving some success in the context of wider issues that cannot be solved by the application of maritime power alone. The navy – particularly its amphibious assets – also played a key role in the relief operations that followed the devastating Haiti earthquake. Much effort is also being expended in developing naval partnerships in line with the general direction of CS-21. The unpredictable but steadily deteriorating situation in the Korean peninsula probably has the greatest potential for all-out conflict and naval exercises with the Republic of Korea Navy have been stepped up. USN salvage and diving assets were also deployed to assist with the recovery of the corvette *Cheonan* in the aftermath of her sinking at the end of March 2010.

Closer to home, the US Coast Guard is making further progress in bringing the troubled 'Deepwater' recapitalisation programme back on track following creation of an 'in house' Acquisitions Directorate in 2007 to assume management of both the previously commercially-lead project and future procurement activity. Three new classes of cutter are being acquired to replace existing elderly tonnage. The largest of these will be the *Bertholf* (WMSL-750) class national security cutters, corvette-sized ships capable of ocean going deployment. The second of up to eight units, *Waesche* (WMSL-751), was commissioned on

Enterprise (CVN-65) entering Northrop Grumman's Newport News facility at the start of her final refit in April 2008. She has now rejoined the fleet for operational service prior to her scheduled decommissioning in 2013. *(Northrop Grumman)*

The US Coast Guard now has two *Bertholf* (WMSL-750) class national security cutters in service following the commissioning of *Waesche* (WMSL-751) on 7 May 2010. A third cutter is under construction. *(US Coast Guard)*

Trinidad and Tobago have also taken delivery of a new flotilla of high-speed patrol craft as a part of a general renewal of the country's maritime assets. This is an image of *Chaconia* in Australian waters before her delivery voyage. *(Austal Ships)*

7 May 2010, whilst the keel of the third ship, *Stratton* (WMSL-752), was laid on 21 July 2009. At the other end of the scale are the 47m-long inshore 'Sentinel' type fast response cutters, essentially variants of the Damen Stan 4708 type that are being licence-built by Bollinger Shipyards. The keel of the first ship was laid on 9 April 2010 and three further vessels out of a total class of up to fifty-eight units were ordered on 15 December 2009. Plans for the intermediate sea-going ship, known as an offshore patrol cutter, are less advanced, with current thinking envisaging the award of three preliminary design contracts from which a final selection would be made.

Construction of the US Coast Guard's inshore 'Sentinel' fast response cutters is now underway. The design is essentially a Damen Stan 4708 variant. *(US Coast Guard)*

OTHER NORTH & CENTRAL AMERICAN NAVIES

Navies in **Mexico** and the other Central American countries remain focused on the acquisition of modern patrol vessels, both to police offshore economic interests and to combat the narcotics trade. Mexico has made available sufficient money to resume series construction of its locally-built offshore vessels, with the third *Oaxaca* class ship *Independencia* (PO-163) being commissioned on 1 June 2010 following the launch of the fourth unit, *Revolución* (PO-164), on 23 November 2009. Displacing around 1,500 tons and with a length of 86m, the ships are equipped with a light helicopter and fast interceptor boat to assist their primary surveillance and seizure roles. Given that the first two ships were delivered as long ago as 2003, it is likely that this new batch will have incorporated improvements over their older sisters. Funding for additional ships in the class, as well as for smaller coastal vessels, has been approved. Meanwhile, Mexico's small front-line surface flotilla of discarded USN escorts is becoming increasingly elderly. It will therefore be interesting to see whether it will take advantage of forthcoming withdrawal of more modern USN FFG-7 type frigates to modernise its force or continue its recent emphasis on domestic construction of less capable vessels.

Also taking delivery of new warships is **Trinidad and Tobago**, which placed a £150m (US$225m) order for three offshore patrol vessels for its coast guard from what is now BAE Systems Surface Ships in April 2007. First of class, *Port of Spain*, commenced delayed sea trials from the company's Portsmouth facility at the start of 2010 and was due to be handed over in the course of the summer. Construction of the other ships has been transferred to the company's Glasgow yards, from where second of class *Scarborough* was launched on 19 November 2009. Similar in concept and role to their Mexican counterparts, these 90.5m-long ships are able to embark an helicopter and fast interceptor craft, as well as up to fifty fully-equipped troops. Top speed is in excess of 25 knots, whilst they are capable of sustaining operations for up to thirty-five days with a range of 5,500nm (10,175km) at economical cruising speed. They will supplement a class of six high-speed patrol craft of aluminium construction

The first of the Trinidad and Tobago Coast Guard's new offshore patrol vessels, *Port of Spain*, departing Portsmouth on sea trials in February 2010. (*Conrad Waters*)

contracted from Australia's Austal in 2008. The final batch of these 30m vessels, which are capable of speeds in excess of 40 knots and have a range of over 1,000nm (1,850km), was delivered by heavy-lift ship in January 2010 following an earlier delivery towards the end of 2009. Operated by a crew of just eleven personnel, armament includes a 20mm cannon and general-purpose machine guns.

MAJOR SOUTH AMERICAN NAVIES – ARGENTINA

Details of the current Argentine naval strength are contained in Table 2.1.5. There has been no material change to fleet composition over the past twelve months. Although British oil exploration in the waters off the Falkland Islands has resulted in renewed sabre-rattling by Argentina's authorities – including threats to send warships to patrol waters near the disputed zone – the navy has far to go to regain the position it enjoyed as, possibly, Latin America's premier fleet at the start of the 1982 Falklands War.

There have, however, been some positive developments recently for the *Armada Argentina*. The modernisation of the TR-1700 submarine *San Juan*

Table 2.1.5: ARGENTINEAN NAVY: PRINCIPAL UNITS AS AT MID-2010

TYPE	CLASS	NUMBER	TONNAGE	DIMENSIONS	PROPULSION	CREW	DATE
Principal Surface Escorts							
Destroyer – DDG	**ALMIRANTE BROWN** (MEKO 360)	4	3,600 tons	126m x 14m x 4m	COGOG, 30 knots	200	1983
Frigate – FFG	**ESPORA** (MEKO 140)	6	1,800 tons	91m x 11m x 3m	Diesel, 27 knots	100	1985
Corvette – FSG	**DRUMMOND** (A-69)	3	1,200 tons	80m x 10m x 3m	Diesel, 24 knots	95	1978
Submarines							
Submarine – SSK	**SANTA CRUZ** (TR 1700)	2	2,300 tons	65m x 7m x 7m	Diesel-electric, 25 knots	30	1984
Submarine – SSK	**SALTA** (Type 209)	1	1,200 tons	54m x 6m x 6m	Diesel-electric, 22 knots	30	1974

Argentina's MEKO 140 light frigate *Gómez Roca* pictured on exercises with the US Navy in March 2010. Completed in May 2004 after a construction period of over ten years, she is currently the most modern Argentine surface unit. *(US Navy)*

is reportedly making good progress at the local Astillero Domecq Garcia shipyard and there are ongoing rumours that work on the sister boats suspended during the 1990s might recommence. More likely in the short term is construction of Fassmer OPV80 type offshore patrol vessels similar to Chile's *Piloto Pardo*. Funding for this project now seems to have been reinstated into the procurement programme after a previous postponement on financial grounds. A total of four ships will be built at Astilleros Tandanor in Buenos Aires starting in August 2010 at an estimated cost of 619m Argentine pesos (c. US$150m). In the meantime, Tandanor is finishing repairs costing around US$75m to the icebreaker *Almirante Irizar* – severely damaged by fire in April 2007 – in time for her operational deployment during the 2011/12 Antarctic summer. Yet more money will be allocated to modernisation of the main Puerto Belgrano naval base, notably refurbishment of its No 2 dock.

Although it has long operated without an aircraft carrier, the naval air arm's complement of eleven Super Étendard strike fighters make it amongst the most potent in the region. A deal has been signed with France to upgrade ten of these to M (*Modernisé*) standard, whilst the French *Mer et Marine* website has speculated that additional French aircraft may be transferred once replaced by Rafale Ms. Six surplus USN Sea King UH-3H helicopters have also been delivered over the past couple of years, more than compensating for the two destroyed in the *Almirante Irizar* fire.

MAJOR SOUTH AMERICAN NAVIES – BRAZIL

The *Marinha do Brasil* is currently at the start of a major modernisation plan driven by the 'END' (*Estratégia Nacional de Defesa*) Brazilian National Defence Strategy, published on 18 December 2008. The navy has expanded its previous 2006-25 programme into the 'PEAMB' organisation and equipment plan to fulfil its part of the overall strategy. This revised plan will be implemented in three phases up until 2030. Whilst, therefore, the fleet composition set out in Table 2.1.6 shows no year-on-year change, the Brazilian Navy is likely to see significant renewal in the medium term as a recapitalisation programme estimated to cost in excess of US$80bn gets underway.

The most significant modernisation project contracted to date has been construction of four new patrol submarines of the French 'Scorpène' type and a prototype nuclear-powered boat under an agreement with DCNS reportedly valued at 6.7bn (c. US$8.5bn) that was first announced in December 2008. A formal contract signed on 3 September 2009 was followed by the start of construction work on the first boat at DCNS Cherbourg on 27 May 2010. The

Table 2.1.6: BRAZILIAN NAVY: PRINCIPAL UNITS AS AT MID-2010

TYPE	CLASS	NUMBER	TONNAGE	DIMENSIONS	PROPULSION	CREW	DATE
Aircraft Carriers							
Aircraft Carrier – CV	SÃO PAULO (FOCH)	1	33,500 tons	265m x 32/51m x 9m	Steam, 30 knots	1,700	1963
Principal Surface Escorts							
Frigate – FFG	GREENHALGH (Type 22-Batch 1)	3	4,700 tons	131m x 15m x 4m	COGOG, 30 knots	270	1979
Frigate – FFG	NITERÓI	6	3,700 tons	129m x 14m x 4m	CODOG, 30 knots	220	1976
Corvette – FSG	INHAÚMA	4	2,100 tons	96m x 11m x 4m	CODOG, 27 knots	120	1989
Corvette – FSG	BARROSO	1	2,400 tons	103m x 11m x 4m	CODOG, 30 knots	145	2008
Submarines							
Submarine – SSK	TIKUNA (Type 209 – modified)	1	1,600 tons	62m x 6m x 6m	Diesel-electric, 22 knots	40	2005
Submarine – SSK	TUPI (Type 209)	4	1,500 tons	61m x 6m x 6m	Diesel-electric, 22+ knots	30	1989
Major Amphibious Units							
Landing Ship Dock – LSD	CEARÁ (LSD-28)	2	12,000 tons	156m x 26m x 6m	Steam, 22 knots	345	1956

Brazilian 'Scorpènes' will be enlarged versions of the submarines already supplied to Chile and Malaysia, with a longer hull providing more fuel and refrigeration space to permit a greater endurance. Although the forward section of the first submarine is being built in France, construction of the other boats will be carried out entirely at a new facility in Brazil being established in alliance with DCNS' local partner, the conglomerate Odebrecht. The first boat will be handed over in 2017 – somewhat later than originally envisaged – with all four of the diesel-electric submarines likely to be in service by 2021. The additional nuclear-powered boat will be reliant on Brazilian-developed nuclear propulsion technology and her delivery date will inevitably be dependent on the speed with which this project advances.

The navy has also been expanding its patrol forces. *Macaé*, the first of the new 500-ton NPA-500 offshore patrol vessels based on the French CMN Vigilante 400 design, was delivered in December 2009. A further five ships of a class that might eventually number as many as twenty-seven units are under construction. Attention is now turning to plans for a larger NPA-1800 oceanic patrol type, with a number of European yards offering designs for the local fabrication of a class that will ultimately comprise between eight and twelve ships. A firm contract for an initial batch of three ships – with options for a further two – is likely to be placed before the end of 2010. However, the real draw for the international shipbuilding community is the much more lucrative programme to recapitalise Brazil's fleet of surface escorts. Amongst a number of potential suppliers are France and Italy, who are touting competing variants of their FREMM design. Both countries have deployed units of the preceding 'Horizon' class to Brazilian waters in recent months in support of their marketing campaigns. Although local construction is likely to be imposed on the

An impression of the stretched 'Scorpène' type submarine ordered for the Brazilian Navy from an alliance of France's DCNS and local conglomerate Odebrecht. Current plans envisage the first of four diesel-electric submarines being handed over in 2017. *(DCNS)*

successful contractor, Brazilian sources suggest that only 40 per cent domestic content will be required.

As the new projects will take time to deliver results, increased efforts are being made to refurbish and improve existing classes, most notably the purchase of upgrades and new torpedoes for the current submarine force. The sole carrier *São Paulo* (the former *Foch*) should also return to fleet service before the end of 2010 following conclusion of repairs and modifications that commenced as long ago as 2005. Initial post-refit sea trials commenced in December 2009 but work on the lateral catapult and condensers was not scheduled to complete until the following summer.[6]

MAJOR SOUTH AMERICAN NAVIES – CHILE

The *Armada de Chile* has possibly been the best equipped and trained of South America's 'ABC' (Argentina-Brazil-Chile) club of leading fleets in recent years, undergoing almost complete renewal in the first decade of the new Millennium. As such, the

Table 2.1.7: CHILEAN NAVY: PRINCIPAL UNITS AS AT MID-2010

TYPE	CLASS	NUMBER	TONNAGE	DIMENSIONS	PROPULSION	CREW	DATE
Principal Surface Escorts							
Frigate – FFG	**ALMIRANTE WILLIAMS** (Type 22-Batch 2)	1	5,500 tons	148m x 14m x 5m	COGOG, 30+ knots	260	1988
Frigate – FFG	**ALMIRANTE COCHRANE** (Type 23)	3	4,200 tons	133m x 16m x 5m	CODLAG, 28 knots	185	1990
Frigate – FFG	**CAPITÁN PRAT** (L class)	2	3,800 tons	131m x 15m x 4m	COGOG, 30 knots	200	1986
Frigate – FFG	**ALMIRANTE RIVEROS** (M class)	2	3,300 tons	122m x 14m x 4m	CODOG, 30 knots	160	1992
Submarines							
Submarine – SSK	**O'HIGGINS** ('Scorpène')	2	1,700 tons	66m x 6m x 6m	Diesel-electric, 22 knots	30	2005
Submarine – SSK	**THOMSON** (Type 209)	2	1,400 tons	60m x 6m x 6m	Diesel-electric, 22 knots	35	1984

principal surface units outlined in Table 2.1.7 are unlikely to see significant change in the short to medium term. Chile has, however, continued to invest in the replacing obsolete secondary tonnage. For example, the former US replenishment tanker *Andrew J Higgins* (T-AO-190) – now renamed *Almirante Montt* – arrived at Valparaiso in April 2010 to replace the obsolescent *Araucano*. At over 40,000 tons full load displacement, she is by far the largest vessel in Chile's fleet. The second Fassmer OPV80 *Piloto Pardo* class offshore patrol vessel *Comandante Toro* was delivered by ASMAR's Talcahuano yard in the summer of 2009.

Previous plans envisaged ASMAR constructing a second pair of offshore patrol vessels but these are now on hold following the shipyard's devastation in the February earthquake. As of the summer of 2010, it appeared that reasonable progress had been made in clearing up the aftermath of the resulting tsunami, most notably refloating the damaged fast attack craft *Chipana* on 1 June. However, permanent rebuilding will take several years and absorb funding previously allocated to fleet modernisation. ASMAR had also been successful in developing an expanding export business and there have been reports that some of this will be transferred to facilities in Argentina as part of a growing rapprochement between these former rivals.

MAJOR SOUTH AMERICAN NAVIES – PERU

Peru's fleet has also undergone a more limited recapitalisation in recent years through the acquisition of surplus Italian *Lupo* class frigates to supplement existing members of the class. Current modernisation plans appear to be focused on the progressive modernisation of the eight members of this class, along with the acquisition of two former USN *Newport* class tank landing ships. Refurbishment of the ships – *Fresno* (LST-1182) and *Racine* (LST-1191) – and an associated delivery of six UH-3H Sea

Chile's SAAR 4 fast attack craft *Casma* and *Angamos* on exercises in the Magellan Strait. The third Chilean member of the class, *Chipana*, was damaged by the February 2010 earthquake and tsunami that devastated the ASMAR facility in Talcahuano, where she was undergoing refit. *(US Navy)*

King helicopters – will cost around US$90m and will doubtless allow retirement of the veteran *Terrebonne Parish* tank landing ships still in service. The even older fleet flagship, *Almirante Grau* (the former Dutch *De Ruyter*), still remains on the fleet list as the last conventionally-armed cruiser in the world. She will reach the seventieth anniversary of her launch in December 2011 and seems a strong candidate for eventual preservation.

The unchanged details of Peru's principal fleet units are set out in Table 2.1.8.

OTHER SOUTH AMERICAN NAVIES

Amongst the other South American fleets, it is **Venezuela's** navy – officially the *Armada Bolivariana de Venezuela* – that is notable in seeing significant investment under President Hugo Chávez's somewhat militaristic regime. The main naval modernisation effort has been focused on the acquisition of more modern patrol ships for both the navy and the coast guard through a €1.7bn (US$2.1bn equivalent) contract for four 'POVZEE' type oceanic patrol vessels and four smaller 'BVL' littoral patrol ships signed with Spain's Navantia in 2005. The first of the BVL type – *Guaicamacuto* – was delivered to the coast guard on 2 March 2010, with a further two vessels expected to enter service by early 2011. The fourth ship is being built in Venezuela with Navantia's technical assistance and will probably take somewhat longer to complete. Of around 1,500 tons

Table 2.1.8: PERUVIAN NAVY: PRINCIPAL UNITS AS AT MID-2010

TYPE	CLASS	NUMBER	TONNAGE	DIMENSIONS	PROPULSION	CREW	DATE
Principal Surface Escorts							
Cruiser – CL	**ALMIRANTE GRAU** (DE RUYTER)	1	12,200 tons	187m x 17m x 7m	Steam, 32 knots	950	1953
Frigate – FFG	**CARVAJAL** (LUPO)	8	2,500 tons	112m x 12m x 4m	CODOG, 35 knots	185	1977
Submarines							
Submarine – SSK	**ANGAMOS** (Type 209)	6[1]	1,200 tons	54m x 6m x 6m	Diesel-electric, 22 knots	30	1980

Notes

1 Peru operates both T209/1100 and T209/1200 submarines. Details refer to the Type 209/1100 variant

Venezuela ordered four littoral patrol ships and four oceanic patrol vessels from Spain's Navantia in 2005. This image shows the first of the smaller littoral patrol type, *Guaicamacuto*, which was handed over on 2 March 2010. *(Navantia)*

displacement and 80m in length, the ships are capable of a maximum speed of 22 knots and are equipped with an Oto Melara 76mm 'Compact' gun as their main armament. The larger, 2,200-ton POVZEE type are 99m long and capable of 25 knots but have a similar main armament. First of class was launched with the name *Caribé* – currently used by a Type 209 submarine – on 24 June 2009 from Navantia's Puerto Real facility near Cadiz. All four vessels were expected to be in the water by July 2010, with deliveries scheduled to commence around the end of the year.

Venezuela has also been reportedly in the market for new submarines but, although negotiations for Russian Project 636 type 'Kilo' boats were thought to be well advanced in 2008, no further announcement has been made. Pending new acquisitions, the navy has been modernising its two existing German-built Type 209/1300 class boats. *Jane's Defence Weekly* has reported that first of class *Sábalo* was returned to the fleet on 11 November 2009 after five years in dock-yard hands. Work on sister boat *Caribé* is also underway and should be completed during 2011. Germany's HDW, which originally constructed the boats, has played a major sub-contracting role in the refits.

Venezuela's regional rival **Colombia** is carrying out a similar domestic modernisation scheme in conjunction with HDW for its own pair of Type 209/1200 boats. Neighbouring **Ecuador** has adopted a different approach, contracting Chile's ASMAR facility in Talcahuano for similar work on its own two Type 209/1300 submarines. It was therefore fortunate that *Shyri* escaped major damage when the shipyard was wrecked in Chile's February 2010 earthquake. However, it would seem difficult for the refit work to continue in the aftermath of the destruction and completion of the contract by another Latin American country, possibly Argentina, would seem a possibility.

Notes

1. Please see *Naval Operations Concept 2010 – Implementing The Maritime Strategy* (Washington DC, US Department of Defense, 2010) at www.navy.mil/maritime/noc/NOC201.pdf.

2. An excellent overview of the reasoning behind the Air-Sea Battle concept is contained in Andrew F Krepinevich's *Why AirSea Battle?* (Washington DC, Center for Strategic and Budgetary Assessments, 2010). It can be found on the CSBA's website at www.CSBAonline.org

3. The required technical specifications of the Arctic patrol vessels have now been drawn up under the terms of a contract awarded to BMT Fleet Technology Canada, an affiliate of the UK's BMT. Equipped with a gun armament and capable of embarking and operating a helicopter up to CH-148 size, they will have a designed service life of twenty-five years. Maximum speed will be at least 17 knots, whilst minimum range will be 6,800nm (12,580km).

4. The new NSPS is reviewed in the broader context of the challenges facing Canadian Procurement in Sharon Hobson's 'Stress tests', *Jane's Defence Weekly* – 26 May 2010 (Coulsdon, HIS Jane's, 2010).

5. See Director, Warfare Integration, *Report to Congress on Annual Long-Range Plan for Construction of Naval Vessels for FY2011* (Washington DC, Office of the Chief of Naval Operations, 2010). The CBO produces a useful analysis of each updated plan – please refer to *An Analysis of the Navy's Fiscal Year 2011 Shipbuilding Plan* (Washington DC, Congressional Budget Office, 2010) which can be found by searching www.cbo.gov. Its analysis suggests that the navy has under-budgeted the plan's costs by just under 20 per cent.

6. The Portuguese language *Poder Naval* website – www.naval.com.br – is an excellent source of information on Brazilian naval developments.

Author:
Conrad Waters

2.2 REGIONAL REVIEW

ASIA AND THE PACIFIC

The defining naval event of the last year so far as Asia's navies were concerned was inevitably the destruction of South Korea's *Po Hang* class corvette *Cheonan* on 26 March 2010. Her sinking off Baengnyeong Island in the Yellow Sea by what a team of international experts subsequently concluded was a North Korean torpedo sent relations on the Korean peninsula to a new low. The desire to avoid all-out conflict with its unstable and heavily-armed neighbour has meant that South Korea's response has inevitably been restrained. However, the event still has a broad significance both for South Korea's naval development and also for navies more generally.

At one level, the incident raises the question as to whether the Republic of Korea Navy's pursuit of oceanic 'blue water' naval ambitions has resulted in it ignoring the threat on its own doorstep. It is certainly embarrassing that a warship that – whilst elderly – was equipped with a range of anti-submarine systems was apparently destroyed in shallow waters by an adversary not generally regarded as being in the forefront of underwater maritime technology. There have already been reports in the Korean press that the navy might need to rebalance its strategy. This might see greater emphasis placed on countering the threat posed by the North Korea's extensive fleet of midget submarines and fast attack craft. At another level, the incident has wider lessons for the broader naval community, adding the risk of underwater attack to the range of asymmetric challenges facing the world's fleets. Certainly, many commentators believe that the importance of maintaining effective anti-submarine

capabilities has been neglected since the end of the Cold War. If the obsolescent equipment maintained by North Korea is capable of causing such destruction with seeming impunity, the threat presented by navies currently acquiring the latest generation of diesel-electric submarines may need to be re-evaluated.

The potential provided by underwater capabilities is certainly being recognised by a growing number of Asian countries. In addition to Australia's plan to double the size of its submarine flotilla to twelve vessels, Vietnam has signed a deal worth a total of up to US$3.2bn in December 2009 for six Project 636 'Kilo' class patrol submarines and associated weaponry. Another Asian maritime power considering the creation of underwater forces for the first time is Thailand. The kingdom is reportedly seeking an initial capability based on two second-hand boats in spite of facing considerable political uncertainties in order to avoid being left behind in what is fast becoming a regional underwater arms race.[1] Meanwhile, neighbouring Malaysia has taken delivery of its own submarine force with the arrival of the first of its two 'Scorpène' class boats, *Tunku Abdul Rahman*, in September 2009. When combined with the refurbishment of Singapore's A-17 *Archer* (former Swedish *Västergötland*) class boats, the series production of Japan's AIP (air-independent propulsion) equipped *Soryu* class and ongoing construction of submarines in both China and South Korea, regional investment in underwater systems is formidable. It is also noteworthy that the core technologies used in nearly all these submarines – if not the boats

themselves – continues to be essentially of European origin, with China seemingly being the principal exception. Reliance on so much imported technology will undoubtedly result in a considerable additional burden in establishing an appropriate local support and maintenance infrastructure if these new underwater assets are to be used effectively.

To some extent, this is one of the largest question marks hanging over the much-vaunted expansion of Asian naval capabilities. Although potent weapons systems have been acquired, it remains a moot point whether the necessary logistical or training back-up is in place to ensure their safe and efficient operation. One particular cause for concern is the amount of tonnage either damaged or written off by accident or fire in recent years. Even the most experienced regional fleets have suffered from this trend. For example, Japan's helicopter-carrying destroyer *Kurama* (DDH-144) suffered damage from a collision and resulting spectacular conflagration in the Kammon Strait on 27 October 2009, thereby following her sister *Shirane* (DDH-143) – hit by an onboard fire in December 2007 – into dockyard hands. More serious was the destruction by fire of the Malaysian Navy's *Newport* class tank landing ship *Sri Inderapura* on 8/9 October 2009 after an inadequate initial response from the ship's duty officers. Whilst such incidents are by no means the sole prerogative of Asia's fleets, it will be interesting to observe whether further increases in the incidence of 'self harm' can be avoided as the extent and tempo of deployments expands.

The shattered stern section of the South Korean corvette *Cheonan* being raised from the waters off Baengnyeong Island in the Yellow Sea on 15 April 2010. The ship's loss to a probable North Korean submarine attack holds significant lessons for both South Korea's and the world's navies. *(AFP)*

Table 2.2.1: FLEET STRENGTHS IN ASIA AND THE PACIFIC – LARGER NAVIES (MID-2010)

COUNTRY	AUSTRALIA	CHINA	INDONESIA	JAPAN	KOREA S	SINGAPORE	TAIWAN	THAILAND
Support/Helicopter Carrier (CVS/CVH)	–	–	–	1	–	–	–	1
Strategic Missile Submarine (SSBN)	–	3	–	–	–	–	–	–
Attack Submarine (SSN)	–	5	–	–	–	–	–	–
Patrol Submarine (SSK/SS)	6	55	2	16	12	4	4	–
Fleet Escort (DDG/FFG)	12	45	6	41	19	6	26	8
Patrol Escort/Corvette (FFG/FSG/FS)	–	30	24	6	25	6	–	11
Missile Armed Attack Craft (PGG/PTG)	–	75	4	6	1	–	c.50	6
Mine Countermeasures Vessel (MCMV)	6	20	12	30	9	4	12	6
Major Amphibious Units (LHD/LPD/LSD)	–	1	4	3	1	4	1	–

Note: Chinese numbers approximate; Taiwanese fast attack craft numbers are fluctuating as new KH-6 class replaces many of the existing 'Hai Ou' type.

The Australian frigates *Darwin* (FFG-7 class) and *Ballarat* (*Anzac* class) pictured at anchor in March 2010 during a fleet concentration period. The two classes represent Australia's principal classes of surface warship. *(Royal Australian Navy)*

MAJOR REGIONAL NAVAL POWERS – AUSTRALIA

The Royal Australian Navy is currently experiencing something of a temporary hiatus in its development. Previous procurement programmes have delivered the current principal fleet units listed in Table 2.2.2, viz. four modernised FFG-7 *Adelaide* air-defence and eight *Anzac* general-purpose frigates, supplemented by six *Collins* class patrol submarines. New construction ordered as a result of the 2000 Defence White Paper and 2006-16 Defence Capability Plan holds out the prospect of potent new destroyers (under project SEA 4000) and amphibious shipping (under project JP2048) in due course.[2] Further expansion is planned over the longer term. In the meantime, completion of the FFG-7's modernisation leaves upgrades to the *Anzac* and *Collins* the principal short-term focus.

Although it will be several years before the new units currently under construction are commis-sioned, 2010 has seen good progress made with these projects. Fabrication of blocks for the three new *Hobart* class destroyers – based on the Spanish Navantia F-100 design – is now underway at three separate locations in Australia. Assembly of completed hull blocks at ASC in Adelaide is scheduled to begin in the summer of 2011 prior to delivery of the first of class by the Air Warfare Destroyer (AWD) Alliance at the end of 2014. Lockheed Martin commenced testing the first completed Aegis weapon system for the ships – destined for *Hobart* – as far back as August 2009. Amphibious construction is also moving ahead. The keel for the first of two *Canberra* class amphibious assault ships derived from Spain's *Juan Carlos I* was laid at Navantia's Fene-Ferrol shipyard on 23 September 2009 prior to an expected 2011 launch. She will be delivered to BAE System's Williamstown facility in Australia during 2012 for final outfitting, followed by her sister some two years later.

The next stage of the Royal Australian Navy's development is heralded by the 'Force 2030' set out in the defence white paper published in May 2009. Its key elements are a doubling of the submarine force through orders for twelve replacements for the existing *Collins* class (project SEA 1000); the eventual replacement of the *Anzac*s on a one-for-one basis by a new anti-submarine frigate (project SEA 5000); and the construction of a new class of twenty offshore combatant vessels to replace existing patrol and mine-countermeasures assets (project SEA 1180). The last two projects have a degree of commonality with the British Royal Navy's planned Type 26 and C3 future surface combatants and it is therefore not surprising that the UK and Australia have held preliminary talks to establish whether there are grounds for collaboration with regards to their respective programmes.

Present modernisation efforts are focused on progressive upgrades to existing fleet units, not least

Table 2.2.2: ROYAL AUSTRALIAN NAVY: PRINCIPAL UNITS AS AT MID-2010

TYPE	CLASS	NUMBER	TONNAGE	DIMENSIONS	PROPULSION	CREW	DATE
Principal Surface Escorts							
Frigate – FFG	**ADELAIDE** (FFG-7)	4	4,200 tons	138m x 14m x 5m	COGAG, 30 knots	210	1980
Frigate – FFG	**ANZAC**	8	3,600 tons	118m x 15m x 4m	CODOG, 28 knots	175	1996
Submarines							
Submarine – SSK	**COLLINS**	6	3,400 tons	78m x 8m x 7m	Diesel-electric, 20 knots	45	1996

the troubled *Collins* class submarines. These have suffered from poor levels of availability through maintenance issues and crew shortages. Only three fully-trained crews are reportedly available at the current time pending completion of plans to step up an additional boat's complement at the end of 2011. The practical value of this initiative has, however, to be questionable given that ongoing equipment defects have meant that it has proved impossible to keep even three boats fully operational for considerable periods over the last couple of years. A well-established programme of enhancements – not least installation of a replacement combat system – is being implemented on a rolling basis across the class to improve operational effectiveness. The support infrastructure available to ASC, which built and now maintains the submarines, is also being upgraded. However, these initiatives are taking time to deliver improvements and an Australian Submarine Program Office (ASPO) was therefore established in February 2010 to improve focus on availability and thereby speed progress. The new organisation was involved in the final stages of the full cycle docking period of *Dechaineux*, which returned to the fleet in May 2010 in a welcome boost to available numbers. The refit included the new Raytheon AN/BYG-1 combat system, provision for US Mk48 heavyweight torpedoes and implementation of a Special Forces delivery capability.

Meanwhile, *Anzac* class frigate enhancements have reached another stage with the commencement of work on *Perth* in January 2010 to upgrade radar and combat management systems under the ASMD anti-ship missile defence programme (project SEA 1448 Phase 2). The most significant element of the upgrade is the installation of CEA Technologies' locally-built, six-faced CEAFAR active phased-array radar and associated CEAMOUNT illuminators to allow simultaneous engagement of multiple targets by Evolved Sea Sparrow Missiles (ESSM). The ship's modernisation will be completed in 2011 and will be extended to all eight of the class under an A$158m (US$140m) programme if sea trials of the first system are successful.

MAJOR REGIONAL NAVAL POWERS – CHINA

After a phase of very rapid integration of new equipment during the middle of the first decade of the new millennium, China's People's Liberation Army Navy (PLAN) has also been experiencing a doubtless temporary slow down in its pace of technological change. It would seem that the navy's recent emphasis has been on testing out its new equipment in an operational context, most notably through frequent deployments of small task groups on anti-piracy operations in the Indian Ocean. This expansion in geographical reach has also been accompanied by a more assertive regional stance, a stance reflected in comments made to the *Financial Times* newspaper by the commander of US forces in the Pacific, Admiral Robert F Willard, in May 2010. Whilst Willard indicated that China's growing regional influence was largely viewed positively, he suggested China's extensive territorial claims were '…generating increasing concern broadly across the region and require address…'. It is certainly the case that there is, at best, a degree of ambivalence towards China's growing military capabilities, which is one of the key factors behind the ongoing regional arms build-up referenced in several parts of this book.

International sensibilities are particularly susceptible to China's increasingly open ambitions to develop an aircraft carrier strike capability, which is currently largely the sole prerogative of the US Navy in the region. There have been ongoing reports of progress with the refurbishment of the former Soviet Project 1143.5/6 *Kuznetsov* carrier, *Varyag*, which has been subject to extensive work since arrival at Dalian in 2002. The ship emerged from a year in dry dock in March 2010 with a modified island structure that

Australia's *Collins* class submarine *Dechaineux* pictured on her return to the fleet in May 2010 after completion of a full-cycle docking period and combat system upgrade. *(Royal Australian Navy)*

Ongoing modernisation of the Royal Australian Navy's *Anzac* class frigates will see them being equipped with CEA Technologies' locally-built CEAFAR active phased-array radar to provide improved self-defence capabilities. This impression gives a good indication of the new radar's purpose. *(CEA Technologies)*

Table 2.2.3: PEOPLE'S LIBERATION ARMY NAVY: PRINCIPAL UNITS AS AT MID-2010

TYPE	CLASS	NUMBER	TONNAGE	DIMENSIONS	PROPULSION	CREW	DATE
Principal Surface Escorts							
Destroyer – DDG	Type 051C **SHENYANG** ('Luzhou')	2	7,100 tons	155m x 17m x 6m	Steam, 29 knots	Unknown	2006
Destroyer – DDG	Type 052C **LANZHOU** ('Luyang II')	2	6,500 tons	154m x 17m x 6m	CODOG, 28 knots	280	2004
Destroyer – DDG	Type 052B **GUANGZHOU** ('Luyang I')	2	6,000 tons	154m x 17m x 6m	CODOG, 29 knots	280	2004
Destroyer – DDG	Project 956E/EM **HANGZHOU** (Sovremenny)	4	8,000 tons	156m x 17m x 6m	Steam, 32 knots	300	1999
Destroyer – DDG	Type 051B **SHENZHEN** ('Luhai')	1	6,000 tons	154m x 16m x 6m	Steam, 31 knots	250	1998
Destroyer – DDG	Type 052 **HARBIN** ('Luhu')	2	4,800 tons	143m x 15m x 5m	CODOG, 31 knots	260	1994
Plus c. 10 additional obsolescent destroyers of Type 051 **JINAN** ('Luda') class							
Frigate – FFG	Type 054A **XUZHOU** ('Jiangkai II')	6	4,100 tons	132m x 15m x 5m	CODAD, 28 knots	190	2008
Frigate – FFG	Type 054 **MA'ANSHAN** ('Jiangkai I')	2	4,000 tons	132m x 15m x 5m	CODAD, 28 knots	190	2005
Frigate – FFG	Type 053 H2G/H3 **ANQING** ('Jiangwei I/II')	14	2,500 tons	112m x 12m x 5m	CODAD, 27 knots	170	1992
Plus c.25-30 additional obsolescent frigates of Type 053 H/H1/H1G/H2 **XIAMEN** ('Jianghu') classes							
Submarines							
Submarine – SSBN	Type 094 ('Jin')	2+	9,000 tons	133m x 11m x 8m	Nuclear, 20+ knots	Unknown	2008
Submarine – SSBN	Type 092 XIA ('Xia')	1	6,500 tons	120m x 10m x 8m	Nuclear, 22 knots	140	1987
Submarine – SSN	Type 093 ('Shang')	2+	6,000 tons	107m x 11m x 8m	Nuclear, 30 knots	100	2006
Submarine – SSN	Type 091 ('Han')	3	5,500 tons	106m x 10m x 7m	Nuclear, 25 knots	75	1974
Submarine – SSK	Type 039A/Type 041 ('Yuan')	2+	2,500 tons	75m x 8m x 5m	AIP, 20+ knots	Unknown	2006'
Submarine – SSK	Type 039/039G ('Song')	10-16	2,300 tons	75m x 8m x 5m	Diesel-electric, 22 knots	60	1999
Submarine – SSK	Project 877 EKM/636 ('Kilo')	12	3,000 tons	73m x 10m x 7m	Diesel-electric, 20 knots	55	1995

Plus c. 25 obsolescent patrol submarines of the Project 033 ('Romeo' Class) and Type 035 ('Ming' Class) designs.

appears to be designed to accommodate fixed multi-function phased-array radar panels similar to those installed in the Type 052C *Lanzhou* class destroyers. Deployment from around 2012 onwards could well be followed by series construction of an indigenous design that would inevitably impact the global balance of maritime power. New maritime aircraft will be required to operate from the ships, with a purchase of Russian SU-33 multi-role fighters or development of a Chinese J-11B derivative the most likely possibilities.[3]

It seems likely that new classes of surface escort will be evolved to accompany any domestically-produced carriers given that, as of yet, there has been no follow up to the six indigenous destroyers of the Type 052B, Type 052C and Type 051C delivered in three batches of two each during 2004-6. Recent surface construction has focused on smaller Type 054 and Type 054A frigates, the latter of which appear to have been ordered in batches of four from shipyards in Shanghai and Guangzhou. Eight of these frigates – along with the two Type 054 class ships – will be in commission by the start of 2011. This will give the PLAN a reasonably numerous force of modern general-purpose surface combatants. Reportedly capable of speeds in excess of 28 knots from a licensed MAN group CODAD (combined diesel and diesel) power plant, both classes benefit from extensive stealth features and a balanced range of weaponry. The later 'A' variants incorporate significant use of the latest Russian-designed sensors. Further construction of this or a modified design can be expected.

There has been little news of further PLAN submarine production following the introduction of small numbers of Type 094 nuclear-powered strategic missile submarines, Type 093 nuclear-powered attack submarines and Type 039/41 diesel-electric patrol submarines in the 2006-8 timeframe. As for the surface fleet, it may be that the success of these new types is being evaluated before advancing to series production of a modified type. This also seems to be the approach taken with amphibious shipping. A solitary Type 071 LPD-type amphibious transport dock was commissioned in 2007 but it is only recently that reports have begun to circulate that a new amphibious vessel had been laid down in the Shanghai HuDong Shipyard that built the lead ship. China also plans to acquire Project 1232.2 'Zubr' landing craft air cushioned (LCAC) heavy hovercraft in a further expansion of amphibious capability.

Further details of current principal fleet units are provided in Table 2.2.3.

MAJOR REGIONAL NAVAL POWERS – JAPAN

Japan's current naval strength is summarised in Table 2.2.4. The Japan Maritime Self Defence Force (JMSDF) arguably remains the dominant regional naval power, albeit it has historically been structured to act as a complement to capabilities provided by US Navy forces deployed in the Pacific rather than a fully-rounded, independent force. The underlying political and military relationship with the United States seems likely to remain a dominant factor in the foreseeable future in spite of occasional friction. However, the last decade has seen something of a shift from the navy's focus on providing powerful anti-submarine forces to protect lines of communication – and help screen US Navy reinforcements – in favour of development of a more balanced fleet. The changed environment caused by the collapse of Soviet power is undoubtedly one of the key factors behind this evolution in structure. Other factors are an increasing willingness to undertake more wide-ranging deployments as unhappy memories of the Second World War fade, coupled with a reappraisal of threats that places more emphasis on the challenge posed by, particularly, North Korea and, possibly, China. Given a largely static defence budget, there has been an emphasis on quality over quantity. In effect, a modest shrinkage in overall fleet size will be outweighed by deployment of more capable units. The most evident manifestation of this new approach has been recent construction of large helicopter-carrying 'destroyers' and AIP-equipped submarines, as well as the modernisation and enlargement of the flotilla of Aegis-equipped air-defence escorts to provide an embryonic theatre ballistic missile defence (TBMD) capability.

Of all these developments, it has been the acquisition of a capacity for TBMD that has been most pressing due to North Korea's active pursuit of both ballistic missile and nuclear weapons programmes. The four older *Kongou* (DDG-173) Aegis destroyers have been upgraded to deploy the enhanced

The Japanese 'helicopter destroyer' *Hyuga* in company with the US Navy aircraft carrier *George Washington* (CVN-73). A sister-ship, *Ise*, will commission during 2011 and larger vessels are planned as part of the Japanese Maritime Self Defence Force's transition to a more balanced fleet. *(US Navy)*

Table 2.2.4: JAPAN MARITIME SELF-DEFENCE FORCE: PRINCIPAL UNITS AS AT MID-2010

TYPE	CLASS	NUMBER	TONNAGE	DIMENSIONS	PROPULSION	CREW	DATE
Support and Helicopter Carriers							
Helicopter Carrier – DDH	**HYUGA** (DDH-181)	1	18,000 tons	197m x 33m x 7m	COGAG, 30 knots	340	2009
Principal Surface Escorts							
Helicopter Destroyer – DDH	**SHIRANE** (DDH-143)	2	7,500 tons	159m x 18m x 5m	Steam, 32 knots	350	1980
Helicopter Destroyer – DDH	**HARUNA** (DDH-141)	1	6,900 tons	153m x 18m x 5m	Steam, 31 knots	370	1973
Destroyer – DDG	**ATAGO** (DDG-177)	2	10,000 tons	165m x 21m x 6m	COGAG, 30 knots	300	2007
Destroyer – DDG	**KONGOU** (DDG-173)	4	9,500 tons	161m x 21m x 6m	COGAG, 30 knots	300	1993
Destroyer – DDG	**HATAKAZE** (DDG-171)	2	6,300 tons	150m x 16m x 5m	COGAG, 30 knots	260	1986
Destroyer – DDG	**TAKANAMI** (DD-110)	5	5,300 tons	151m x 17m x 5m	COGAG, 30 knots	175	2003
Destroyer – DDG	**MURASAME** (DD-101)	9	5,200 tons	151m x 17m x 5m	COGAG, 30 knots	165	1996
Destroyer – DDG	**ASAGIRI** (DD-151)	6 (2)	4,300 tons	137m x 15m x 5m	COGAG, 30 knots	220	1988
Destroyer – DDG	**HATSUYUKI** (DD-122)	10 (1)	3,800 tons	130m x 14m x 4m	COGOG, 30 knots	200	1982
Frigate – FFG	**ABUKUMA** (DE-229)	6	2,500 tons	109m x 13m x 4m	CODOG, 27 knots	120	1989
Submarines							
Submarine – SSK	**SORYU** (SS-501)	2	4,200 tons	84m x 9m x 8m	AIP, 20 knots+	65	2009
Submarine – SSK	**OYASHIO** (SS-590)	11	4,000 tons	82m x 9m x 8m	Diesel-electric, 20 knots+	70	1998
Submarine – SSK	**HARUSHIO** (SS-583)	3 (2)	3,300 tons	77m x 10m x 8m	Diesel-electric, 20 knots+	75	1990
Major Amphibious Units							
Landing Platform Dock – LPD	**OSUMI** (LST-4001)	3	14,000 tons	178m x 26m x 6m	Diesel, 22 knots	135	1998

Note: Figures in brackets refer to trials or training ships.

Table 2.2.5: RECENT JMSDF WARSHIP PROCUREMENT

FINANCIAL YEAR	2006		2007		2008		2009		2010	
	NUMBER	COST[1]	NUMBER	COST[1]	NUMBER	COST[1]	NUMBER	COST[1]	NUMBER	COST[1]
Destroyer (DDH/CVH)	1	US$1,025m	0	–	0	–	0	–	1	US$1,200m
Destroyer (DD)	0	–	1	US$785m	1	US$725m	2	US$1,525m	0	–
Submarine (SSK)	1	US$590m	1	US$560m	1	US$535m	0	–	1	US$555m
Minesweeper (MCMV)	1	US$165m	0	–	1	US$165m	1	US$160m	0	–
Auxiliary Ships	0	–	1	US$175m	0	–	1	US$300m	0	
Other Expense[2]	–	US$330m	–	US$330m	–	US$85m	–	US$5m	–	US$10m
Total	3	US$2,110m	3	US$1,850m	3	US$1,510m	4	US$1,990m	2	US$1,765m

Notes:

1 Japanese yen converted into US$ at a fixed rate of Japanese yen 100 = US$1.05.

2 Relates largely to update of Aegis destroyers for TBMD role, including purchase of SM-3 missiles.

The Japanese destroyer *Kurama* and the South Korean container ship *Carina Star* anchored in Japan's Kammon Strait after a collision and fire during the night of 27 October 2009. Severe damage to *Kurama*'s bow is clearly visible. *(AFP – Jiji Press)*

Standard SM-3 missile at yearly intervals during 2007-10. *Kirishima* (DDG-174) will be the last to complete the relevant modifications prior to trials in the second half of 2010. The two more recent *Atago* (DDG-177) class destroyers, the only other Aegis ships in the JMSDF, would also seem likely candidates for enhancement but this has yet to be confirmed. In the meantime, Japan made up for a failed trial of an SM-3 interception by *Chokai* (DDG-176) in November 2008 with the successful destruction of a separating ballistic missile target by *Myoko* over the US Navy's Pacific missile ranges on 28 October 2009. However, the overall ballistic defence effort, which includes the use of land-based Patriot PAC-3 missiles for local defence, has been expensive. Total costs to March 2010 are in the region of US$8bn, of which c. US$2bn relates to Aegis upgrades and the purchase of SM-3 missiles.

Peak expenditure on Aegis destroyer modernisation has now passed. However, as demonstrated by Table 2.2.5, recent warship procurement funding of around US$1.5bn to US$2.0bn p.a. has only proved sufficient to purchase an average of three warships each year. Although future plans will have to await publication of a delayed 'Mid Term Defense Program' document, it seems inevitable that fleet size will fall significantly. Indeed, a gap in destroyer procurement in FY2005 has meant that 2010 was unusual in so far as no major new surface ship joined the fleet. However, the new helicopter-carrying destroyer/light aircraft carrier *Hyuga* (DDH-181) that was commissioned in March 2009 will be joined by a sister, *Ise* (DDH-182), in the first half of 2011. The 2010 budget makes provision for acquisition of a larger variant (19,500 tons compared with 14,000 tons standard displacement) that will probably form one of a pair intended to replace the two existing *Shirane* class helicopter destroyers. The 2010 budget makes provision for their early retirement, ostensibly to release crew for other ships. However, it is possible that the damage referenced in the opening paragraphs has also played a part in this decision.

Current surface construction is largely focused on the 19DD (DD-115) destroyer class, four of which were approved between 2007 and 2009. The first of these ships was laid down by Mitsubishi Heavy Industries on 17 July 2009. Displacing around 5,000 tons in standard condition and equipped with COGAG propulsion, these ships will reinforce the established eight-strong escort flotillas centred on the

The remaining first-generation JMSDF destroyers are being paid off early prior to arrival of their carrier-like replacements. This is *Hiei* pictured alongside the US Navy destroyer *Mustin* (DDG-89) on 11 June 2010 during a photo opportunity celebrating the fiftieth anniversary of the Japanese-US alliance. *(US Navy)*

helicopter carriers and Aegis destroyers. Submarine procurement remains focused on the AIP-equipped *Soryu* class, the second of which – *Unryu* – was delivered by Kawasaki Heavy Industries on 25 March 2010. Whilst the FY2009 defence budget omitted a submarine purchase in a blow to Japan's two submarine builders, a further boat was included in the 2010 plan. Japan has historically maintained a youthful submarine fleet, with boats leaving front-line service after only sixteen years in the fleet. There is scope to slow the production 'drumbeat' if the budget requires, albeit at industry's expense.

MAJOR REGIONAL NAVAL POWERS – SOUTH KOREA

The Republic of Korea Navy's principal units are listed in Table 2.2.6. The main addition to the fleet over the past year has been the third Type 214A submarine, *An Jung-Geun*, which was delivered by Hyundai Heavy Industries (HHI) on 1 December 2009. A contract for the licensed production of a second batch of six of these AIP-equipped boats was agreed with Germany's HDW during 2008. Construction is being shared between HHI and its rival Daewoo, which was allocated the first of the new batch. HHI subsequently gained a contract for the second boat in July 2009. It seems likely that fabrication will continue at annual intervals prior to transition to the indigenous KSS-III design.

The deployment of AIP-equipped submarines is part of the navy's broader focus on developing 'blue water' capabilities that took a more tangible form on 1 February 2010 with the formal inauguration of the 7th Mobile Fleet, heralded as the navy's first rapid deployment force. It is eventually intended to comprise two squadrons, each headed by a KDX-III *Sejongdaewang-Ham* Aegis-equipped destroyer supported by three of the earlier and smaller KDX-II destroyer type. Submarines and maritime patrol aircraft will also be assigned to the force as necessary. The navy's second KDX-III class ship, *Yulgok Yi l*, had not yet been delivered when the new fleet was created but should have completed sea trials before the end of 2010. A third ship will be delivered during

Table 2.2.6: REPUBLIC OF KOREA NAVY: PRINCIPAL UNITS AS AT MID-2010

TYPE	CLASS	NUMBER	TONNAGE	DIMENSIONS	PROPULSION	CREW	DATE
Principal Surface Escorts							
Destroyer – DDG	KDX-III **SEJONGDAEWANG-HAM**	1	10,000 tons	166m x 21m x 6m	COGAG, 30 knots	300	2008
Destroyer – DDG	KDX-II **CHUNGMUGONG YI SUN-SHIN**	6	5,500 tons	150m x 17m x 5m	CODOG, 30 knots	200	2003
Destroyer – DDG	KDX-I **GWANGGAETO-DAEWANG**	3	3,900 tons	135m x 14m x 4m	CODOG, 30 knots	170	1998
Frigate – FFG	**ULSAN**	9	2,300 tons	102m x 12m x 4m	CODOG, 35 knots	150	1981
Corvette – FSG	**PO HANG**	22	1,200 tons	88m x 10m x 3m	CODOG, 32 knots	95	1984
Corvette – FS	**DONG HAE**	3	1,100 tons	78m x 10m x 3m	CODOG, 32 knots	95	1982
Submarines							
Submarine – SSK	KSS-2 **SON WON-IL** (Type 214)	3	1,800 tons	65m x 6m x 6m	AIP, 20+ knots	30	2007
Submarine – SSK	KSS-1 **CHANG BOGO** (Type 209)	9	1,300 tons	56m x 6m x 6m	Diesel-electric, 22 knots	35	1993
Major Amphibious Units							
Amph. Assault Ship – LHD	LPX **DOKDO**	1	18,900 tons	200m x 32m x 7m	Diesel, 22 knots	425	2007

2012. Construction work has started on a major new naval base on Jeju Island in the Korea Strait that is eventually intended to form the fleet's main operating base from the middle of the decade onwards.

The navy would like to acquire more Aegis-type ships to bolster its surface flotillas. Having first attempted to secure approval of funding for more of the costly KDX-III class ships, its focus appears to have shifted to a smaller KDX-IIA type equipped with the AN/SPY-1F-based lightweight Aegis system used in Norway's *Fridtjof Nansen*. However, it was far from certain that this project would find favour before the *Cheonan* incident and looks even less likely afterwards. It would therefore not be surprising if greater emphasis is placed on development of smaller types such as the new FFX patrol frigate, a smaller 2,300 tons standard displacement patrol frigate more focused on operations in coastal areas. HHI was awarded a contract to construct the prototype of an initial batch of six vessels in December 2008, which are intended to replace the existing *Ulsan* from around 2015. However, many more will be needed to replace the *Dong Hae* and *Po Hang* class corvettes – that are already starting to decommission – on a like for like basis. Another programme likely to benefit from North Korea's apparent aggression is construction of the 400-ton PKX fast attack craft. Two additional ships will join the existing *Yoon Young-Ha* in the second half of 2010 and more are under construction. Recent reports suggest that plans to acquire new anti-submarine helicopters have also been given added urgency.

The destruction of *Cheonan* has had a negligible impact on the regional naval balance given that the ship was of a type that is already starting to be phased out. However, it is an enormous shock to a force that has generally maintained the upper hand in encounters with its North Korean neighbour, with which the South remains technically at war. Whilst the precise details of the incident have been subject to some dispute, what is clear is that *Cheonan* was patrolling South Korean territorial waters off Baengnyeong Island on the evening of 26 March 2010 when split in half by an underwater explosion. The two halves sank rapidly in shallow water and only fifty-eight of the 104 crew onboard survived. The ship's wreckage was subsequently recovered in a major salvage operation assisted by US Navy forces and subjected to an examination that included international experts from Australia,

A view of the first South Korean KDX-III destroyer *Sejongdaewang-Ham* at sea in company with the Type 209 patrol submarine *Lee Eokgi*. A further two vessels are under construction to form the core of the newly inaugurated 7th Mobile Fleet's 'blue water' squadrons. *(US Navy)*

The Hyundai Heavy Industries-built South Korean Coast Guard salvage vessel *3009*, which features an innovative hybrid diesel-electric propulsion system. In common with many Asian navies. South Korea's navy is backed up by a powerful coast guard. *(Hyundai Heavy Industries)*

Sweden, the United Kingdom and the United States. Their investigations concluded that the explosion was the result of the detonation of a homing torpedo below and to the left of the ship's gas turbine room. The resulting shockwave and bubble effect caused the ship to split apart around the access trunks to the machinery spaces. The discovery of torpedo parts matching a North Korean heavyweight CHT-0D torpedo at the site strongly suggested the North's involvement, a conclusion reinforced by analysis of the movements of 'Sango' diesel-electric and midget submarines used by that country around the time of the incident.[4] However, the conclusion has not been universally accepted, with some Chinese sources suggesting an accidental mine explosion as a more likely explanation.

Whilst the impact of *Cheonan*'s loss will be most keenly felt by the navy, it also has implications for the Korean Coast Guard's search and rescue assets. In common with the coast guards of several other Asian countries, not least Japan, this is a large and capable force with assets that would be the envy of many minor navies. Its most significant recent addition is a new 3,000-ton salvage ship delivered by HHI in February 2010. It carries a small-calibre gun and is capable of helicopter operation. The vessel is significant in featuring a hybrid diesel-electric propulsion system. For low-speed operation, propulsion is by means of electric power produced by the ship's generators, with the main diesels only being used at higher

speeds. The system is being touted as a cost-effective and environmentally-friendly design suitable for meeting Asia's growing need for effective 'constabulary' vessels.

OTHER REGIONAL FLEETS

Brunei: Further details are emerging about the new coastal patrol vessels being acquired from Germany's Lürssen in replacement for the cancelled deal for *Nakhoda Ragam* corvettes from the UK's BAE Systems. It appears that four of the new *Itjihad* class will be built to replace the previously planned ships but that they will be considerably smaller and less sophisticated. Overall length is in the region of 40m, whilst armament will comprise a light gun possibly supplemented by surface-to-surface missiles. They will be joined by a class of larger offshore patrol vessels, which will be fitted with a 57mm gun and be capable of helicopter operation.

Indonesia: The Indonesian Navy's recent history has been marked by a struggle to maintain effective maritime security throughout its country's extensive waters against a backdrop of modest naval expenditure. This has resulted in something of a conflict between the desire to maintain a reasonably effective front-line fleet to achieve a degree of balance with neighbouring fleets whilst funding sufficient patrol and surveillance assets to police the vast Indonesian archipelago. The compromise it adopted has been to

purchase small numbers of high-quality warships from overseas countries and to acquire larger numbers of less-capable vessels for second-line duties. These latter ships are increasingly domestically produced, with state-owned PT PAL of Surabaya the leading local shipyard engaged in this endeavour.

The front-line fleet is inevitably dominated by the four Sigma type *Diponegoro* class corvettes recently built by the Dutch Damen shipyards. The last of these, *Frans Kaisiepo*, was completed in March 2009 but not formally commissioned until 9 February 2010. Current plans envisage additional corvettes being licence-built by PT PAL. Shipyards in Italy and Russia as well as the Netherlands are reportedly in contention for a technology transfer deal that could be signed before the end of 2010. The remainder of the surface flotillas continue to comprise the six former Dutch *Leander/Van Speijk* class frigates first commissioned in the 1960s, as well as the three more modern *Fatahillah* class corvettes. The underwater flotilla of two ageing Type 209/1300 submarines has been an ongoing priority for modernisation but various plans for the acquisition of new and second-hand submarines have been repeatedly deferred for lack of money.

There has been more progress with renewal of patrol and amphibious forces, albeit delivery of locally-built c.100-ton PC-36 and PC-40 coastal patrol boats has not been sufficient to cater for all requirements. The navy's flotillas of patrol vessels are

Indonesia's offshore patrol forces are dominated by obsolescent corvettes of former East German origin acquired after the reunification of Germany. This is *Wiratno* (ex *Perleberg*) on exercises with the Royal Australian Navy in April 2010. *(Royal Australian Navy)*

Malaysia's first submarine, *Tunku Abdul Rahman*, pictured during sea trials. She arrived in Malaysian waters in September 2009. *(DCNS)*

therefore a rather motley collection, including vessels originating from Australia, South Korea and the former East Germany. The latest additions are two *Waspada* class fast attack craft donated by Brunei. Amphibious forces are, however, starting to show greater signs of homogeneity. The first domestically produced multi-role amphibious transport dock, *Banjarmasin*, was handed over by PT PAL on 28 November 2009, joining two Korean-built sister-ships (and a 'hospital ship' half-sister) in Indonesian service. A fourth ship, *Banda Aceh*, was launched on 19 March 2010 and should enter service in 2011. Displacing 7,300 tons in standard condition, the class is capable of deploying up to 218 troops by two personnel landing craft and up to five embarked helicopters. Maximum speed is just 15 knots but a maximum range of 10,000nm (18,500km) is possible from the diesel propulsion system. The next priority appears to be the construction of a class of smaller tank landing ships to replace the ancient US wartime LST-1 that will shortly be decommissioned. At least one of these ships served in the 1944 D-Day landings in Normandy.

Malaysia: The Royal Malaysian Navy faces similar challenges to its Indonesian counterpart in so far as it also has to balance its desire to operate the most capable types of surface ships and submarines against the need to maintain a large fleet of less sophisticated vessels to patrol Malaysia's relatively extensive territorial waters. In general terms, however, it has benefited from a comparatively positive funding regime when set against its larger neighbour: Malaysia's defence budget is around 80 per cent of Indonesia's in spite of having little more than a tenth of its population. It has therefore managed to achieve more, particularly in terms of maintaining a modern and effective force of major fleet units.

The most significant recent development has been the establishment of a small, two-boat flotilla of Franco-Spanish 'Scorpène' type submarines. The first, *Tunku Abdul Rahman*, was handed over by builders DCNS in January 2009, arriving in Malaysian waters in September of that year. Subsequent sea trials have not been altogether straightforward, as defects in the high-pressure air system caused a temporary prohibition on diving that extended sea trials. However, the issue appears to have been resolved quickly and the second of class, *Tun Razak*, is expected to arrive at the Sepanggar submarine base established to support the class in early summer 2010. A c. US$35m contract

The Royal New Zealand Navy has completed its Project Protector fleet modernisation programme with the arrival of the offshore patrol ships *Otago* and *Wellington* from BAE Systems Australia. These views show *Otago* sailing in New Zealand waters for the first time during April 2010 in company with two of the inshore patrol vessels delivered during 2009. *(NZDF)*

for a simulator and associated training services was signed with DCNS in April 2010. The programme has involved capital costs in excess of US$2bn, whilst ongoing support costs have been reported at around US$80m per year.

The planned procurement of a second batch of two *Lekiu* class frigates under a technology transfer arrangement with BAE Systems that involved local assembly has now been cancelled. Future surface construction is therefore likely to be focused on further MEKO A-100 type *Kedah* class offshore patrol vessels. The previously troubled contract for the first batch of six ships now appears to be back on track. Delivery of the final four vessels – all assembled locally – commenced in June 2009 and has continued at approximately six-monthly intervals, with fifth of class *Kelantan* commissioning on 8 May 2010. Up to twenty-seven ships were originally planned so additional orders seem likely. The navy also requires a replacement for the destroyed *Sri Inderapura*, leading to hopes that the previously postponed multi-purpose support ship programme for a new LPD-type vessel might be restarted.

New Zealand: The Royal New Zealand Navy has completed its fleet re-capitalisation, with the much delayed delivery of offshore patrol ships *Otago* and *Wellington* marking completion of the problematic NZ$500m (US$350m) Project Protector. Four inshore patrol vessels and the multi-role support vessel *Canterbury* were handed over previously, supplementing the two *Anzac* frigates in the fleet. An ongoing defence review scheduled to report in September 2010 will decide on future procurement, including the extent of mid-life frigate modernisation and potential support ship replacements.

Singapore: The Republic of Singapore has always placed a heavy emphasis on maintaining an effective military, as reflected in defence expenditure that is substantially higher than neighbours such as Indonesia and Malaysia. The country's surface forces are arguably the most modern and powerful in South East Asia, with the navy's six *Formidable* class multi-role frigates, four *Endurance* class

amphibious transport docks and supporting flotillas of corvettes and minehunters providing a capability matched only by the larger fleets. The four modernised but elderly *Challenger* (former Swedish A-12 *Sjöormen*) submarines are arguably the weak link in the maritime structure. However, the imminent arrival of the two refurbished *Archer* (former Swedish A-17 *Västergötland*) class boats that have been retrofitted with AIP should improve the situation. It is likely that work on both boats will be completed by 2011, providing Singapore with technology currently fielded only by Japan and South Korea within the region.

The extent of recent force upgrades suggests that there is little immediate scope – or need – for further naval investment. However, Sweden's decision to progress with development of its new A-26 submarine design could attract Singapore in the medium term, particularly the heavy regional investment in underwater technology previously referenced. This might also suggest further investment in

other anti-submarine equipment, although the six S-70B Sea Hawk helicopters purchased to operate from the frigates have only recently been accepted into service.

Taiwan: The Republic of China Navy continues its relative quantitative and qualitative decline against the rival People's Liberation Army Navy. Indeed, the disparity between the two forces – particularly in terms of underwater forces – is now so great that it seems only US Navy involvement would be able to counter the PLAN's dominance if conflict were to erupt. Modernisation that has taken place seems to have been limited and somewhat half hearted, with projects such as the acquisition of new submarines repeatedly stalled. The major development during the last year was the deployment of the first squadron of new 170-ton 'Kuang-Hua' (KH-6) fast attack craft in May 2010, comprising the first ten production vessels handed over. Deliveries appear to be taking place in batches of two, with a total of twelve out of

Right and opposite: The Royal Thai Navy's *Sichang* tank landing ship *Surin* on exercise with the US and other regional navies during February 2010. These are currently the main modern tonnage available to Thailand's well-regarded Marine Corps but a new *Endurance* class LPD is under construction in Singapore. *(US Navy)*

thirty planned vessels – plus the original prototype – being handed over by early June 2010. The class will eventually replace the existing 'Hai Ou' class developed from the Israeli 'Dvora' design in three of the five fast attack squadrons. Taiwan may also be one of a number of countries interested in acquiring surplus US FFG-7 frigates as the class is retired, particularly since it already operates eight locally-built ships of the class commissioned between 1993 and 2004. The possibility of an upgrade along the lines implemented to Australia's *Adelaide*s would be an additional consideration.

Thailand: Whilst ongoing political unrest in Thailand has reduced economic growth due to its impact on investor and consumer confidence, defence expenditure is rising sharply from the low point reached in the early years of the millennium, putting Thailand on broad parity with neighbouring states such as Indonesia and Malaysia. Whether this expenditure – which appears to be at least partly a political bribe to keep the military 'on side' with the current regime – proves to be sustainable will only be determined with time. However, it appears to be sufficient at present to allow the start of a much-needed modernisation of the Royal Thai Navy.

At present, the navy's structure appears unbalanced. For example, the sole aircraft carrier provides a potentially unique regional capability but lacks an effective air wing and is rarely sent to sea. The fleet of surface vessels is focused around obsolescent Chinese designs supplemented by some Western equipment, whilst the lack of a submarine flotilla is at variance with other force structures in the region. The Royal Thai Marine Corps is well regarded but lacks much in the way of modern tonnage beyond the two *Sichang* tank landing ships. It therefore seems appropriate that the most advanced new construction programme is the US$150m order for an *Endurance* class LPD, which is currently under construction by Singapore's ST Marine for delivery in 2012. A second ship may follow. The prospect of more effective surface patrol forces is held out by the licence-built construction of a BAE Systems designed offshore patrol vessel that is similar to Trinidad and Tobago's *Port of Spain*. Equipped with Thales radar and electronics and armed with a 76mm gun, she is likely to be the prototype for an extended class and replaces previous plans for further construction of the *Pattani* type. Series production of the smaller, locally designed T-991 class patrol craft is already well-established, continuing a longstanding line of indigenous coastal patrol craft.

Vietnam: The Vietnam People's Navy is fast becoming a significant regional maritime player with considerable investment in Russian-type equipment. In addition to the establishment of a submarine flotilla previously referenced, the country will soon take delivery of its first modern frigates with the arrival of two Project 1166.1 'Gepard' type vessels from Tartarstan's Zelenodolsk shipyard. Ordered back in 2006, the two ships were launched in December 2009 and March 2010 prior to undertaking the long journey northwards along the River Volga for pre-delivery trials in the Baltic. Both are expected to arrive in Vietnam before the end of 2010. Meanwhile, negotiations for a second pair are reportedly underway, with licence-built construction in Vietnam a possibility. They will reinforce Project 1241.1 'Taruntul' and Project 1241.2 'Pauk' corvettes in the coastal defence role.

Notes

1. A brief overview of Thailand's long-considered acquisition plans for submarines is contained in Jon Grevatt's and Tim Fish's 'Royal Thai Navy pushes for submarines', *Jane's Defence Weekly* – 24 February 2010 (Coulsdon, HIS Jane's, 2010).

2. A good reference for current and planned Australian procurement projects is the *Defence Capability Plan 2009* (Canberra, Defence Material Organisation, 2009). A copy can be accessed at www.defence.gov.au/mo/

3. The best source of information on ongoing PLAN developments – including regular updates on *Varyag*'s modernisation – is possibly the China Air and Naval Power blog, which can be found at china-pla.blogspot.com. Dawei Xia's sinodefence.com provides a more structured overview of the Chinese military.

4. Please refer to *Investigation Result on the Sinking of ROKS 'Cheonan'* (Seoul, The Joint Civilian-Military Investigation Group, 2010). It can be accessed by searching the South Korean government's official multi-language website, www.korea.net

Author:
Conrad Waters

2.3 REGIONAL REVIEW

THE INDIAN OCEAN AND AFRICA

Although partly upstaged by events in the waters off the Korean peninsula, this vast and diverse region continues to give rise to the greatest global concerns in terms of its inherent instability and potential for all-out conflict. At one end of the spectrum, ongoing piracy off the Horn of Africa continues as a high profile but essentially low level irritant. At the other, Iran's apparent desire to continuously ratchet up its essentially confrontational international agenda against a backdrop of internal political repression seems unlikely to have a happy ending. Another longstanding but recently dormant hazard to regional stability flashed back to life on 31 May 2010. A botched operation by Israel Navy commandos to enforce its government's naval blockade of the Gaza Strip resulted in nine civilian deaths and many more injuries. The fatalities occurred when the commandos encountered fierce resistance from activists on board the Turkish-owned *Mavi Marmara* – part of a humanitarian convoy attempting to break the blockade – as they attempted to seize the ship in international waters. The incident put further strain on the previously strong relationship between Turkey and Israel and increases the latter's regional isolation. This is by no means a helpful development as Israel continues to weigh its response to Iran's developing nuclear programme.

Given this toxic backdrop, it is not surprising that the region's military expenditure continues to be reasonably healthy, albeit Middle Eastern and North African nations will have been hit by the decline in oil prices during the latter part of 2008 and early 2009. According to SIPRI, two of the world's top ten military spenders – Saudi Arabia and India – are located in the region and both have seen above-average rises in defence budgets during that time. The greatest impact from a maritime perspective has clearly been seen in India, which has started to reverse a period of relative neglect to stand on the threshold of becoming a serious global naval power. It is, however, interesting to note the difficulty it has faced in translating more robust financial support into improvements in force structure. Indeed, delays to projects such as the indigenous construction of 'Scorpène' submarines might actually result in a short-term decline in capabilities in certain areas until the fruits of investment are felt. There are undoubtedly some valuable lessons to be learned here about the timeframe between cause and effect so far as changing military budgets are concerned.

The delays in the arrival of new construction will be all the more keenly felt by India given that the challenge of piracy has continued to result in an unprecedented level of naval deployments to the Indian Ocean. Indeed, the waters off the Horn of Africa must, at times, have something of the air of an international fleet review as warships from as far away as Scandinavia, China and Japan mingle with the units of navies that have maintained a longer-standing presence in the region. The motivations behind these deployments are somewhat ambiguous; whilst the praiseworthy desire to protect trade and combat potential terrorism is likely at the forefront of many minds, aspirations to extend influence and develop the capability for extended maritime deployments are inevitably also present. The increased naval presence does seem to be achieving some, inevitably patchy, success in neutralising pirate attacks and destroying their equipment, albeit it seems difficult to envisage a comprehensive solution to the scourge until political stability in Somalia is restored.

One of the more disappointing aspects of the current situation is the limited African response to the problem. Whilst some neighbouring countries have provided logistical facilities and even participated in legal process, the ability or willingness to join the naval effort to combat the menace has not been present. Perhaps most disappointing of all has been the lack of a South African commitment to assist international efforts given both previous hopes for the country's broader engagement across the continent and also the fact that it is one of the few African countries with the maritime potential to make such a contribution. Some of the background to South Africa's somewhat hesitant steps to what many commentators believe is its natural role as a regional maritime power is provided in Leon Engelbrecht's addendum to this regional review in Chapter 2.3A.

Opposite: Anti-piracy activities off the Horn of Africa are giving parts of the Indian Ocean the air of an international fleet review. Here the US Navy destroyer *Farragut* (DDG-99) is pictured next to a burning skiff she has just destroyed in a successful disruption operation in March 2010. *Farragut* was acting as flagship of the multinational Combined Task Force CTF-151 at the time. *(US Navy)*

Table 2.3.1: FLEET STRENGTHS IN THE INDIAN OCEAN, AFRICA AND THE MIDDLE EAST – LARGER NAVIES (MID-2010)

COUNTRY	ALGERIA	EGYPT	INDIA	IRAN	ISRAEL	PAKISTAN	SAUDI ARABIA	SOUTH AFRICA
Support/Helicopter Carrier (CVS/CVH)	–	–	1	–	–	–	–	–
Attack Submarine (SSN/SSGN)	–	–	1	–	–	–	–	–
Patrol Submarine (SSK/SS)	2	4	16	3	3	5	–	3
Fleet Escort (DDG/FFG)	–	6	21	–	–	8	6[2]	4
Patrol Escort/Corvette (FFG/FSG/FS)	6	4	8	6	3	–	4	–
Missile Armed Attack Craft (PGG/PTG)	12	30[1]	12	24	10	6	9	3
Mine Countermeasures Vessel (MCMV)	–	14	8	–	–	3	7	3
Major Amphibious (LPD)	–	–	1	–	–	–	–	–

Notes:

1 Egyptian fast attack craft numbers approximate.

2 Status of one Saudi Arabian fleet escort doubtful following grounding damage.

Bangladesh's long-term ambitions to modernise and upgrade its fleet are being given a shot in the arm by the transfer of surplus Royal Navy tonnage. The survey ship *Roebuck* was subject to a 'hot transfer' but the former *Leeds Castle* and *Dumbarton Castle* have required significant refurbishment on the Tyne before handover. *(Derek Fox)*

INDIAN OCEAN NAVIES

Bangladesh: The Bangladesh Navy has had long-held ambitions to modernise and upgrade its fleet. This includes an aspiration to follow in the footsteps of its South East Asian neighbours and acquire a submarine flotilla. Little tangible progress has been made in realising any of these objectives, although the new political regime headed by the Awami League that was elected at the end of 2008 appears to be giving greater prioritisation to the modernisation process. Two 'Castle' class offshore patrol vessels and the former survey ship *Roebuck* have been acquired from the UK, apparently partly with the assistance of British international development aid funding, whilst negotiations have commenced with China for the purchase of at least two F-22P frigates of a similar design to those acquired by Pakistan. Light helicopters, missile upgrades and additional offshore patrol ships are reportedly also on the shopping list. However, the hoped-for submarines are somewhat further away, with current pronouncements suggesting that an underwater capability will not be acquired until the end of the decade.

India: India's Navy is already the region's dominant indigenous maritime force and plans are well underway to build on this status. Whilst construction delays are impacting the speed of expansion, Table 2.3.2 provides details of an extremely capable force.

Greatest strides have, perhaps, been made in the procurement of front-line surface escorts. This process has essentially involved three lines of development, viz.

■ The construction of indigenous Project 15 and derivative Project 15A and Project 15B destroyers from 1987 onwards. So far three ships have been delivered, with a further three in the final stages of construction and an additional four approved. The design and development of these destroyers is described in more detail in Chapter 3.2.

■ The development of an indigenous line of Project 17 stealth frigates. The lead ship, *Shivalik*, was commissioned on 29 April 2010 and she should be followed by sister *Satpura* around the end of the year. Displacing around 5,300 tons in standard displacement, the ships follow traditional Indian practice of incorporating a mixture of Western and Russian technology but are possibly most closely related to the Russian-built Project 1135.6 *Talwar* class. A follow-on programme for a further seven Project 17A ships at a reported cost

India's Russian-built Project 1135.6 *Talwar* class frigate *Tabar* (F44) sails in company with the Australian frigate *Anzac* (FFH-150) during 2005. Three further ships of the class are under construction at the Yantar yard in Kaliningrad, of which two have already been launched. *(Royal Australian Navy)*

Table 2.3.2: INDIAN NAVY: PRINCIPAL UNITS AS AT MID-2010

TYPE	CLASS	NUMBER	TONNAGE	DIMENSIONS	PROPULSION	CREW	DATE
Aircraft Carriers							
Aircraft Carrier (CV)	**VIRAAT** (HERMES)	1	29,000 tons	227m x 27/49m x 9m	Steam, 28 knots	1,350	1959
Principal Surface Escorts							
Destroyer – DDG	Project 15 **DELHI**	3	6,700 tons	163m x 17m x 7m	COGAG, 32 knots	350	1997
Destroyer – DDG	Project 61 ME **RAJPUT** ('Kashin')	5	5,000 tons	147m x 16m x 5m	COGAG, 35 knots	320	1980
Frigate – FFG	Project 17 **SHIVALIK**	1	5,300 tons	143m x 17m x 5m	CODOG, 32 knots	255	2010
Frigate – FFG	Project 1135.6 **TALWAR**	3	4,000 tons	125m x 15m x 5m	COGAG, 30 knots	180	2003
Frigate – FFG	Project 16A **BRAHMAPUTRA**	3	4,000 tons	127m x 15m x 5m	Steam, 30 knots	350	2000
Frigate – FFG	Project 16 **GODAVARI**	3	3,850 tons	127m x 15m x 5m	Steam, 30 knots	315	1983
Frigate – FFG	**NILGIRI** (LEANDER)	3	3,000 tons	114m x 13m x 5m	Steam, 28 knots	300	1974
Corvette – FSG	Project 25A **KORA**	4	1,400 tons	91m x 11m x 5m	Diesel, 25 knots	125	1998
Corvette – GSG	Project 25 **KHUKRI**	4	1,400 tons	91m x 11m x 5m	Diesel, 25 knots	110	1989
Submarines							
Submarine – SSK	Project 877 EKM **SINDHUGHOSH** ('Kilo')	10	3,000 tons	73m x 10m x 7m	Diesel-electric, 17 knots	55	1986
Submarine – SSK	**SHISHUMAR** (Type 209)	4	1,900 tons	64m x 7m x 6m	Diesel-electric, 22 knots	40	1986
Submarine – SSK	Project 641 **VELA** ('Foxtrot')	2	2,500 tons	91m x 8m x 6m	Diesel-electric, 16 knots	75	1967
Major Amphibious Units							
Landing Platform Dock – LPD	**JALASHWA** (AUSTIN)	1	17,000 tons	173m x 26/30m x 7m	Steam, 21 knots	405	1971

India's sole carrier *Viraat*, the former Royal Navy *Hermes*, pictured on exercises with the US Navy in 2007. She has completed an extensive refit at Cochin that should allow her to remain in service until 2015, by which time replacements should have been delivered. *(US Navy)*

approaching US$10bn was approved in June 2009. Construction will be shared between Mumbai's Mazagon Dock Ltd (MDL) and Kolkata's Garden Reach Shipbuilders & Engineers Ltd (GRSE), which will be modernised to permit modularised construction.

■ The import of additional stealth frigates of the Project 1135.6 *Talwar* type from Russia. Three ships were delivered by St Petersburg's Baltic Shipyard during 2003-4 and a second batch of three is under construction at the Yantar yard in Kaliningrad. The first of this new batch, *Teg*, was launched in November 2009, being followed by the second ship, *Tarkash*, on 23 June 2010.

These fleet escorts will be supplemented by the delivery of indigenously-built patrol frigates and offshore patrol vessels for secondary roles. The most significant are the Project 28 anti-submarine corvettes, also being built by GRSE. The first of an initial batch of four ships, yard no. 3017, was launched as *Kamorta* on 19 April 2010. Delivery of the batch is planned for 2012-15 and could be followed by eight, improved Project 28A types. Low-end capabilities will be provided by the *Saryu* offshore patrol ships contracted to Goa Shipyard Ltd; naval variants of two similar *Sankalp* patrol ships already delivered to the Indian Coast Guard.

Emphasis on coastal surveillance and patrol has been reinforced by the Mumbai terrorist atrocities, suggesting that these ships and the smaller *Car Nicobar* fast patrol craft will be given a degree of priority. Indeed, *Jane's Defence Weekly* has reported that the navy's new Maritime Doctrine specifically emphasises the coastal security role alongside more established power projection, sea control and second nuclear-strike duties.

India's submarine projects are generally progressing less well. On the plus side, the first indigenous strategic nuclear submarine, *Arihant*, was launched on 26 July 2009. She has now commenced sea trials prior to induction by the end of 2011. Armament will be twelve K-15 ballistic missiles that are reported to be capable of delivering a nuclear warhead to c. 700km. It has been reported that at least two further units are under construction. Their eventual deployment will provide India with an effective second-strike nuclear capability, achieving a further step in the country's deterrence strategy. Underwater forces will also be reinforced by consummation of the long-awaited lease of the Project 971 'Akula' class nuclear-powered attack submarine *Nerpa* from Russia, which will be named *Chakra* in Indian service. Her delivery was delayed by a fatal accident that killed twenty personnel during initial sea trials at the end of 2008 but repairs have now been completed and she should enter service by

the end of 2010. However, the project to build 'Scorpène' submarines at MDL is running badly behind time and over budget, with the first boat not now scheduled for delivery before the end of 2014. The current sixteen-strong force of patrol submarines will therefore shrink, with the two remaining Project 641 'Foxtrot' class slated for withdrawal during 2010-11 and the older members of the Type 209 *Shishumar* and Project 877 ('Kilo') *Sindhughosh* classes soon approaching their twenty-fifth birthdays. Russia's Zvezdochka has previously completed mid-life refits on four of the last-mentioned class and started work on a fifth, *Sindhurakshak*, in June 2010. More of the class will also be equipped with the Klub S (SS-N-27) cruise missile.

India's naval aviation capabilities also look fragile in the face of delays to the Project 71 indigenous aircraft carrier and, particularly, the refurbishment of the former Soviet *Admiral Gorshkov*. India now appears to be confident that the latter, to be renamed *Vikramaditya*, will be delivered by the end of 2012, although a re-negotiated US$2.3bn price tag is more than double what was initially envisaged and arguably as much as the cost of a new ship. The first Mig-29K squadron destined to operate from the new ship has already stood up in India and the new refurbishment contract was accompanied by an order for a second batch. The sole existing carrier *Viraat* – the former Royal Navy *Hermes* – completed an extensive refit at Cochin in September 2009 that should allow her to remain in service until 2015, thus covering the gap until the new ships arrive.[1] However, the real problem is lack of suitable jet aircraft: the Mig-29ks cannot operate from *Viraat* and crashes have reduced the navy's complement of Sea Harrier FRS51 fighters to around only a dozen airframes.

Significant efforts are being devoted to modernising naval infrastructure to support naval expansion. In addition to the dockyard upgrades already mentioned, further funds are being provided to expand the new west coast naval base established at Kawar under Project Seabird. This will allow major fleet units to be withdrawn from the crowded and vulnerable facilities at Mumbai.

Pakistan: Although Pakistan's armed forces remain amongst the largest in the world, the imperative of focusing on the army and paramilitary forces to counter both internal unrest and potential external threats has meant that its navy has faced a steady qualitative and numerical decline against the Indian

Table 2.3.3: PAKISTAN NAVY: PRINCIPAL UNITS AS AT MID-2010

TYPE	CLASS	NUMBER	TONNAGE	DIMENSIONS	PROPULSION	CREW	DATE
Principal Surface Escorts							
Frigate – FFG	**ZULFIQAR** (F-22P)	2	3,000 tons	118m x 13m x 5m	CODAD, 29 knots	185	2009
Frigate – FFG	**TARIQ** (Type 21)	6	3,600 tons	117m x 13m x 5m	COGOG, 32 knots	180	1974
Submarines							
Submarine – SSK	**HAMZA** (AGOSTA 90B/AIP)	1	2,100 tons	76m x 7m x 6m	AIP, 20 knots	40	2008
Submarine – SSK	**KHALID** (AGOSTA 90B)	2	1,800 tons	68m x 7m x 6m	Diesel-electric, 20 knots	40	1999
Submarine – SSK	**HASHMAT** (AGOSTA)	2	1,800 tons	68m x 7m x 6m	Diesel-electric, 20 knots	55	1979

Navy, its main regional rival. Its submarine flotilla, traditionally the essential fall back of a weaker fleet looking to counterbalance a neighbour's maritime supremacy, has been particularly hard hit. However, efforts are being made to address the imbalance. Previous reports of negotiations to acquire German-designed Type 214 AIP-equipped boats have recently been supplemented by talk of negotiations with China as a potential supplier. This might well prove a more realistic option given ongoing financial constraints. In the meantime, it has been confirmed that a second member of the three-strong 'Agosta 90B' *Khalid* class will receive DCNS's MESMA AIP system on next refit, strengthening Pakistan's regional lead with this technology.

China is fast becoming the supplier of choice for Pakistan's armed forces, with the navy currently in the course of receiving four F-22P frigates based on the Type 053H3 'Jiangwei II' design. The lead ship, *Zulfiqar*, was commissioned on 19 September 2009 with sister *Shamsheer* following three months later. The third class member will be in service before the end of 2010 but the final ship, being built locally at Karachi Shipyard & Engineering Works, will take longer. The new equipment was tested in a major exercise in March 2010 when a former *Leander* class frigate – reportedly the previous *Zulfiqar* (ex *Apollo*) – was destroyed in an operation that also involved submarine and aircraft missile firings. It seems probable that Pakistan will seek to receive more ships from this source, possibly of the improved Type 054/054A classes. In the interim, the navy has settled on the acquisition of surplus USN FFG-7 frigates as a temporary stopgap. The first transfer agreed is that of *McInerney* (FFG-8) and she is scheduled to be handed over in a reported US$65m deal on 31 August 2010. The Pakistan Naval Air Arm is also benefiting from the steady arrival of modernised US P3-C maritime patrol aircraft under a contract for eight additional aircraft agreed in 2006.

Pakistan has wasted little time putting the first of four new Chinese F-22P frigates into service. Here *Zulfiqar* is pictured behind the Australian frigate *Stuart* during operations in the Indian Ocean in February 2010. *(Royal Australian Navy)*

The acquisition of former US Navy units is another means by which Pakistan is looking to bolster its naval strength. The planned transfer of *McInerney* (FFG-8) at the end of August 2010 is likely to be followed by other ships to replace obsolescent Type 21 frigates. *(US Navy)*

The three *Nakhoda Ragam* class corvettes built for Brunei by BAE Systems but never delivered could be bought by Algeria. Two ships of the class are pictured here on trials in Scottish waters during 2003. *(BAE Systems)*

AFRICAN NAVIES

As always, naval developments amongst the majority of Africa's coastal countries are relatively thin on the ground, with most procurement focused on the country's northern and southern fringes. Elsewhere, **Nigeria's** navy will celebrate its fifty-fifth anniversary in 2010. It continues to revive previously unserviceable platforms, as well as acquiring limited numbers of new platforms, mostly aimed at strengthening its ability to patrol the littorals. For example, Singapore-based Suncraft International delivered two Malaysian-built 38m Sea Eagle fast patrol vessels in 2009, adding to the six 17m Manta Mk 2 ASD interceptor craft delivered from 2008 onwards. Two Israeli Shaldag fast patrol craft have also been ordered for delivery from mid-2010. The small Naval Air Arm has been inducting new light helicopters. A small group of naval personnel completed Special Forces training and a newly-formed special boat squadron deployed on operations. The navy remains actively engaged in operations in the strife-torn Niger Delta Region, as well as combating piracy and crude oil theft but maintainability issues and inadequate seamanship skills pose ongoing challenges.[2]

The North African coastline remains something of an exception to the continent's overall picture of depressed procurement activity, with **Algeria** seemingly leading the charge. Delivery of two additional 'Kilo' submarines from St. Petersburg's Admiralty yard that were ordered in 2006 was expected in the course of 2010, whilst an ongoing competition for new surface ships has been attracting interest from shipbuilders across Europe. Press reports suggest that the Italian version of the Franco-Italian FREMM

A computer-generated graphic of the new 'Ambassador III' FMC fast missile craft design being built for Egypt by VT Halter Marine. The keel of the first of four vessels was laid in April 2010. *(VT Halter Marine)*

design may be the preferred contender but contracts have yet to be signed. Algeria has also been linked to the *Nakhoda Ragam* corvettes that have been put up for sale by Brunei, a transaction that would make

The first of the *Baynunah* corvettes being built by an alliance of France's CMN and Abu Dhabi Shipbuilding pictured on preliminary sea trials from CMN's Cherbourg shipyard in January 2010. A further five ships are under construction in the Middle East. (CMN)

most sense if a British bid for the new frigate construction programme was ultimately successful.

Neighbouring **Morocco** is further ahead with its plans for new surface-ship construction, with fabrication of the single French FREMM variant and three Dutch Sigma corvettes contracted in 2008 now underway. The first of the Dutch-built ships should be launched before the end of 2010 to meet a scheduled 2011 delivery date. The remaining ships will arrive in 2012/13. Work has also started on **Egypt's** new 'Ambassador III' fast attack craft, with the keel of the first of what will now be four ships following a March 2010 contract amendment laid at VT Halter Marine's Pascagoula, Mississippi, yard on 7 April 2010. With a length of 62m and featuring stealth technology, these fast, highly-manoeuvrable ships will feature an extensive range of anti-air, anti-surface and electronic warfare capabilities that is reflected in a project cost of over US$800m. Whilst the new ships will undoubtedly make a potent contribution to Egypt's maritime strength on delivery from mid-2012 onwards, the country still faces a huge problem in modernising an increasingly elderly fleet. It will therefore be interesting to see whether its navy takes advantage of the decommissioning of German Type 206A submarines and US Navy FFG-7 frigates to reinforce its capabilities in these areas.

Information on South African naval developments is contained in Chapter 2.3A.

MIDDLE EASTERN NAVIES

Although, overall, the Middle East continues to exhibit an unfortunate degree of instability, heavy commitments to existing naval construction programmes in the region means that little new procurement has been announced. Most news flow is therefore focused on progress with previously announced contracts.

The most ambitious naval power in the region is probably the **United Arab Emirates**, which was one of the few countries to announce new construction during 2009-10. Italy's Fincantieri has been the main beneficiary. It announced an initial order for an *Abu Dhabi* class derivative of the Italian Navy's 'Comandante' offshore patrol vessel design, together with an option for a second vessel, in August 2009. This was followed by a subsequent order for two 55m patrol craft, with options for the local build of two more, in January 2010. As is increasingly the fashion, these vessels will incorporate a considerable amount of stealth technology but do not seem to be particularly fast, with reported speed being 'in excess of 20 knots'. This requirement appears to be met by the *Baynunah* missile-armed corvette programme being realised by Abu Dhabi Shipbuilding in alliance with France's CMN. The lead ship of these fast and powerfully-armed vessels commenced sea trials from CMN's Normandy facility in January 2010 and should be delivered by mid-2011. Attention will then switch to the five remaining vessels being built in Abu Dhabi, which are scheduled for launch from the middle of 2010 onwards.

Meanwhile, **Oman's** order for sophisticated offshore patrol vessels from what is now BAE Surface Ships has under Project Khareef also been making progress. The first of three ships, *Al Shamikh*, was launched in July 2009 and is expected to commence sea trials imminently. She is claimed to be the first vessel constructed at Portsmouth Dockyard for a non-UK naval requirement. Oman is also understood to be in the market for three simpler patrol ships, with yards in Korea, India and the Netherlands reportedly in contention for the deal.

The major driving factor behind the investment programmes in the Persian Gulf is undoubtedly uncertainty over **Iran's** future intentions, with the country's aggressive anti-American rhetoric being matched by significant defence spending. So far as naval forces are concerned, most attention has been focused on the deployment of the indigenous frigate *Jamaran*, which was commissioned at Iran's Bandar Abbas naval base in February 2010. Derived from the country's British-built Vosper Mk5 light frigates delivered in the early 1970s – of which three still remain in service – she displaces around 1,500 tons and is claimed to be capable of speeds in excess of 30 knots. Armament comprises a range of domestic copies of Western designs, supplemented by imported or licence-built Chinese equipment, most notably C-802 surface-to-surface missiles. A second member of this so-called 'Mowj' class is in the later stages of construction. In truth, however, these new vessels are unlikely to pose much of a threat to more advanced Western designs, with Iran's investment in powerful batteries of land-based surface-to-surface missiles of Chinese origin, supplemented by midget submarines, mines and swarms of fast attack craft, likely to pose the most potent threat to US and allied forces should conflict erupt around the Strait of Hormuz.

One of the countries most likely to be impacted by any stepping up of Iranian belligerence is **Saudi Arabia**. However, the country's substantial defence budget has been largely channelled into land and air-based projects, with discussion on fleet renewal yet to produce anything in the way of tangible results. Whilst the Western Fleet on the Red Sea is relatively modern, the *Badr* class corvettes and *Al Siddiq* fast attack craft that form the core of the Eastern Fleet in the Persian Gulf will need replacement soon in a potential boom for Western arms suppliers. Indeed, it is somewhat surprising that the Kingdom has delayed renewal of these components of the Royal Saudi Navy given the overall instability of the security situation.

Nobody could, however, claim that **Israel** looks on developments in Iran with anything other than the utmost seriousness. To some extent, this is increasing the importance of the Israel Navy in the overall Israel Defence Force, with the three Type 800 *Dolphin* class boats taking on a particular strategic significance. The boats have been subject to ongoing rumours that they are equipped with nuclear-armed cruise missiles to provide a seaborne 'second strike' deterrent and recent deployments to the Red Sea are seen as a tacit warning to Iran. Indeed, the *Sunday Times* has recently speculated that a permanent presence close to the Persian Gulf could be contemplated. A further two members of the class are currently under construction by HDW with financial assistance from the German government and Israel would like to order a sixth if funding can be agreed. Germany is also said to be the likely source of future surface warships after the international version of the USN's *Freedom* (LCS-1) was ruled out on cost grounds, with a development of the *Deutsche Marine's* K-130 type seen as one possible alternative.[3]

Notes

1. A report on the completion of the refit was contained in the 17 August 2009 edition of India's *The Hindu* newspaper. The article, entitled 'INS *Viraat* refit complete, gears up for golden jubilee' can be found by searching www.thehindu.com.

2. The editor is grateful to Mrityunjoy Mazumdar for contributing the information on the Nigerian Navy contained in this section of the review.

3. An excellent overview of the recent evolution of the Israel Navy is contained in Yaakov Katz's 'Navy on a new level', *Jane's Defence Weekly* – 10 March 2010 (Coulsdon, HIS Jane's, 2010), pp 23-8.

Author:
Leon Engelbrecht

THE SOUTH AFRICAN NAVY

It is difficult to discern South Africa's military, let alone naval, intentions. The most recent White Paper on Defence (WPD) was published fourteen years ago in 1996 and a follow-up Defence Review (DR) was completed in 1998. A direct result of this was the acquisition – from 1999 – of the four German-built MEKO A200SAN 'Valour' class patrol frigates and three 'Heroine' class Type 209 diesel-electric submarines at a cost of R9.690bn (US$1.6bn) and R8.152bn (US$1.4bn) – in 2008 Rand – respectively that form the core of the current fleet (please see Table 2.3A.1 for more details on current fleet strength). Both the policy and the naval acquisitions, delivered between 2005 and 2007, have been criticised on a number of grounds. The documents, in particular, are steeped in a naiveté that was common in South Africa in the mid-1990s, just after the fall of the Berlin Wall, the end of Apartheid and the start of the Mandela administration. It was an era of unbounded optimism when – in the newly-governing African National Congress (ANC) – there was a determination to do things in another way.

A CHANGE IN STRATEGIC DISPOSITION

The last white South African government had maintained a strategic offensive posture and exercised a pre-emptive capability. It had developed nuclear weapons, supported insurgent movements in neighbouring states and destabilised the region as a countermeasure to steps taken to end minority rule. The new government would be different – and it would be seen to be different. The ANC re-established a defence secretariat and staffed it with a mixture of personnel that included left-wing intellectuals schooled in peace studies and the turning of swords in ploughshares. Their motto might have been '*If you want peace, prepare for peace*'. Violence must be met with negotiation.

This approach was pursued with zeal in both national and foreign policy: if white and black South Africans could resolve their differences amicably and

An AgustaWestland Super Lynx helicopter onboard the South African Navy's 'Valour' class frigate *Amatola*. Current force structure is largely based on decisions taken in the 1998 Defence Review. (*Leon Engelbrecht*)

avoid race war, then so could the warring factions of Savimbi and Dos Santos in Angola, Arab and Israeli in the Middle East and Republican and Loyalist in Northern Ireland. Only in Northern Ireland did this approach meet with success, most likely because a critical mass disposed to peace existed. In the defence realm, policy eschewed the offensive, especially pre-emptive strike. The new military would concentrate on territorial defence and would be equipped accordingly. That is one reason why the frigates subsequently acquired still lack any form of land-attack capability, despite this being a standard requirement in many peer-group navies.

Various ministers of defence have promised a strategic update since 2004 but none of these have yet reached Parliament. The current incumbent at the Department of Defence, Lindiwe Sisulu, has promised a new defence review focussing on the 'role of defence in the developmental state' but has given no specifics of what this might mean, especially for naval acquisition. In her second annual budget vote in early May 2010 she noted that major changes, '…both dramatic and evolutionary, have taken place in the defence environment over the past 15 years'. The policy review will '…of necessity take this into consideration and will be informed by a clear-eyed assessment of what we want our foreign policy to achieve, the potential threats facing us, and socio-economic interests in what is a very uncertain era of growing competition among new major powers'.

'The new environment requires new thinking and new approaches,' Sisulu said. 'We had a Defence Workshop from 19 to 21 March 2010 to review the work done in this respect and are of the view that we need to give this added impetus … for the SANDF [South African National Defence Force] and particularly the SA Army to remain successful, it will have to take into account the complexities of African politics. The size of the continent, its geographic and climate complexity, as well as the lack of transport infrastructure, problems engendered by economic under-development and the diverse military challenges it may encounter, will necessitate the SANDF to be well and appropriately equipped and trained for both its external and internal roles as prescribed by the Constitution.' There was no mention whatsoever of naval matters. Complicating the picture is the appointment of Mpumi Mpofu as the new Secretary for Defence, the Department of Defence's (DoD) top civil servant. A former transport department boss but defence outsider, her views on both subjects are completely unknown.

For the moment, therefore, South Africa remains reliant on the dated 1996 and 1998 documents, as well as on two others that need urgent review. These are a white paper on peacekeeping published by the Department of Foreign Affairs in 1999 and a separate white paper on the defence industry. The former foresaw a modest peacekeeping commitment, capped at perhaps one infantry battalion. No major air or sea deployments were contemplated and an expeditionary capability was eschewed – the very word 'expeditionary' being deemed highly politically incorrect. Within a few years, however, these premises were obsolete and South Africa had three battalions and also air as well as naval elements deployed, the latter on Lake Tanganyika in support of the United Nations and African Union effort in Burundi.

That deployment has given rise to the Maritime Reaction Squadron (MRS), a small force of naval infantry and patrol boats. These were initially existing *Namacurra* class harbour patrol boats. However, in the last two years new boats as well as a base and command-and-control facilities have been acquired at a cost of R89m (US$13m) under Project Xena. Another lesson from Burundi was that 'expeditionary' was not a dirty word, hence an ambition to acquire a 'strategic support ship' (SSS), in effect an amphibious transport dock (LPD) or amphibious assault ship (LPD/LPH) that can carry a reinforced motorised/mechanised infantry battalion and a mixed squadron of medium utility, light utility and attack helicopters (Project Millennium). However, acquiring this capability will not come cheap and – by all accounts – the South African military is already currently grievously under-funded.

LESSONS FROM HISTORY

Indeed, South Africa has a long tradition of skimping on defence – and especially naval – spending, with more important social needs and a low threat environment the usual reasons for this. Despite all its potential wealth, the comment that 'South Africa has much poverty and there is a definite upper limit to what the country is prepared to spend on defence', is as true today as when it was first uttered by then defence minister Oswald Pirow in September 1938. Pirow also held that it was a 'certainty' that South Africa and its nearest neighbours could never become the main theatre of a major war. 'Due to the geographical position, South Africa's maximum effort will not have to be made until six months after the outbreak of hostilities. This allowed a period for intensive preparation ... [although] the manpower resources when compared with those of even second-class powers are very limited. Our geographical position is such that large-scale gas or air attack on the civil population need not be seriously considered.'

Just thirteen months later, the German 'pocket battleship' *Admiral Graf Spee* sank two ships off Angola, rounded the Cape and sank another off Inhambane, Mozambique, the next month. Captain Hans Langsdorff then returned to the Atlantic to sink two more off Angola. With its six 11in (283mm) guns the *Graf Spee* could have done considerable damage to any of South Africa's ports, had Langsdorff chosen to do so. The South African Naval Service, forerunner to the current navy, had just three officers and three ratings in full-time service, and a naval force had effectively to be improvised from scratch. In the interim, South Africa had to look to Britain's Royal Navy for its maritime defences.

Today the Royal Navy is long gone and the task of protecting South Africa's exclusive economic zone (EEZ) is the sole preserve of is small Navy and Air Force. The task of enforcing South Africa's neutrality is not as far-fetched as it may seem. For example, should tension between the US and Iran over nuclear weapons come to blows, one or the other may attempt a blockade or to interdict 'unfriendly' maritime traffic. The Indian Ocean has four main entrances – through the Suez Canal and Red Sea; through the Strait of Malacca and Indonesian waters; via the Tasman Sea south of Australia or around the Cape of Good Hope. When the Arab-Israeli wars of the 1960s and 1970s closed the Suez Canal, nearly all maritime trade headed for the east coast of the United States and to Europe had to sail around the Cape and

South Africa's harbours were a frequent stopping point. The Red Sea can easily be blocked during any conflict in the Indian Ocean basin by dropping a few naval mines, or deploying a submarine, Special Forces, or – for those so-inclined – suicide bombers.

The *Graf Spee* was involved in commerce raiding, an activity similar to crime and one that policing will displace rather than prevent. The traditional weapon of the weaker naval power, commerce raiders will tend to operate in areas where the risk to them is lowest. Australia and several Asian nations have navies and air forces powerful enough to displace commerce raiders elsewhere – this might be off South Africa's shores unless it, too, can deter them. After war came in 1939, South Africa improvised a navy – the Seaward Defence Force – but German U-boats, sea mines and raiders still remained a menace.

Turning to crime proper, Somali former fishermen have, in the last few years, raised piracy from an irritation to almost a strategic threat. Equipped with small motor-craft, machine guns and rocket-propelled grenades, they have made passage of an ever-larger swathe of the Indian Ocean a dangerous undertaking, befuddling the international fleet deployed there to safeguard trade – including that to and from South Africa. Already incidents have been reported as far south as the Mozambique Channel and as far east as just offshore India.

Africa, let alone South Africa, has so far taken little part in policing the scourge beyond the role of Kenya and the Seychelles in prosecuting – or offering to prosecute – captured pirates. Djibouti and the Seychelles currently also offer shore facilities to the international anti-piracy fleet. Egypt and South Africa, nations with capable navies and a commercial – as well as a strategic reason to act – have been strangely lethargic. It is known South Africa has been asked repeatedly by the European Union (EU), Germany and France to support the international counter-piracy effort. The last two have even offered to President Jacob Zuma to pay for fuel and victuals. It is understood they still await an answer. The Navy meanwhile says they are ready to deploy, but the government says they are not. They also say the EU, the UN World Food Programme, France and Germany have not gone through the 'right channels' but the former say they have.

BUDGET ISSUES

The National Treasury, that parsimonious holder of South Africa's purse-strings, in its Estimates of

TABLE 2.3A.1: SOUTH AFRICAN NAVY: PRINCIPAL UNITS AS AT MID-2010

TYPE	CLASS	NUMBER	TONNAGE	DIMENSIONS	PROPULSION	CREW	DATE
Principal Surface Escorts							
Frigate – FFG	**AMATOLA** (MEKO A200 SAN 'Valour')	4	3,600 tons	121m x 16m x 4m/6m	CODAG, 28 knots	100	2006
Submarines							
Submarine – SSK	**MANTHATISI** (Type 209/1400 'Heroine')	3	1,600 tons	62m x 8m x 6m	Diesel-electric, 22 knots	30	2005
Fast Attack Craft[1]							
Fast Attack Craft – PGG	**ISAAC DYOBHA** (SAAR 4)	3	450 tons	62m x 8m x 3m	Diesel, 32+ knots	50	1977
Mine Warfare Vessels[2]							
Minehunter – MCMV	**UMKOMAAS** ('River')	3	380 tons	48m x 9m x 3m	Diesel, 16 knots	40	1981

Notes:

1 Now re-rolled as offshore patrol vessels without missile armament.

2 Now largely operate as inshore patrol vessels.

The 'Warrior' fast attack craft *Isaac Dyobha* on a training exercise in Table Bay during March 2009. Three of these ships remain in service as offshore patrol vessels. *(Leon Engelbrecht)*

The Type 209/1400 'Heroine' class submarine *Charlotte Maxeke* (S102) alongside in Cape Town Harbour in September 2008. The acquisition of three Type 209 submarines and four MEKO 200 'Valour' class frigates were the key naval decisions arising out of the 1998 Defence Review. *(Leon Engelbrecht)*

National Expenditure (ENE) for the year 1 April 2010 to 31 March 2011 describes the South African Navy's main task for the next three years as bedding down its four new Project Sitron frigates and three Project Wills diesel-electric submarines. That may be easier said than done. DoD briefings to Parliament show the Navy is substantially under-funded and add that the Treasury has declined requests to obtain the cash needed to operate the vessels.

The ENE puts the actual 2010/11 defence budget at just R30.7 billion, about R1.3 billion less than last year's estimate of R32 billion. The document also includes budget estimates for 2011/12 (R33.3 billion) and 2012/13 (R36.4 billion). But – of this – only 7.8 per cent (R2.2 billion) is going to the sea service this financial year, with R2.3 billion provisionally allocated next year and R2.5 billion in the year after that. Many in the South African Navy consider this further proof of an 'agricultural' or landward mentality in government that blithely presumes safe passage on the high seas. This is despite South Africa being one of the top twelve sea-trading nations, depending on the oceans for 95 per cent of its imports and exports. In addition 30 per cent of the global crude oil trade passes by its shores, taking Middle Eastern oil west and Angolan oil east.

Just how small a part of state expenditure defence spending is can be seen from the total government budget of R818bn or some 30.3 per cent of the country's Gross Domestic Product (GDP). Defence spending amounts to less than 1.3 per cent of GDP or less than four cents out of every rand the government spends. The DoD in March 2010 briefed the lower house of parliament's Portfolio Committee on Defence and Military Veterans that it was under-funded by at least R7.335bn for the current year.

However – based on a glimpse at a previous attempt at updating the WPD and DR found in the DoD's 2007/8 annual report – the under-funding problem might be greater and more damaging than those referenced in the parliamentary briefing. The annual report quotes a still unpublished 'Defence Update' as arguing that – should the defence budget keep increasing at a rate linked to inflation, as is currently the case – the SANDF would only '…be partially able to meet ordered commitments…' and '…significant risks and limitations would exist…'. A Credible Force Design (CFD) that would include new naval assets would simply not be achievable. 'The best possible output within the budget, with the best balance of forces, would be sought. Certain defence capabilities are reduced and other defence capabilities are completely lost.'

The annual report continued that – at that time –

The prototype river patrol boat acquired for the Maritime Reaction Squadron under Project Xena. The possible acquisition of more potent amphibious capabilities under Project Millennium remains fluid. *(Leon Engelbrecht)*

the defence planners foresaw the CFD largely attained by FY2025/6 and fully attained by FY2030/1. However, that would have required a 'significant change' to the defence budget planned for 2008/9 to c. R41.3bn or about R7bn more than could be expected. The unpublished Defence Update also envisaged the defence allocation should reach c. R45.7bn in FY2017/18, continuing around this level until FY2023/4, when it should stabilise at around R46.4bn (all figures quoted in 2007 Rand). Such increases seem unlikely as the Treasury tartly responded that the DoD must do more with less. However, a change of heart is, perhaps, not quite as unlikely as in previous years. Parliament last year passed the Money Bills Amendment Procedure and Related Matters Act – despite concerns from the Treasury – to give lawmakers the power to amend money bills. The defence portfolio committee of the 3rd Parliament also recommended to the 4th Parliament (elected in April 2009) that the military budget should be mandate-driven rather than confined to the strictures of Treasury – a point also made in the ill-fated Defence Update.

ALL AT SEA

For the present time – FY2010/11 – Sisulu has said that the SANDF and, consequently, the South African Navy, will have to live within their budget. This means that the South African Navy will have to cope with an overall shortfall of R687m, of which R440m would have been allocated to operations. It has also emerged that the DoD had submitted proposals for additional funding in late 2009 but that these had been rejected. They had included

The first South African 'Heroine' class submarine *Manthatisi* (S101) pictured in German waters shortly before departing for her home country. Arriving in South Africa from 2006, they will provide the navy's core sub-surface capability for the foreseeable future. *(Thyssen Krupp Marine Systems)*

Table 2.3A.2: SOUTH AFRICAN NAVY: HISTORIC AND PLANNED PATROL HOURS

INDICATOR	PROGRAMME	PAST			CURRENT	PROJECTIONS		
		FY2006/7	FY2007/8	FY2008/9	FY2009/10	FY2010/11	FY2011/12	FY2012/13
Number of sea hours on patrol in South African maritime zones per year	Maritime Defence	9,949	9,648	8,236	11,000	10,000	9,000	9,000

Note: South African Navy patrol hours.
Source: Treasury ENE, February 2010.

R186m to operate the 'Valour' class frigates and 'Heroine' class submarines this year and R204.6m next year, as well as a further R225m for FY2012/13.

The ENE tabulates the operational navy as:

- A surface combat capability consisting of four frigates (the 'Valour' class), one combat support vessel (*Drakensberg*), three offshore patrol vessels (the 'Warrior' class), three inshore patrol vessels (the 'River' class) and a maritime reaction squadron in each annual operational cycle;
- A sub-surface combat capability of three submarines (the 'Heroine' class) in each annual operational cycle;
- Two mine-countermeasures systems in each annual operational cycle to ensure safe access to South African harbours and where mine clearance may be required; and
- An ongoing hydrographic survey capability to ensure safe navigation in charting areas and to meet international obligations.

It adds that the South African Navy will '…focus on the preparation and maintenance of the approved force structure elements (deployable assets) and the associated force structure (supporting elements), including the associated human resources at the required readiness levels, to meet maritime defence commitments in a sustained manner …'. The ENE continues: 'It will also focus on finalising all activities for the full acceptance and integration of the strategic defence package (SDP) frigates, helicopters and submarines. The South African Navy's naval capabilities will continue to be prepared for government peace support operations and engagements in Africa…' The SDP was the controversial R47bn (c. US$8bn) arms deal signed in 1999 as a result of the 1998 DR that saw South Africa acquire the submarines and frigates already referenced, as well as twenty-four BAE Systems Hawk Mk120 lead-in fighter trainers, twenty-six Saab Gripen advanced

Amatola pictured on a rare international deployment to the UK in the summer of 2007. The navy's operating budget is insufficient to maintain a local seagoing presence. *(Conrad Waters)*

light fighter aircraft and thirty AgustaWestland A109M light utility helicopters. However, the helicopters referred to here are the four AgustaWestland 300 Super Lynx rotorcraft that were subsequently and separately ordered at a cost of £80m (US$120m) for the South African Air Force (SAAF) to operate off the frigates and delivered in July 2007.

Other than bedding down not-so-new equipment the South African Navy is also tasked with patrolling the country's 3,924km coastline (inclusive of the Prince Edward Islands) and its 1,553,000km² EEZ. This area is just larger than South Africa itself. However, the budget squeeze means that the South African Navy will only spend 10,000 hours at this task during the current year. For the next two years, the figure is even less, as Table 2.3A.2 makes clear. On average that means the navy will be able to put to sea just one ship or submarine at a time if it is to maintain a presence at sea every day of the year – just one vessel, perhaps two, to police a sea area equivalent in size to the world's twenty-fifth largest nation.

Imagine attempting to police a large city, let alone country, with one vehicle. Even with air support, the task is well nigh impossible.

Not that much air support is available, either in quantity or quality. The SAAF is also facing its own budgetary problems, being R1.2bn under-funded for this year, all of it operational. The service is tasked with supporting the South African Navy, as the latter has no air wing of its own. A March 2010 briefing implied this will be difficult given that just over half the optimal number of maritime patrol flying hours have been allocated, It is also noteworthy these are being flown by five Douglas C47 Dakota aircraft delivered to the SAAF from 1943 and fitted with a minimal sensor suite.

FUTURE PLANS

More positively, the ENE does not just contain troubling news. It notes that a 'higher than average' increase in spending in the Maritime Defence programmes over the next three years is '…due to the additional allocations received for … initiating programmes to acquire a hydrographic vessel and off-shore patrol vessels.' These acquisition programmes are known as Projects Hotel and Biro respectively. A lot has been written about both in recent years, much of it contradictory. Indeed, in the continued absence of a policy framework and government (as opposed to naval) comment on future acquisitions, it is difficult to make definitive statements on the subject.

What is known is that the South African Navy anticipates a replacement hydrographic survey vessel as well as new patrol vessels by 2015, when the existing ships are scheduled to retire. The SSS previously mentioned is slated for 2017. In addition the Navy may need a replacement combat support ship in 2020. By then the *Drakensberg*, launched in 1987, will be somewhat long in the tooth, albeit the ship is currently undergoing a midlife upgrade under Project Brutes. Current planning envisages the frigates receiving midlife upgrades in 2025 (the four frigates were launched in 2002 and 2003 and commissioned in 2006 and 2007 with expected lifetimes of between thirty and forty years).

For the moment, Project Biro appears to be the priority. The South African Navy – in a December 2008 media briefing – said that the service was, at the time, planning the acquisition of three offshore patrol vessels (OPVs) and three inshore patrol vessels (IPVs) as part of Biro. However, navy chief Vice Admiral Johannes Mudimu also stressed that, while the sea service had its own hopes on the time line, this decision was 'in the final analysis' one for the government. Despite expectations of orders being placed by late 2009, by June 2010 the state arms acquisition agency Armscor was not known to have issued any requests for information or proposals to industry. At the time Biro was portrayed as a one-for-one replacement of the three remaining re-roled 'Warrior' class missile fast attack craft, as well as of the three ex 'River' class mine-countermeasure vessels (MCMVs), the former now without their Israeli 'Gabriel' surface-to-surface missiles and the MCMVs with now-antiquated unmanned underwater vehicles.

The Navy Chief Director of Maritime Strategy, Rear Admiral Bernard Teuteberg, added that the South African Navy would seek to have the Biro vessels built in South Africa. This will, perhaps, be the case for the new hydrographic vessel as well, as long as the final specification is close enough to that of the OPV to allow it. Size-wise the OPVs were expected to measure between 80m and 85m in length, and the IPVs from 53m to 55m. According to Teuteberg, 'The OPV must be able to carry a helicopter. The moment you talk about carrying a helicopter, you're talking of a ship 80-85 metres. The size of the IPVs by contrast is a function of the sea conditions, available money and so forth.'

Teuteberg also stated that the OPV would carry a 76mm gun and the IPV a 30mm cannon. Neither would be fitted with missiles. The OPVs would also carry autonomous underwater vehicles (AUVs) acquired as part of Project Mapantsula, a requirement for an off-board, containerised mine-countermeasures system, if and when needed. The AUVs can also be carried aboard the 'Valour' class frigates should this be necessary. Mapantsula buys into the international trend that specialised but pricey MCMVs are now obsolete. The system is likely in the class of Atlas Elektronik Sea Otter mine-hunting system and Sea Fox mine disposal weapon displayed at the Sea Power for Africa Symposium in March 2009.

The admiral added that the Navy was working on convincing its regional partners to purchase similar OPVs, a theme raised again at the Sea Power for Africa Symposium, as well as at a *defenceWeb* maritime security conference in October of that year. He explained that using the same hulls would extend the production run and bring down unit costs, while using the same communications equipment and engineering plant will allow for greater efficiency and economic viability. Southern African Development Community navies would be better able to patrol their waters jointly or severally and could further gain from maintaining a centralised training system as well as spares holding. 'Why maintain spares in each county when you can hold it in one location so all can share… That makes it more economically viable.'

It is not clear what the acquisitions would cost. A consideration of available literature shows that an average armed OPV costs about R400m (c. US$60m) and an IPV half that, giving Biro, as depicted here, a potential R1.8bn (US$260m) price-tag. By comparison the former Department of Environmental Affairs and Tourism paid R150m for a Damen-built unarmed offshore environmental protection vessel, the *Sarah Baartman*, in 2003.

Isaac Dyobha alongside at Simon's Town with decommissioned *Daphne* class submarines in the background. She will be replaced by the new class of offshore patrol vessels planned under Project Biro. *(Leon Engelbrecht)*

It appears the original Biro requirement was for

The second 'Valour' class frigate *Isandlwana* on manoeuvres. Potential modernisation includes a larger gun and the acquisition of land-attack capable missiles, anti-submarine torpedoes and upgraded radar. *(Leon Engelbrecht)*

nine OPVs. Several retired admirals have questioned the need for the IPVs, saying their sea experience had taught them that the minimum length of vessels suitable for South Africa's harsh seas, some of the most violent in the world, was around 85m. There are now indications the requirement has turned a full circle and the Project Biro requirement is again for nine OPV and no IPV. There is also the suggestion the vessels will carry the Denel Dynamics 'Mokopa' precision guided missile in the anti-surface role. This is a domestic 10km-range, 2m-long, 50kg weapon just emerging from a development programme protracted by … under-funding.

Looking at other acquisition plans, not much more is known about Project Hotel other than that it will replace the *Hecla* class survey ship *Protea*, now thirty-eight years old, with a vessel similar to a Biro type OPV. It will also see the establishment of a mobile hydrographic survey team. Further into the future, the situation regarding the Project Millennium SSS also remains fluid. There is as yet, no mention of it in the ENE and government has not recently spoken on the subject. The Drakensberg currently has a limited amphibious capacity and has exercised with the MRS, the Special Forces and the Army's 9 South African Infantry battalion – the land service's designated sea-landing battalion – in that

role. Questions that remain to be answered therefore include whether the navy replace *Drakensberg* with a new combat support ship or if underway replenishment will become a function of the SSS, whether the requirement can be satisfied by just one ship and what overall size and configuration might be adopted. In 2007, *Aviation Week* reported that an amphibious ship derived from the *Mistral* type that France's DCNS was offering would cost c. €350m or R3.7bn at then exchange rates.

Equally opaque are the upgrade plans for the submarines and frigates. Perhaps the submarines will, in time, gain air-independent propulsion, mines and guided missiles, the latter maybe with a land-attack capability. As for the frigates, there has been talk of up-gunning the main armament from 76mm to 155mm, acquiring land-attack capable missiles and unmanned aerial vehicles. The fact that the ships are fitted for – but not with – torpedoes may also be addressed. A radar upgrade and improved versions of the domestic Denel Dynamics 'Umkhonto' infrared terminally-guided short-range point air-defence missile are probabilities. Also on the cards is the gradual acquisition of weapons systems for the Project Maulstic Super Lynx helicopters acquired for the frigates. The SAAF and South African Navy are said to be keen on fitting the

'Mokopa' to the rotorcraft, although not as the lead customer (which would require a substantial outlay). Torpedoes are also probable, giving the frigate system an actual anti-submarine capability should that ever be needed.

So far as maritime surveillance is concerned, the SAAF plans to retire the venerable Dakota in 2015, and has registered Project Saucepan to acquire about thirteen maritime patrol and maritime security aircraft-cum-transports by 2016. In early 2010, the air force revisited its future transport/maritime requirement in light of the country's cancellation of a contract to buy eight Airbus Military A400M transporters (Project Continent). However, by June 2010, this still had to be put to the national Cabinet and details were not yet in the public domain.

Notes

1. With little currently in publication on the South African National Defence Force, readers wanting further information on current naval developments are best served by the two official military sites – www.dod.mil.za and www.navy.mil.za – as well as the broader coverage provided by *defenceWeb* at www.defenceweb.co.za. Reference can also be made to Rear Admiral CH Bennett & Rear Admiral AG Soderlund *South Africa's Navy* (Simon's Town, South African Navy, Naval Publications Unit, 2008) for a wider historical context.

Author:
Conrad Waters

2.4 REGIONAL REVIEW

EUROPE AND RUSSIA

The European economies were arguably amongst those worst hit by the recent global recession. Continued economic instability, particularly within the Euro-zone, suggests that recovery will be slow and hesitant. Many European governments are therefore faced with the need to slash unsustainable levels of public expenditure if they are to put their finances back on a more sustainable footing. Given this backdrop, the outlook for defence and, therefore, naval expenditure is inevitably uncertain and cutbacks look set to be the order of the day. To date, much of this pain has been deferred, not least because of a political desire to sustain key defence projects and – as a result – industrial jobs in the depths of the economic crisis. However, this is now less of an imperative as business conditions pick up and deficit reductions assume greater priority. Consequently, 2011 is likely to be a difficult year for many European navies.

Of course, the pain will not be equally felt. For example, the health of public finances in the European countries varies quite considerably. The willingness to protect defence and associated industrial capabilities in comparison with the priority accorded to social programmes is another relevant factor. Germany's *Deutsche Marine* is facing particularly heavy cutbacks alongside the rest of the country's armed forces in spite of the government maintaining a relatively resilient fiscal position. Yet another consideration is the timing of military projects. Italy's *Marina Militare* is fortunate to have completed the renewal of its core surface components with the delivery of the carrier *Cavour* and its *Andrea Doria* air-defence frigates. Similarly, construction of the British Royal Navy's *Queen Elizabeth* strike carriers might now be so far advanced that contractor penalties would outweigh any benefits from any potential cancellation. Conversely, the postponement until 2012 of the decision whether to build a second, *deuxième porte-avions* (PA2), carrier for France's *Marine Nationale* looks less likely to yield a positive result in an era of budget cutbacks.

Last year's *Seaforth World Naval Review* made reference to the evolution of Europe's navies from Cold War structures to forces more capable of global deployment in support of stabilisation or expeditionary missions. It seems likely that this evolution will continue in spite of budgetary strain. There is a general understanding across the continent that the region's naval forces are likely to see much greater involvement in long-distance stabilisation missions than hitherto. This has been demonstrated by the positive and successful response to the requirements of the EU NAVFOR Somalia's Operation 'Atalanta' anti-piracy mission off the Horn of Africa. The extent to which this mission has been supported by warships from fleets not previously deployed beyond European waters has been particularly notable. It also seems likely that procurement of the more flexible types of warship best suited for these types of operations will be looked upon relatively favourably during the forthcoming round of defence reviews. For example, the previously mentioned reductions in German fleet strength have fallen most heavily on coastal forces, with construction of new F-125 stabilisation frigates much less impacted.

Meanwhile, developments in Russia continue to suggest that the depletion of the country's defence industrial base in the aftermath of the Soviet Union's collapse will continue to hinder reconstitution of an effective fleet. The programme to renew the submarine-based element of the country's nuclear deterrent is being accorded the highest priority yet is making only hesitant progress in the face of repeated technical problems. The transition to serial production of new submarines and light frigates is also much slower than previously anticipated, whilst plans for further refurbishments of Soviet-era vessels have an air of desperation given the extent to which their basic technology lags behind current Western designs. Whilst significant naval export contracts are still being gained, these tend to be focused on older designs that lack the most recent refinements. The possible acquisition of *Mistral* class amphibious ships from France's DCNS is possibly the clearest indication as to just how poorly local industrial capabilities must be viewed by the country's leaders, even accepting the fact they would represent a new type of ship in Russian service. However, it is interesting to recall that France has a history of supporting and modernising Russian naval industry that extends back to the days of the Tsars. Consequently, their involvement in a project that would involve the licensed construction of an extended class might just provide the impetus local industry needs to embark upon a much required rejuvenation.

European navies continue to reap the benefits of previously authorised programmes: the British Royal Navy's Type 45 destroyer *Dauntless* and lead *Astute* class submarine are pictured off the Scottish coast in this March 2010 view. However, the economic environment means that the future will be much more difficult. *(BAE Systems)*

TABLE 2.4.1: FLEET STRENGTHS IN WESTERN EUROPE – LARGER NAVIES (MID-2010)

COUNTRY	FRANCE	GERMANY	GREECE	ITALY	NETHERLANDS	SPAIN	TURKEY	UK
Aircraft Carrier (CVN)	1	–	–	–	–	–	–	–
Support/Helicopter Carrier (CVS/CVH)	1	–	–	2	–	1	–	3
Strategic Missile Submarine (SSBN)	4	–	–	–	–	–	–	4
Attack Submarine (SSN)	6	–	–	–	–	–	–	8
Patrol Submarine (SSK)	–	4	8	6	4	4	14	–
Fleet Escort (DDG/FFG)	18	15	14	16	6	10	16	24
Patrol Escort/Corvette (FFG/FSG/FS)	15	[5]	3	8	–	–	6	–
Missile Armed Attack Craft (PGG/PTG)	–	10	20	–	–	–	27	–
Mine Countermeasures Vessel (MCMV)	14	19	9	12	10	6	20	15
Major Amphibious (LHD/LPD/LPH/LSD)	4	–	–	3	2	3	–	7

Note: Five new German K-130 corvettes have been completed but need to complete gearing repairs before they are fully operational.

The first French Navy FREMM type frigate, *Aquitaine*, in the course of being floated out of her building berth at DCNS's Lorient facility in the spring of 2010. Orders for a further three ships were confirmed in October 2009. *(DCNS)*

MAJOR REGIONAL NAVAL POWERS – FRANCE

France's *Marine Nationale* continues to develop in line with the force structure set out in the 2008 White Paper on defence and national security. This essentially envisages a surface fleet comprised of eighteen fleet escorts supported by broadly similar numbers of less-capable surveillance frigates and offshore patrol vessels. This will be supplemented by an amphibious force built around four *Mistral* type amphibious assault ships. The submarine flotilla will include four strategic missile submarines and six nuclear-powered attack submarines, with the existing *Rubis* boats being replaced by *Suffren* class on a one-for-one basis. The current fleet, listed in Table 2.4.2, is already constituted in broad alignment with this plan, whilst procurement decisions taken over the past twelve months have also been taken in accordance with its objectives.

The most important announcement was made on 8 October 2009, when an order placed with DCNS for a further three FREMM (*frégate multi-mission*) escorts at the end of the previous September was made public during a ceremony marking first steel-

TABLE 2.4.2: FRENCH NAVY: PRINCIPAL UNITS AS AT MID-2010

TYPE	CLASS	NUMBER	TONNAGE	DIMENSIONS	PROPULSION	CREW	DATE
Aircraft Carriers							
Aircraft Carrier – CVN	CHARLES DE GAULLE	1	42,000 tons	262m x 33/64m x 9m	Nuclear, 27 knots	1,950	2001
Principal Surface Escorts							
Frigate – FFG	FORBIN	2	7,000 tons	153m x 20m x 5m	CODOG, 29+ knots	195	2008
Frigate – FFG	CASSARD (FAA-70)	2	5,000 tons	139m x 15m x 5m	CODAD, 30 knots	250	1988
Frigate – FFG	TOURVILLE (FASM-67)	2	6,100 tons	153m x 16m x 5m	Steam, 32 knots	300	1974
Frigate – FFG	GEORGES LEYGUES (FASM-70)	7	4,800 tons	139m x 15m x 5m	CODOG, 30 knots	240	1979
Frigate – FFG	LA FAYETTE	5	3,600 tons	125m x 15m x 5m	CODAD, 25 knots	150	1996
Frigate – FSG	FLORÉAL	6	3,000 tons	94m x 14m x 4m	CODAD, 20 knots	90	1992
Frigate – FS[1]	D'ESTIENNE D'ORVES (A-69)	9	1,300 tons	80m x 10m x 3m	Diesel, 24 knots	90	1976
Submarines							
Submarine – SSBN	LE TRIOMPHANT	4	14,400 tons	138m x 13m x 11m	Nuclear, 25 knots	110	1997
Submarine – SSN	RUBIS	6	2,700 tons	74m x 8m x 6m	Nuclear, 25+ knots	70	1983
Major Amphibious Units							
Amph. Assault Ship – LHD	MISTRAL	2	21,500 tons	199m x 32m x 6m	Diesel-electric, 19 knots	160	2006
Landing Platform Dock – LPD	FOUDRE	2	12,000 tons	168m x 24m x 5m	Diesel, 20 knots	225	1990

1 Now officially reclassified as offshore patrol vessels.

cutting on the second ship of the class, *Normandie*. The award completes France's planned purchase of eleven of these Franco-Italian ships, the last two of which will be specialised FREDA (*frégate de défense aérienne*) variants. The programme's cost is running significantly over original estimates. Figures from France's national auditors, the *Cour des Comptes*, suggest that the price of the eleven-ship project will be €7.8bn (US$9.75bn) or €710m (US$890m) per vessel compared with original plans to buy seventeen ships for €9.1bn. Production will continue through to 2022, providing considerable future security for DCNS' principal construction facility for surface ships at Lorient. The shipyard floated out the first of these 6,000-ton ships on 29 April 2010 prior to a formal ceremony attended by French President Nicolas Sarkozy on 4 May.

Also expected to hit the water during 2010 is the third of the LHD-type *Mistral* class amphibious assault ships, *Dixmude*, which was laid down at STX France's Saint Nazaire shipyard on 20 January 2010. Known as a *bâtiment de projection et de commandement* (BPC) in French service, she was ordered under France's economic recovery plan in 2009 and will replace the existing *Foudre* in 2012. As well as their primary amphibious role, the class will also be used to support future training cruises for naval cadets following the withdrawal of the former helicopter cruiser *Jeanne d'Arc* at the conclusion of her final training mission at the end of May 2010. The veteran cruiser was reported to have sailed 1.76 million nautical miles (3.26 million kilometres) during her 46-year operational career, during which time she visited eighty-five different countries.[1]

Other ships being withdrawn from service include two of the 'Tripartite' class minehunters – *Persée* and *Verseau* – as well as growing numbers of the P400 large patrol craft. *La Fougueuse* of this latter class was decommissioned during the spring of 2009 and is set to be followed by sister-ships *L'Audacieuse* and *La Boudeuse* during 2010. The remaining seven vessels slated for withdrawal by 2016. Never an entirely satisfactory design and used largely to patrol the waters of France's overseas colonies, they have apparently suffered from the lower level of maintenance available at these distant locations. Their steady demise will present the *Marine Nationale* with a major headache, as replacements have yet to be ordered. In the short term, the use of some of the remaining A-69 corvettes in the patrol role will

provide a stop-gap solution, with DCNS hoping to sell the navy its 'Gowind' design as a longer-term successor. To this end – and to assist export prospects – DCNS is to self-fund construction of an offshore patrol variant of the design for loan to the French Navy for three years from the end of 2011.

Underneath the water, the fourth *Le Triomphant* class strategic nuclear submarine *Le Terrible* has continued a series of trials as she moves steadily towards formal commissioning. A successful test firing of her principal weapons system – the M-51 nuclear missile – was carried out whilst the boast was submerged off the Brittany peninsula on 27 January 2010. Intended to replace the existing M-45 submarine launched ballistic missile in French service, the new system has a greater, 8,500km, range than its predecessor and is reportedly capable of delivering a greater number of independently targetable warheads. Current plans envisage production of fifty M-51 missiles under a €3bn (US$3.75bn) contract with EADS; they will be retrofitted to the earlier boats of the class by 2014.

The next major procurement decision is whether to proceed with the PA2 aircraft carrier. The decision appears quite finely balanced given current economic conditions. However, the sole existing carrier *Charles de Gaulle*'s lengthy absence from the fleet during 2007-9 when a scheduled refit had to be extended due to the discovery of defective couplings between two of the ship's steam turbines and their respective gearboxes may have strengthened the hands of those suggesting a second carrier is necessary. In the meantime, *Charles de Gaulle* has now returned to operational service after an extensive post-refit workup that saw her lose two Rafale M fighters in a tragic mid-air collision on 24 September 2009 that cost the life of one of the pilots.

MAJOR REGIONAL NAVAL POWERS – ITALY

The Marina Militare's principal fleet units are summarised in Table 2.4.3. With *Cavour* and the two *Andrea Doria* class air-defence frigates of the Franco-Italian 'Horizon' class now in operational service, the main focus is replacement of the rest of the navy's fleet escorts with the follow-on FREMM multi-mission class. Six out of ten planned *Carlo Bergamini* frigates have been ordered to date to replace the

Italy's 'Horizon' class air-defence frigate *Andrea Doria*. She was deployed to South American waters in the first half of 2010 to support potential Italian defence exports to Brazil. *(Italian Navy)*

The French Navy paid farewell to one of its longest serving and best-loved ships in 2010 with the decommissioning of the helicopter cruiser *Jeanne d'Arc*. These views were taken during her last training cruise. *(French Navy)*

Table 2.4.3: ITALIAN NAVY: PRINCIPAL UNITS AS AT MID-2010

TYPE	CLASS	NUMBER	TONNAGE	DIMENSIONS	PROPULSION	CREW	DATE
Aircraft Carriers							
Aircraft Carrier – CV	**CAVOUR**	1	27,100 tons	244m x 30/39m x 9m	COGAG, 29 knots	800	2008
Aircraft Carrier – CVS	**GIUSEPPE GARIBALDI**	1	13,900 tons	180m x 23/31m x 7m	COGAG, 30 knots	825	1985
Principal Surface Escorts							
Frigate – FFG	**ANDREA DORIA**	2	7,100 tons	153m x 20m x 5m	CODOG, 29+ knots	190	2007
Destroyer – DDG	**DE LA PENNE**	2	5,400 tons	148m x 16m x 5m	CODOG, 31 knots	375	1993
Frigate – FFG	**MAESTRALE**	8	3,100 tons	123m x 13 x 4m	CODOG, 30+ knots	225	1982
Frigate – FFG	**ARTIGLIERE**	4	2,500 tons	114m x 12m x 4m	CODOG, 35 knots	185	1994
Frigate – FS	**MINERVA**	8	1,300 tons	87m x 11m x 3m	Diesel, 25 knots	120	1987
Submarines							
Submarine – SSK	**TODARO** (Type 212A)	2	1,800 tons	56m x 7m x 6m	AIP, 20+ knots	30	2006
Submarine – SSK	**PELOSI**	4	1,700 tons	64m x 7m x 6m	Diesel-electric, 20 knots	50	1988
Major Amphibious Units							
Landing Platform Dock – LPD	**SAN GIORGIO**	3	8,000 tons	133m x 21m x 5m	Diesel, 20 knots	165	1987

increasingly elderly *Maestrale* and *Artigliere* classes. However, construction of the class, which feature significant differences in detail from their French half sisters, has been delayed by around a year to 2013 to allow improvements to radar and missile systems. These have been reported as including modification of the ship's EMPAR multifunction radar to incorporate active-array technology, as well as the installation of longer-range Aster 30 surface-to-air missiles in addition to the Aster 15 weapons originally specified.[2] As such, the modified ships, which will be built in anti-submarine and general purpose variants, could initially gain more potent air-defence capabilities than the previous 'Horizon' class specifically designed for this task. Current plans envisage ordering the remaining four ships by 2013 but this will inevitably be subject to budgetary factors. Italy has high hopes of selling the design to the Brazilian Navy, with high-profile visits by both *Andrea Doria* and *Cavour* – the latter *en route* to Haiti to provide humanitarian assistance – to Brazil in the first half of 2010 doubtless intended to showcase Italian technological superiority.

Construction planned for the next decade includes a new series of offshore patrol vessels to replace the existing *Minerva* corvettes and *Cassiopea* patrol ships, more modern replenishment vessels and an upgraded amphibious flotilla. It is hard to envisage funding being found to meet all these requirements and some existing ships might have to serve longer than planned. The highest priority is being accorded to the construction of new amphibious assault ships, for which design funding has now been provided. It is envisaged that two 20,000-ton LHD type ships will be constructed to take the place of the much smaller existing *San Giorgio* LPDs, with the first of the new ships entering service by 2015. A third ship, possibly built to an LHA configuration without a well dock, might be ordered at a later date in replacement of the existing carrier *Giuseppe Garibaldi*.[3]

A notable feature of recent *Marina Militare* operations has been the steadily increasing scope of international deployments. In addition to the Atlantic missions of *Cavour* and *Andrea Doria* already referenced, warships have been despatched in support of Operation 'Atalanta' anti-piracy duties in the Indian Ocean and to the maritime component of the UNIFIL stabilisation force off Lebanon. These deployments are in addition to the longer standing commitment to Multinational Force Observer (MFO) duties in the Red Sea, where Italian patrol boats of the *Esploratore* class have also now completed over ten years service. Italian submarines are also increasingly voyaging further afield, with the Type 212A boat *Sciré* following in her sister *Salvatore Todaro*'s footsteps with a five-month Atlantic mission to the United States that also saw port calls in Spain and the Azores.

MAJOR REGIONAL NAVAL POWERS – SPAIN

Spain's *Armada Española* is expected to take delivery of two significant new ships in the second half of 2010 with the planned commissioning of the LHD-type strategic projection ship *Juan Carlos I* and the fleet replenishment tanker *Cantabria*. With a length of 231m and a full load displacement slightly in excess of 27,000 tons, the former ship will be the largest vessel in the Spanish Navy and has been designed to act as a substitute aircraft carrier to the existing *Principe de Asturias* as well as in her primary amphibious role. Preliminary sea trials commenced in September 2009. However, teething troubles with the ship's propulsion system required the replacement of one of the two diesel engines that, along with a single gas turbine, provides power for her electric pods. The repairs, as well as modifications to the pods themselves, were subsequently tested in a further set of highly successful sea trials between 24 May and 2 June 2010 that saw the ship achieve over one knot more than her official 21-knot design speed. Meanwhile, *Cantabria* completed her own final sea trials between 28 November and 2 December 2009 prior to expected formal hand over in July 2010. A doubled-hulled vessel some 174m in length, she is designed to supply fuel, water and stores to a naval task group and is also equipped with extensive hospital facilities.

A list of current major fleet units is set out in Table 2.4.4. The navy has undergone a qualitative revolution in recent years and previously announced projects look set to deliver further force enhancements. In addition to the construction of a fifth F-100 type frigate, the most significant ongoing programme is the construction of four S-80 class AIP-equipped submarines to an indigenous design that builders

Table 2.4.4: SPANISH NAVY: PRINCIPAL UNITS AS AT MID-2010

TYPE	CLASS	NUMBER	TONNAGE	DIMENSIONS	PROPULSION	CREW	DATE
Aircraft Carriers							
Aircraft Carrier – CVS	**PRINCIPE DE ASTURIAS**	1	16,700 tons	196m x 24/32m x 7m	COGAG, 25 knots	555	1988
Principal Surface Escorts							
Frigate – FFG	**ÁLVARO DE BAZÁN** (F-100)	4	6,300 tons	147m x 19m x 5m	CODOG, 28 knots	200	2002
Frigate – FFG	**SANTA MARIA** (FFG-7)	6	4,100 tons	138m x 14m x 5m	COGAG, 30 knots	225	1986
Submarines							
Submarine – SSK	**GALERNA** (S-70/AGOSTA)	4	1,800 tons	68m x 7m x 6m	Diesel-electric, 21 knots	60	1983
Major Amphibious Units							
Amph. Assault Ship – LHD	**JUAN CARLOS I**	1	27,100 tons	231m x 32m x 7m	IEP, 21 knots	245	2010
Landing Platform Dock – LPD	**GALICIA**	2	13,000 tons	160m x 25m x 6m	Diesel, 20 knots	185	1998

Navantia hope will have considerable export potential. The first metal for fourth and final boat – S-84 – was cut on 19 January 2010, whilst outfitting of modules for the first of class will start towards the end of 2010 prior to a 2012 launch. With a length of 71m, a hull diameter of 7.3m and a surface displacement of 2,200 tons, they are relatively large for a diesel-electric patrol submarine, being quite similar in size to the Russian Project 636 'Kilo' type.

Navantia are also building four BAM (*buque de acción maritima*) offshore patrol vessels as replacements for existing elderly corvettes and patrol ships. Two of these have already been launched, with the third and fourth following in October 2010 and March 2011 respectively. The first will also be delivered around the latter date. Original plans envisaged construction of a further eight members of the class but an anticipated order for a second batch of four has been delayed by Spain's budget crisis, which is amongst the worst in Europe. With plans for additional submarines already cancelled and an order for a sixth F-100 frigate also deferred, the medium-term outlook for future procurement looks relatively bleak. Replacement of the existing FFG-7 type frigates with a new F110 design, as well as acquisition of F-35B Lightning II fighters in place of existing AV-8B Harriers, is required from around 2020 but this will inevitably depend on an improvement in government finances.

MAJOR REGIONAL NAVAL POWERS – UNITED KINGDOM

Still the largest and most potent of all the European fleets, the British Royal Navy's future direction is inextricably tied to the strategic defence review being conducted by the United Kingdom's new Conservative-Liberal Democrat administration

The Spanish Navy welcomed the new LHD-type strategic projection ship *Juan Carlos I* and the fleet replenishment tanker *Cantabria* to the fleet during the course of 2010. Both ships are pictured on sea trials during the latter half of 2009. *(Navantia)*

The British Royal Navy is saying goodbye to its remaining Batch II Type 42 destroyers as new ships join the fleet, with *Nottingham* being decommissioned in February 2010. This leaves *Liverpool*, which deployed as air-defence escort to *Ark Royal* during the Auriga exercises, as the sole remaining example of the type in the fleet. *(Conrad Waters)*

under the leadership of the new Secretary of State for Defence, Liam Fox. The backdrop of a significantly over-committed procurement budget and the need to find additional savings that currently look to be in the order of 10-20 per cent of the existing budget over the four years to 2015 suggest significant revisions to the existing force structure set out in Table 2.4.5, as well as to future procurement plans. The need for the two new *Queen Elizabeth* aircraft carriers currently under construction has attracted considerable speculation, not least from other branches of the armed forces looking to protect their own future plans. However, the project is already well underway and seems to enjoy considerable political support, not least because of its industrial and political significance. The maintenance of a submarine-based nuclear deterrent has already been expressly confirmed, by implication supporting ongoing construction of the current *Astute* class.

In the meantime, the fleet is at last starting to see the replacement of existing obsolescent units by modern and capable designs. The first Type 45 destroyer, *Daring*, was formally commissioned on 23 July 2009, with second of class *Dauntless* following on 3 June 2010. The third ship, *Diamond*, will be delivered to the Royal Navy before the end of 2010 following successful completion of sea trials, by which time the sixth and final member of the class,

Duncan, should have been launched. *Dauntless* is due to host the first firing trials of the Sea Viper surface-to-air missile system from a member of the class in the autumn of 2010. The system's development hit an embarrassing hitch towards the end of 2009 with the emergence of two successive failures during qualification testing that were ultimately traced back to manufacturing defects in its Aster missiles. However, subsequent test firings carried out by *Andrea Doria*, her French sister *Forbin* and the British trials barge *Longbow* in June 2010 have been highly successful. If trials on *Dauntless* also go to plan, the way will be paved for official introduction into Royal Navy service by the end of the year.

Underwater forces should be boosted by the arrival of the new nuclear-powered attack submarine, *Astute*, which commenced sea trials on 14 November 2009 prior to planned commissioning in the summer of 2010. A detailed overview of her design and development is contained in Chapter 3.1. However, transfers have not all been one way, with scheduled withdrawals of the veteran Type 42 destroyer *Nottingham* and the lead *Trafalgar* class submarine being supplemented by the survey ship *Roebuck* and the minehunter *Walney*. The last two ships fell victim to a miniature defence review at the end of 2009 which will also result in the premature disposal of naval helicopters to release additional

resources for operations in Afghanistan. Plans for future helicopter operations propose the transfer of all RAF Merlin helicopters to support Royal Navy commando operations in replacement of the existing Sea Kings. This will produce a combined Merlin fleet of thirty anti-submarine and twenty-eight transport helicopters, supplemented by twenty-eight of the new Lynx Wildcats.

Future surface construction is likely to be focused on the new Type 26 frigate design, which – for some reason or other – is now being referred to as a 'combat ship' in official press releases. A £127m, four-year design development contract for the new type was signed just before the election and subsequently emerged unscathed from a review of contracts by the new government. If all goes well, the contract will result in an order for the first of a class of c. ten ships around 2014. They will enter operational service on an annual basis from 2021 onwards to replace existing Type 22 and Type 23 frigates. Baseline figures for the new frigates suggest they will be slightly smaller than the Type 45 destroyers, with a length of around 140m and a full load displacement of slightly less than 7,000 tons. It is envisaged that significant amounts of equipment will be transferred from existing ships, most notably modernised Type 23 frigates, to keep costs to an acceptable level.

Operationally, the Royal Navy has benefited from

Table 2.4.5: BRITISH ROYAL NAVY: PRINCIPAL UNITS AS AT MID-2010

TYPE	CLASS	NUMBER	TONNAGE	DIMENSIONS	PROPULSION	CREW	DATE
Aircraft Carriers							
Aircraft Carrier – CVS	**INVINCIBLE**	2 (1)	22,000 tons	210m x 31/36m x 8m	COGAG, 30 knots	1,100	1980
Principal Surface Escorts							
Destroyer – DDG	**DARING** (Type 45)	2	7,400 tons	152m x 21m x 5m	IEP, 30 knots	190	2008
Destroyer – DDG	**MANCHESTER** (Type 42-Batch 3)	4	5,200 tons	141m x 15m x 4m	COGOG, 30+ knots	290	1982
Destroyer – DDG	**EXETER** (Type 42 – Batch 2)	1	4,800 tons	125m x 14m x 4m	COGOG, 30 knots	290	1980
Frigate – FFG	**CORNWALL** (Type 22 – Batch 3)	4	5,300 tons	148m x 15m x 5m	COGOG, 30+ knots	250	1988
Frigate – FFG	**NORFOLK** (Type 23)	13	4,900 tons	133m x 16m x 5m	CODLAG, 30 knots	185	1990
Submarines							
Submarine – SSBN	**VANGUARD**	4	16,000 tons	150m x 13m x 12m	Nuclear, 25+ knots	135	1993
Submarine – SSN	**ASTUTE**	1	7,800 tons	93m x 11m x 10m	Nuclear, 30+ knots	100	2010
Submarine – SSN	**TRAFALGAR**	6	5,200 tons	85m x 10m x 10m	Nuclear, 30+knots	130	1983
Submarine – SSN	**SWIFTSURE**	1	4,900 tons	83m x 10n x 9m	Nuclear, 30+ knots	115	1973
Major Amphibious Units							
Helicopter Carrier – LPH	**OCEAN**	1	22,500 tons	203m x 35m x 7m	Diesel, 18 knots	490	1998
Landing Platform Dock – LPD	**ALBION**	2	18,500 tons	176m x 29m x 7m	IEP, 18 knots	325	2003
Landing Ship Dock – LSD (A)	**LARGS BAY**	4	16,200 tons	176m x 26m x 6m	Diesel-electric, 18 knots	60	2006

Note: Figures in brackets refer to ships in extended reserve.

the permanent return of the aircraft of Joint Force Harrier from Afghanistan, allowing the resumption of more frequent carrier deployments. The Auriga 2010 exercises have seen a carrier task group comprising the recently refitted *Ark Royal*, the similarly modernised Type 42 destroyer *Exeter* and four other British, American and French warships undertake extended operations along the eastern freeboard of North America. These included combined exercises with an amphibious task group headed by the LPD *Albion* during the latter stages of the deployment. Elsewhere, the navy has been heavily committed to security and anti-piracy operations in the Persian Gulf and Indian Ocean, counternarcotics activities in the Caribbean and maintaining an ongoing presence in the South Atlantic. Humanitarian successes included the Falkland Island patrol vessel *Clyde*'s recovery of a family from a sinking yacht that had hit an iceberg in May 2010 and the frigate *Chatham*'s rescue of the crew from a cyclone-stricken Somali merchant ship during the same month. *Albion* was even diverted to Santander in Spain to bring home stranded soldiers returning from Afghanistan – as well as vulnerable civilian tourists – during the suspension of air traffic across northern Europe that followed an Icelandic volcanic eruption.

MID-SIZED REGIONAL FLEETS

Germany: As heralded in the Introduction, Germany's *Deutsche Marine* is amongst the first to experience the impact of Europe's new financial straightjacket. A surprise announcement at the start of June 2010 heralded the simultaneous decommissioning of all six remaining Type 206A patrol submarines, more than halving Germany's underwater forces at a stroke. Revised plans will see the navy move to a concept of using two crews for each remaining submarine in service, which will edge back upwards to a new total of six boats when the two additional members of the Type 212A class join their existing sisters around 2012/13. The reductions in force level appear to be only the initial instalment of a series of more extensive savings that could also see reductions in service personnel and further withdrawals of operational units.

At the moment, principal surface procurement programmes look relatively secure. The five K-130 *Braunschweig* class corvettes only await repairs to defective gearing before being brought into service and are ideal for expeditionary operations in the littoral that the navy is becoming increasingly involved in. However, plans for a follow-on K-131 design to replace the remaining fast attack craft of the Type 143A *Gepard* class are looking less likely to

survive the axe, possibly resulting in the premature disposal of these ships and the closure of their base at Warnemünde. The new F-125 stabilisation frigates are also designed to address the navy's new strategic objectives and are also significant for the survival of the country's shipbuilding base. They, along with the three modern F-124 air-defence frigates and four slightly older F-123 ships seem set for a continuing place in the fleet. However, it is possible to envisage the early decommissioning of some of the eight older F-122 *Bremen* class frigates, even though they have recently benefited from modern combat systems upgrades.

Greece: The sorry and convoluted saga of the Hellenic Navy's renewal of its underwater forces was apparently drawing towards a satisfactory conclusion in the first months of 2010 after an agreement was reached with Thyssen Krupp Marine Systems (TKMS) on the future of the Neptune II and Archimedes projects. The former contract, signed in May 2002, envisaged modernisation of the navy's four Type 209/1200 *Poseidon* class boats with the installation of AIP and new combat systems. The latter award – first signed in February 2000 – was based on the construction of four new Type 214 AIP-equipped submarines to replace the older Type 209/1200 *Glavkos* submersibles in Greek service. Both programmes encountered problems in their execution, with particular heat being generated by Greek claims of poor performance by the first Type 214 boat, the German-built *Papanikolis*, during sea trials. TKMS eventually cancelled both contracts in September 2009 over the non-payment of over €500m reportedly owed to the company. The subsequent settlement should see the Neptune II programme terminated with the modernisation of just one boat, *Papanikolis* offered for sale to other countries and two new Type 214 submarines built by Hellenic Shipyards to add to the three already built by this TKMS subsidiary. The deal should result in a submarine flotilla of five Type 214 and one modernised Type 209/1200 boats when the revised strategy is completed.[4] Meanwhile, TKMS is likely to withdraw from the Greek market with the planned sale of Hellenic Shipyards to Abu Dhabi's MAR group.

There had previously been considerable speculation that the dispute was driven as much by shortages of cash at the Greek Ministry of Defence as technical considerations, a conclusion supported by the subse-

The Type 26 frigate – officially known as a 'combat ship' – represents the future of the Royal Navy escort fleet. A four-year design development contract for the new type was let in 2010 for a class that should enter operational service from around 2021. (*BAE Systems*)

quent emergence of very significant financial problems at the heart of the Hellenic Republic. These seem certain to curtail future naval procurement plans, most notably the planned acquisition of six FREMM type frigates from France's DCNS. It therefore seems likely that surface forces will remain focused on the four MEKO 200 *Hydra* and six modernised *Elli* (former Dutch *Kortenaer*) class frigates, with the four remaining *Elli*s looking vulnerable to potential early deletion. The navy has already taken steps to dispose of some of its oldest units, with the two remaining *Niki* (former *Thetis*) corvettes *Doxa* and *Eleftheria* paid off at the naval base on Crete on 22 April 2010. Decommissioning of the elderly US-built coastal minesweepers has also recommenced with the withdrawal of *Kissa* at Salamis on 21 June 2010. It remains possible that two further former US Navy *Osprey* class mine-hunters will be transferred by way of balance.

Maintenance of powerful flotillas of fast attack craft remain a priority given both geographical considerations and underlying tensions with neighbouring Turkey, which has been steadily building up its own forces. Five of the seven *Roussen* class vessels built under licence from the UK's VT Group shipbuilding arm (now BAE Systems Surface Ships) should be fully operational before the end of 2010. Meanwhile mid-life modernisation of the fifteen 'La Combattante' II and III series vessels is progressing with the re-delivery of *Blessas* and *Mikonios*, to the fleet in October 2009. The second and third of the four CMN Cherbourg built 'La Combattante' III craft to complete modernisation, they have emerged with Thales' Tacitos combat management system, as well as upgraded radar and countermeasures systems.

The Netherlands: The Royal Netherlands Navy is starting to see force levels stabilise, as previously-announced cutbacks have now been largely implemented. This leaves the fleet focused on six principal surface escorts of the *De Zeven Provinciën* and *Karel Doorman* 'M' classes, four *Walrus* patrol submarines and the landing platform docks *Rotterdam* and *Johan de Witt*. These will be supplemented over the next two years by the four new offshore patrol vessels of the *Holland* class and the newly ordered JSS joint logistic support ship that is being built to replace the elderly replenishment vessel *Zuiderkruis*.

The JSS is an interesting hybrid concept that is attracting significant interest from a number of other mid-ranking navies looking to combine amphibious

An unusual aerial view of a Greek *Roussen* class fast attack craft. Although the Hellenic Navy is suffering from the country's financial crisis, maintaining a modern fleet of coastal forces is being given a priority as a result of geographic and political considerations. *(BAE Systems)*

An impression of the new JSS joint logistics support ship ordered for the Royal Netherlands Navy. Combining amphibious and logistical support capabilities in a single hull, the design is attracting attention from other second-tier fleets. *(Thales Nederland)*

and logistical support capabilities in a single hull. Specifically designed as a multi-function platform capable of operating in both low- and high-intensity operations, it can undertake maritime support, strategic sea lift and sea basing missions in both open and coastal waters. This combination demands a large ship. Accordingly, the JSS will have an overall length of 205m, a beam of 30m and a full load displacement approaching 28,000 tons. In addition to providing a full replenishment service, this size allows a helicopter deck capable of operating two Chinook-sized helicopters simultaneously, storage capacity for up to six helicopters and sufficient space for 2,000 lane metres of vehicles and 150 surplus personnel in addition to the standard 150-strong crew. Features such as roll on/roll off facilities for vehicles, a 40-ton capable elevator and crane and a stern gate to facilitate landing craft transfers are incorporated to support amphibious missions. The design also incorporates a high level of damage resistance, a number of close-in weapons systems and the innovative Thales integrated mast also incorporated in the *Holland* class design. In common with much other recent Dutch naval construction, preliminary fabrication is being carried out at Damen Schelde Naval Shipbuilding's facility at Galati in Romania prior to final fitting out in the Netherlands. However, over 75 per cent of the c. €365m construction cost will be spent in the Netherlands, as compared with c.15 per cent in Romania.

Current plans envisage the JSS being delivered in 2014 and becoming fully operational the following year. She will be preceded into service by the four *Holland* class ships, with which good progress has been achieved over the past year. The first of these 3,750-ton ships was launched by Queen Beatrix of the Netherlands at Damen's Vlissingen yard on 2 February 2010. It seems likely that she will commence sea trials around the end of the year. Construction of the fourth and final ship commenced in Romania on 9 April 2010. The ships are noteworthy in being fitted with an advanced radar and electronics capability built around the integrated mast previously referred to but incorporating only a light gunnery-based armament.

Turkey: The considerable progress made by Turkey in developing the indigenous content of its large and relatively modern fleet is outlined in detail in Chapter 2.4A. A notable development in 2010 was the despatch of a Turkish Naval Task Force

The Turkish MEKO 200 type frigate *Turgutreis*. She was part of the Turkish Naval Task Force that deployed throughout the Mediterranean in 2010, the first such operation in recent memory. *(Devrim Yaylalı)*

comprising two MEKO 200 type frigates, two 'G' class FFG-7 type frigates and the replenishment tanker *Akar* on a Mediterranean flag waving exercise. Reported to be the first such mission carried out in recent years, the two month deployment saw visits to ten ports in countries as far apart as Algeria, Egypt, Italy, Spain and Tunisia as part of a programme demonstrating the advances in capability the Turkish Navy has achieved.

OTHER REGIONAL FLEETS

Black Sea and Mediterranean: There has been little in the way of recent tangible developments amongst Turkey's Black Sea neighbours following the delivery of refurbished equipment from Belgium and the UK to bolster, respectively, the surface forces of the **Bulgarian** and **Romanian** navies in the second half of the last decade. Indeed, the need to return defence budgets to balance is likely to be the overriding priority over the next few years, a fact made explicit in the then Bulgarian defence minister Nickolay Mladenov's remarks when he attended celebrations in August 2009 to mark the 130th anniversary of the navy's foundation. Bulgaria's defence ministry, particularly, is struggling due to the need to pay the costs of a deal with EADS' Eurocopter subsidiary that

included the supply of six AS656 Panther light helicopters to the navy. Consequently, it is unlikely to find money for plans that previously envisaged the construction of new corvettes any time soon. A possible exception to this picture of inactivity is **Ukraine**, which has undergone a political rapprochement with the Russian Federation that has seen the latter's lease of the key Sevastopol naval base extended for at least a further twenty-five years. Ukraine had previously expressed an interest in acquiring former US Navy ships. However, technical co-operation with Russia, including discussions on the completion of the long laid-up Project 1164 *Slava* class cruiser *Ukraina* – most likely for Russian service – is now the order of the day. Ukraine also has plans for a new class of light corvettes to recapitalise its surface forces. A design that could, reportedly, be used for a series of ten ships was completed towards the end of 2009, with a contract for an initial batch of four awarded to the Chernomorsky Shipyard at Nikolayev on 10 December 2009. Fabrication on the first vessel commenced in the first half of 2010 prior to a scheduled 2012 launch.

Elsewhere, to the south of the region, **Malta** has completed an upgrade to its small maritime squadron, commissioning four new 21m patrol boats built by Australia's Austal on 18 March 2010. The new ships will replace some of the existing American and East German-built boats in Maltese service and complement the larger *Diciotti* and 'Sentinel' types acquired over the past few years.

North Sea and Atlantic: **Ireland's** Naval Service has been one of many smaller navies impacted by the recent financial crisis and plans for much-needed offshore patrol vessels to replace the three remaining elderly P-21 ships class appear to have been delayed. It appears that Babcock's Appledore yard is front runner for a contract that initially involves the construction of two Aker Marine-designed vessels for delivery from 2014 but funding has yet to be released. In the meantime, the most modern patrol vessel currently serving in Ireland's eight-strong fleet, the Appledore-built *Niamh*, has made a rare deployment to South America to celebrate Irish involvement in the continent's early nineteenth century struggle for liberation from Spanish rule. The voyage included visits to Brazil, Argentina, Chile, Panama, Mexico and the United States and saw the most southerly point ever reached by an Irish Naval Service ship with a passage through the Magellan Strait.

Portugal's *Marinha Portuguesa* has been fortunate to complete the bulk of planned fleet upgrades before the full extent of financial austerity begins to bite. *D Francisco de Almeida* (formerly *Van Galen*), the second *Karel Doorman* 'M' class frigate acquired from the Netherlands was handed over on 15 January 2010. She arrived in Lisbon in early March after training and work up, bringing the fleet up to a planned complement of five front-line frigates. Similarly, renewal of the submarine flotilla progressed towards its close with the provisional acceptance of the initial Type 209(PN) boat *Tridente* from TKMS's HDW subsidiary at Kiel on 17 June 2010. Sister-ship *Arpão* should also be delivered within the next twelve months. Attention will then turn to renewal of the country's patrol forces, although it looks questionable whether plans for a total of ten NPO2000 *Viana do Castelo* offshore patrol vessels and a further five coastal patrol craft remain affordable. Lead ship *Viana do Castelo* was christened on 24 July 2009 prior to commencement of sea trials in the first half of 2010, whilst the second ship *Figueira da Foz* is also well advanced. Meanwhile, long held plans for a LPD-type amphibious transport look set for further delay in the current environment.

Portugal's first Type 209 (PN) AIP-equipped submarine *Tridente* was delivered on 17 June 2010. *(HDW)*

The two **Belgian** 'M' class frigates are being kept busy on international operations, with *Louise-Marie* set to commence a second Operation 'Atalanta' deployment to the Indian Ocean in the second half of 2010. The ships will be retrofitted with Thales' Seastar and Gatekeeper sensors between 2011 and 2013 to retain commonality with the two remaining Dutch ships of the class under a contract announced in February 2010.

Scandinavia and the Baltic: The Scandinavian navies are continuing their transition from a largely regional defence role to force structures more capable of conducting global operations. **Norway** is arguably most advanced with this process and the successful *Fridtjof Nansen* programme is described in detail in Chapter 3.4. The Royal Norwegian Navy will also soon start to take delivery of the delayed *Skjold* fast attack craft, with delivery of the first operational member of the class *Storm* scheduled for August 2010 and all six ships likely to be in service before the end of 2011. However, full operational capability is likely to be delayed until 2012-13. By then communications systems upgrades will have been completed and the NSM surface-to-surface missiles that form a principal part of their armament installed.[5] Meanwhile, **Sweden** is making steady progress in bringing the five larger but conceptually similar *Visby* class corvettes into service, with *Helsingborg* and *Härnösand* being handed over for operational duties in December 2009. They subsequently participated in two week's sea training with the Royal Navy's Flag Officer Sea Training (FOST) organisation in May. Again, however, full operational capability is still some way off, as systems such as surface-to-surface missiles and mine clearance capability will not be available until 2012. Meanwhile, design work continues on the A-26 submarine prior to expected approval for the construction of two boats in the second half of 2010. Displacing 1,900 tons and with a length of 63m, the A-26 will be equipped with the Stirling AIP system and could be capable of operation by a crew of as few as seventeen submariners. The contract is vital for the continuation of

A Royal Norwegian Navy *Skjold* class fast attack craft on sea trials. The first operational member of the class, *Storm*, should commission in August 2010 and all six will be in service by the end of 2011. *(Royal Norwegian Navy)*

Above and below: Denmark is making good progress with construction of its three *Ivar Huitfeldt* class air-defence frigates. Derived from the existing *Absalon* design, the lead ship is pictured in this artist's impression and in the course of being floated out on 11 March 2010. *(Danish Defence Acquisition & Logistics Organisation & Thales Nederland)*

Below: Approval for the construction of two A-26 Kockums-designed submarines for the Swedish Navy is expected during 2010. *(Kockums)*

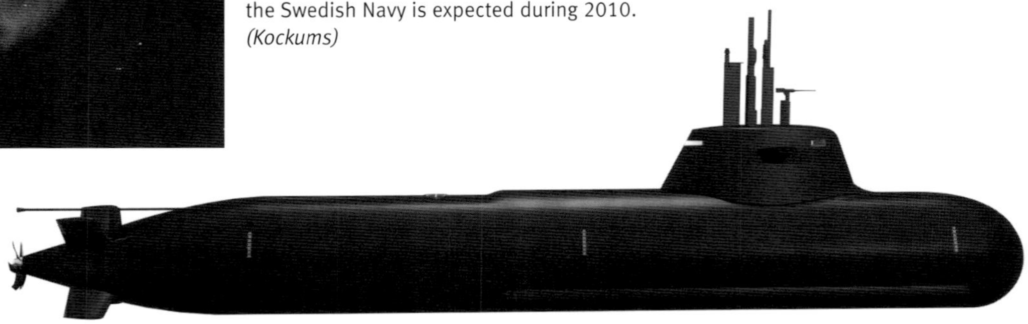

Above: The Royal Danish Navy's three existing *Niels Juel* class frigates were withdrawn from service 'on block' on 18 August 2009. *(Canadian Navy)*

Kockums's submarine activities and could also be of interest to other navies requiring modern submarines, most notably Norway and Singapore.

Elsewhere in the region, **Denmark** is making good progress with completion of its *Ivar Huitfeldt* air-defence frigates, the first of which was floated out on 11 March 2010. They will replace the much smaller *Niels Juel* class that were retired 'on block' on 18 August 2009. Fitted with APAR multifunction radar and the associated Thales SMART-L array, the new vessels will be a powerful reinforcement to NATO's European growing number of air-defence ships. However, their delivery during 2012-13 will also be marked with a degree of sadness, as they will be amongst the last ships built by the giant Odense Steel Shipyard. The historic facility is being closed to new orders by owners AP Moller Maersk due to the impossibility of competing profitably with Far Eastern yards. Meanwhile, **Finland's** naval ambitions are less extensive but delivery of *Katanpää*, the first of three new Italian-built minehunters, is expected by the end of 2010, following launch in June 2009. Their arrival will complement a series of investments that also encompass the delivery of four *Hamima* fast attack craft between 1998 and 2006, supplemented by mid-life modernisations for the four older *Rauma*

Left and opposite: Russia's cruiser *Varyag* passing under the Golden Gate Bridge on a rare visit to San Francisco in June 2010. The Russian fleet is maintaining a recent trend of a high level of international activity. *(Mrityunjoy Mazumdar)*

class vessels. The latter work will commence in August 2010 for completion by 2013. Minelaying capabilities have already been upgraded through refits of the two *Hämeenmaa* class vessels.

Naval developments amongst the other European Baltic states have been somewhat less impressive in the face of economic conditions, with **Latvia** particularly struggling to fund the deployment of the five 'Tripartite' minehunters acquired from the Netherlands in full. Nearby **Poland's** navy is increasingly facing issues of block obsolescence in the face of priority given to army and air force programmes, with the pair of FFG-7 Frigates and four operational *Sokól* (the former Norwegian *Kobben*) submarines requiring replacement or extensive modernisation. The former should have been replaced by the new MEKO A-100 derived Project 621 'Gawron' type corvettes but stop start progress on the prototype vessels suggests that she will not be completed until the latter half of the decade. The 2010-18 defence modernisation plan therefore envisages life extensions of at least some of the principal units until around 2017 to provide time for new projects to commence.

RUSSIA

The Russian Navy continues to display contradictory signals. At one level a high degree of operational activity is being maintained, with current deployments probably as ambitious as anything that has been seen since the end of the Cold War. Notable highlights over the past twelve months have included the despatch of the cruisers *Pyotr Veliky* from the Northern Fleet and *Moskva* from the Black Sea Fleet for drills with ships of Russia's Pacific Fleet that culminated in the giant Vostok 2010 strategic exercise during June and July. There has also been an increasing level of interface with Western fleets as the legacy of the Georgian invasion starts to dissipate. Well-established multinational liaisons such as the FRUSUK and BALTOPS exercises have been supplemented by increased bilateral engagements, including a rare visit of the cruiser *Varyag*, Russia's Pacific Fleet flagship, to San Francisco in June 2010. The navy has also been gaining operational experi-

ence through its contribution to anti-piracy operations off the Horn of Africa, including a successful mission in May 2010 to rescue Russian sailors seized with the tanker *Moscow University*. These deployments have largely been carried out by gas-turbine powered units of the *Udaloy* and *Neustrashimy* classes as they are the most reliable and amongst the more modern surface vessels in the Russian fleet.

The real question is how this level of activity will be maintained in the future given only limited new construction to replace Russia's increasingly elderly collection of Soviet-style ships. Excluding strategic nuclear forces, post Soviet-era warship construction appears to be largely focused on four principal design streams, viz.

■ **Project 2235.0 Frigates:** Intended to be Russia's principal future surface ship, up to twenty of these 4,500-ton frigates are planned. First of class, *Admiral Sergei Gorshkov*, was laid down at United Industrial Corporation's Severnaya yard at St Petersburg in 2006. She is currently scheduled for launch in 2010, somewhat earlier than previously planned. Work on a second ship, *Admiral Kasatonov*, commenced in November 2009. Press reports suggest that the design is based on the Project 1135.6 *Talwar* class built for India.

■ **Project 2038.0 Corvettes:** Effectively light frigates built for general-purpose operations in the littoral, this class is arguably furthest advanced of Russia's major warship programmes. The lead ship, *Steregushchy*, has been operational since 2008 and second-of-class, *Soobrazitelny*, was floated out at the Severnaya Shipyard in March 2010 prior to sea trials planned for the end of the year. At least three further ships are at various stages of fabrication. Nevertheless, there is a considerable way to go before a planned total of twenty of these 2,000-ton ships is reached.

- **Project 677 Patrol Submarines:** Known as the 'Lada' class, these are the follow-on to the current Project 636 'Kilo' class that comprises a large proportion of Russia's underwater strength. The first boat, *St Petersburg*, was launched as long ago as 2004 but was involved in around five years of extended sea trials before being formally delivered to the Russian fleet in April 2010. At least two further boats are under construction at the Admiralty Shipyard in St Petersburg. A total of at least six is planned.
- **Project 885 Nuclear-Powered Attack**

Submarines: Laid down as long ago as 1993, the first 'Yasen' class submarine, *Severodvinsk*, has been delayed by lack of funding, technical issues and priority given to the Project 955 'Borey' class strategic missile submarines. She was finally rolled out of her building hall at the Sevmash yard in Severodvinsk in June 2010. Work on a second boat, *Kazan*, commenced in July 2009.

Whilst this programme would appear to provide a sensible route map to the fleet recapitalisation, it can be seen that overall progress has been relatively slow. As such, it seems unlikely that new ships will be delivered quickly enough to replace existing ships falling due for retirement.

Whilst the mooted alliance with France for the construction of *Mistral*-type amphibious assault ships offers one potential way forward, ongoing refit and refurbishment of existing designs is therefore also a necessity, however inefficient. For example, 2010 saw the return to operational service of the *Udaloy* type destroyer *Admiral Kulakov* after completion of a refit programme that originated back to the early 1990s. Looking forward, reports suggest that the navy's sole aircraft carrier, *Admiral Kuznetsov*, will commence a long refit from 2012 onwards to allow her to remain in service until a new carrier design is commissioned. Work is likely to commence at the Sevmash yard once the refit of India's *Vikramaditya* is completed.

United Industrial Corporation's Severnaya Shipyard launched the second Project 2038.0 light frigate *Soobrazitelny* for the Russian Navy in March 2010. Progress with the deployment of new surface and submarine designs has generally been slow. *(United Industrial Corporation)*

TABLE 2.4.6: RUSSIAN NAVY: SELECTED PRINCIPAL UNITS AS AT MID-2010

TYPE	CLASS	NUMBER[1]	TONNAGE	DIMENSIONS	PROPULSION	CREW	DATE
Aircraft carriers							
Aircraft Carrier – CV	Project 1143.5 **KUZNETSOV**	1	60,000 tons	306m x 35/73m x 10m	Steam, 32 knots	2,600	1991
Principal Surface Escorts							
Battlecruiser – BCGN	Project 1144.2 **KIROV**	1 (1)	25,000 tons	252m x 29m x 9m	CONAS, 32 knots	740	1980
Cruiser – CG	Project 1164 **MOSKVA** ('Slava')	3	12,500 tons	186m x 21m x 8m	COGAG, 32 knots	530	1982
Destroyer – DDG	Project 956/956A **SOVREMENNY**	c. 5	8,000 tons	156m x 17m x 6m	Steam, 32 knots	300	1980
Destroyer – DDG	Project 1155.1 **CHABANENKO** ('Udaloy II')	1	9,000 tons	163m x 19m x 6m	COGAG, 29 knots	250	1999
Destroyer – DDG	Project 1155 **UDALOY**	c.8	8.400 tons	163m x 19m x 6m	COGAG, 30 knots	300	1980
Frigate – FFG	Project 1154 **NEUSTRASHIMY**	2	4,400 tons	139m x 16m x 6m	COGAG, 30 knots	210	1993
Frigate – FFG	Project 1135 **BDITELNNY** ('Krivak I/II')	c.4	3,700 tons	123m x 14m x 5m	COGAG, 32 knots	180	1970
Frigate – FFG	Project 2038.0 **STEREGUSHCHY**	1	2,200 tons	105m x 11m x 4m	CODAD, 27 knots[2]	100	2008
Frigate – FFG	Project 1161.1 **TATARSTAN**	2	2,000 tons	102m x 13m x 4m	CODOG, 27 knots	100	2002
Submarines							
Submarine – SSBN	Project 955 **YURY DOLGORUKY** ('Borey')	1	17,000+ tons	170m x 13m x 10m	Nuclear, 25+ knots	110	2010
Submarine – SSBN	Project 941 **DONSKOY** ('Typhoon')	1 (2)	33,000 tons	173m x 23m x 12m	Nuclear, 26 knots	150	1981
Submarine – SSBN	Project 677BDRM **VERKHOTURYE** ('Delta IV')	6	18,000 tons	167m x 12m x 9m	Nuclear, 24 knots	130	1985
Submarine – SSBN	Project 677BDR **ZVEZDA** ('Delta III')	‹5	12,000 tons	160m x 12m x 9m	Nuclear, 24 knots	130	1976
Submarine – SSGN	Project 949B ('Oscar II')	c.5	17,500 tons	154m x 8m x 9m	Nuclear, 30+ knots	100	1986
Submarine – SSN	Project 971 ('Akula I/II')	c.10	9,500 tons	110m x 14m x 10m	Nuclear, 30+ knots	60	1986
Submarine – SSK	Project 677 **SAINT PETERSBURG** ('Lada')	1	2,700 tons	72m x 7m x 7m	Diesel-electric, 21 knots	40	2010
Submarine – SSK	Project 877/636 ('Kilo')	c.20	3,000 tons	73m x 10m x 7m	Diesel-electric, 20 knots	55	1981
Major Amphibious Units							
Landing Platform Dock – LPD	Project 1174 **IVAN ROGOV**	1	14,000 tons	157m x 24m x 7m	Gas, 19 knots	240	1978

Notes:

1 Table only includes main types & focuses on operational units: bracketed figures are ships being refurbished or in maintained reserve.

2 Some sources state CODOG propulsion.

The most immediate headache faced by Russia's naval planners is not, however, related to conventional forces but the increasingly pressing problem of how to keep the seaborne element of the country's nuclear deterrent operational. At the moment, a rolling programme of life extension overhauls for the six existing Project 677 BDRM 'Delta IV' ballistic missile submarines that first entered service in 1985 has maintained a credible strategic flotilla. However, this programme is drawing to a close with the planned completion of the sixth and final modernisation – on K-407 *Novomoskovsk* – by the end of 2010. The clock is therefore ticking. Long term plans have envisaged current strategic nuclear submarines being replaced by the Project 955 'Borey' class armed with the new RSM-56 'Bulava' (NATO: SS-NX-30) ballistic missile. Construction of the submarines themselves has progressed well – trials of first of class *Yury Dolgoruky* commenced in June 2009 and a further three out of a planned total of eight boats are under construction following commencement of work on *Svyatitel Nikolay* at the start of 2010. Unfortunately, tests of the 'Bulava' missile from the modified 'Typhoon' class submarine *Dimitry Donskoy* have been far from successful, with further test failures in July and December 2009 meaning that at least seven of a total of twelve or thirteen trials have suffered from significant mishaps. A further series of test launches from both *Dimitry Donskoy* and *Yury Dolgoruky* planned for the end of 2010 is likely to have a significant impact on the project's entire future.

Notes

1. For French speaking readers, an affectionate description of *Jeanne d'Arc*'s lengthy career can be found on the *Mer et Marine* website – www.meretmarine.com.

2. A full review of the development of multifunction radar is contributed by Norman Friedman in Chapter 4.1. A good overview of the planned changes to the previous Italian FREMM configuration is contained in 'Italy's FREMM will be a Year Late, Better-Armed', *Defense News* – 7 December 2009 (Springfield, VA, Army Times Publishing, 2009), p 6.

3. Please refer to Andy Nativi's 'Sea Base – Italy launches a versatile amphibious ship program', *Defense Technology International* – June 2010 (Washington DC, McGraw Hill Companies Inc, 2010), pp 36-7.

4. *Jane's Defence Weekly* has provided excellent ongoing commentary on the whole Greek submarines saga. The conclusion was summarised in Theodore L Valmas and Tim Fish's 'Greece to acquire Type 214 subs to resolve TKMS dispute', *Jane's Defence Weekly* – 24 March 2010 (Coulsdon, HIS Jane's, 2010), p 5.

5. The author is grateful to Commander (SG) Geir Mykleby, Royal Norwegian Navy, Programme Manager for the *Skjold* class and NSM, for his update on this project.

Author:
Devrim Yaylalı

2.4A Fleet Review

THE TURKISH NAVY

Occupying an important strategic position in the Eastern Mediterranean and controlling transit to the Black Sea through command of the Bosporus and Dardanelles, Turkey has long been a leading regional naval power. Whilst enjoying a much lower profile than many other European fleets, the Turkish Navy has steadily evolved in the decades since the end of the Second World War and now comprises a balanced force encompassing major surface combatants, fast attack craft, mine-warfare vessels and submarines (please refer to Table 2.4.1). The fleet's recent progress has been marked by increasingly ambitious international deployments – largely in conjunction with NATO allies – and steady development of indigenous construction and associated technology. Although much local shipbuilding has been based on imported, largely German, designs, local industrial capability has now become sufficiently sophisticated to allow the development of purely national warship programmes. The chapter focuses on the more significant advances currently being achieved.

RECENT OPERATIONS

2009 was a particularly busy year for the Turkish Navy. For the first time, the navy operated a warship south of Suez continuously throughout the whole year. Increased piracy along the coast of Somalia and the hijacking of several Turkish-flagged or owned merchant ships were the key reasons behind the deployment of Turkish warships to the region. In total, four former USN FFG-7 frigates, locally know as the 'G' class – *Giresun, Gaziantep, Gediz* and *Gökova* – were sent to the Gulf of Aden. These ships operated either as part of NATO's SNMG-2 task force or in CTF-151, created by the US Navy in order to form an international taskforce to combat piracy in the Indian Ocean. From May to August 2009, Rear Admiral Caner Bener held the command of CTF-151. This was the first time that a high-ranking officer from the Turkish Navy had commanded a multinational task force outside the scope of NATO.

Above and opposite: The Turkish Navy has constructed a powerful regional fleet focused around a core of licence-built German designs. The *Kiliç* class fast attack craft *Atak* and the MEKO 200 TN frigate *Fatih* are pictured here. *(Devrim Yaylalı)*

In 2010, the regional presence of Turkish warships was maintained, with two more 'G' class deployments – of *Gelibolu* and *Gediz* – being made to the shores of Somalia to contribute to anti-piracy efforts. Between August 2009 and May 2010 Turkish warships neutralised seventy-eight pirates on ten different occasions.

On average, each of the frigates sent to the region, spent 150 days away from home, of which as many as 120 days were spent underway. Each warship covered a distance of up to 30,000 nautical miles during this time.

'G' CLASS FRIGATE MODERNISATION

It is noteworthy that all the ships sent on anti-piracy missions have been from the 'G' class. One reason why this class has been favoured instead of the MEKO 200 frigates is likely to have been the longer range of the former. However, another reason may be the 'G' class frigate combat management system modernisations that these ships have recently received. Under this programme, the Turkish Navy has aimed at transforming the class's war-fighting potential through installation of a fully-integrated weapons control capability featuring enhanced tracking capacity, automatic threat detection and improved tactical data links. At the heart of these plans lies GENESIS (*Gemi Entegre Savas Idare Sistemi*), an open-architecture combat management system.

The development of GENESIS was initially started by the navy's own research and development organisation, the Turkish Naval Research Center

Table 2.4A.1: TURKISH NAVY: PRINCIPAL UNITS AS AT MID-2010

TYPE	CLASS	NUMBER	TONNAGE	DIMENSIONS	PROPULSION	CREW	DATE
Principal Surface Escorts							
Frigate – FFG	BARBAROS (MEKO 200 TN II A/B)	4	3,400 tons	118m x 15m x 4m/6m	CODOG, 32 knots	195	1995
Frigate – FFG	YAVUZ (MEKO 200 TN I)	4	3,000 tons	116m x 14m x 4m/6m	CODAD, 27 knots	190	1987
Frigate – FFG	'G' GAZIANTEP (FFG-7)	8	4,100 tons	136m x 14m x 5m/8m	COGAG, 30 knots	220	1977
Frigate – FFG[1]	TEPE (KNOX)	[2]	4,300 tons	134m x 14m x 5m/8m	Steam, 27 knots	285	1969
Frigate – FS	BURAK (A-69)	6	1,300 tons	80m x 10m x 3m/5m	Diesel, 23 knots	90	1976
Submarines							
Submarine – SSK	'AY' ATILAY (Type 209/1200)	6	1,200 tons	61m x 6m x 6m	Diesel-electric, 22 knots	40	1976
Submarine – SSK	PREVEZE (Type 209/1400)	4	1,600 tons	62m x 6m x 6m	Diesel-electric, 22 knots	45	1994
Submarine – SSK	GÜR (Type 209/1400)	4	1,600 tons	62m x 6m x 6m	Diesel-electric, 22 knots	45	2006
Fast Attack Craft							
Fast Attack Craft – PGG	KILIÇ	9	550 tons	62m x 9m x 3m	Diesel, 38+ knots	45	1998
Fast Attack Craft – PGG	YILDIZ	2	450 tons	58m x 8m x 3m	Diesel, 38+ knots	45	1996
Fast Attack Craft – PPG	DOĞAN	8	450 tons	58m x 8m x 3m	Diesel, 38+ knots	45	1977
Fast Attack Craft – PTG	KARTAL (JAGUAR)	8	200 tons	43m x 7m x 3m	Diesel, 42 knots	35	1966
Mine Warfare Vessels[2]							
Minehunter – MCMV	'AYDIN' ALANYA	6	700 tons	55m x 10m x 3m	Diesel, 14 knots	50	2005
Minehunter – MCMC	EDINCIK (CIRCÉ)	5	500 tons	51m x 9m x 3m	Diesel, 15 knots	50	1972

Notes:

1 This class is in the course of being withdrawn from service and numbers might be out of date.

2 There are also a number of coastal and inshore mine-countermeasures vessels of obsolescent US design. Other fleet components include large numbers of patrol vessels – many operated by the Coast Guard – and a considerable complement of LST, LCT and LCM type amphibious craft.

Command (ARMERKOM). ARMERKOM defined the system's specifications and subsequently undertook initial design, system development and integration work to achieve a prototype. When the project had reached a sufficient level of maturity, it was handed over to private defence companies for further development and production. This kind of co-operation between military and civilian institutions had no precedent in Turkey. The key company involved in this process was Havelsan, the leading systems integrator in the Turkish defence industry. Under the contracts agreed, Havelsan has carried out the system development, integration, hardware and software testing of the GENESIS system and will provide the necessary training and maintenance services throughout the system's lifespan. Havelsan has also signed a co-operation deal with America's Raytheon to market the GENESIS project worldwide, a potentially significant development given the number of USN FFG-7 frigates transferred to other fleets.

After the conclusion of 'G' class frigate combat management system modernisation, four of these frigates will also receive an eight-cell Mk 41 Vertical Launching System (VLS) and gain RIM-162B Evolved Sea Sparrow Missile (ESSM) firing capability. To support the ESSM missiles, Thales Netherlands' SMART-S Mk2 radars will be installed. According to Thales, SMART-S is a 2,000-4,000 MHz, E/F-band (US S band) 3D volume search radar for anti-air and anti-surface warfare applications with a range of up to 25km. It is optimised for operation in littoral conditions. The Mk-92 Mod2 fire-control system on board the four ships will be upgraded. There is an ongoing project to replace the existing transmitters of the Mk92 Mod2s with a new solid state transmitter that supports both ESSM and SM-2 missiles.

Once completed, these planned upgrades will increase the 'G' class's threat detection range, shorten their reaction times and increase the effective radius of their weapons. Modernisation will therefore make them effective 21st-century warships. Equally important, however, the programme demonstrates Turkey's ability to develop and integrate modern combat systems – a major step in the development of a truly indigenous warship that is now taking shape in the MILGEM project.

THE MILGEM CORVETTE PROJECT

The MILGEM programme is the most important Turkish naval shipbuilding project of all. MILGEM is an acronym of the Turkish word *Milli Gemi* (National Ship). This high-priority project is pivotal, as it will form the foundation of the experience and know-how required for the design, production and integration of a complex warship through local means. The programme is also critical in defining the future of the customer/producer relationship between the Turkish Navy (as end-user and the builder of the first two ships), the Under-secretariat for Defence Industries (as procurement agency) and

The 'G' (FFG-7) class frigate *Gediz*. Much used in support of anti-piracy operations off the Horn of Africa, the class are receiving new indigenous combat management systems under the MILGEM project. *(US Navy)*

the country's private shipyards (as suppliers). The successful conclusion of this project will mark a new era for naval shipbuilding in Turkey, shaping both the local warship construction industry and major future projects such as the TF-2000 air-defence frigate.

The history of MILGEM goes back to the late 1990s. In 1996 the Turkish Navy declared that it wanted to procure eight corvettes under project MILGEM. As the name shows, the maximum possible Turkish contribution was desired from the beginning. After delays due to severe economic crises, MILGEM was brought into life by Defence Industry Executive Committee (DIEC) in February 2000. Initial acquisition numbers were eight platforms plus four optional. However, despite the fact that twelve shipyards acquired the Request for Proposal, only two submitted proposals. Both of these were found to be invalid due to deficiencies in their bid bonds.

Thus it seemed for a couple of years as if the MILGEM project would be put on ice. However, in 2004 – in an unprecedented move – a dedicated design office was created for MILGEM by the Turkish Navy. The MILGEM Project Office (MPO) – which is located at Istanbul Naval Shipyard – was tasked with all design and construction activities regarding the ship. After the MPO started to design the ship, the Under-secretariat for Defence Industries, the main defence procurement agency in Turkey, started a bidding process in co-operation with the Turkish Navy for various sub systems for the ship. In parallel, a series of workshops were organised to arouse the interest of the commercial shipbuilding, machinery and supporting industries. This was necessary in order to obtain the high degree of local contribution that was required.

Thus MILGEM grew from being more than just a simple shipbuilding programme, as significant subsystems, equipment and sensors are being produced for the first time for MILGEM. For example the hull-mounted sonar to be used in MILGEM class warships was developed by the Science and Technological Research Council for Turkey (TUBITAK): this is the first ever sonar designed and constructed in Turkey. Similarly, the fire-control radar for the main gun developed by defence electronics group Aselsan is the first to be developed and produced locally. The aim is for many systems and sensors developed for MILGEM to be used in future shipbuilding projects.

The MILGEM class corvettes have a 99m mono-

Two computer-generated images of the prototype MILGEM (national ship) corvette *Heybeliada*. This most important Turkish shipbuilding project should pass an important milestone towards the end of 2010 when the first ship commences sea trials. *(Thales Nederland)*

hull, with many stealth features incorporated into the design of the ship. The planned displacement is around 2,000 tons. The principal armament is one 76mm Oto Melara gun, eight RGM-84 Harpoon surface-to-surface missiles and two Mk-32 twin torpedo launchers. For self-defence the ship is armed with a 21-cell RIM-116 RAM launcher, as well as two STAMP remote-controlled stabilised weapon stations. Facilities are provided for the operation of a helicopter of S-70B Seahawk size, whilst the principal search radar is the SMART-S Mk2 being retrofitted to some of the G class. CODAG propulsion will allow sprint speeds of around 29 knots. See Table 2.4.2 for further details of MILGEM and other current surface construction.

F-511 *Heybeliada* – the first ship of the class – was launched on 27 September 2008. She is currently in dry dock being fitted out. Sea acceptance trials are scheduled for the late summer of 2010. Fabrication of the second ship F-512 *Büyükada* is also underway, with a planned launching date during summer 2011. Further ships will be built in private yards, with a total class of up to twelve ships envisaged.

The success or the failure of the MILGEM programme, will directly influence the procurement model for the next major combat ship project, the TF-2000 air-defence frigate. The Turkish Navy has a requirement for a dedicated anti-air-warfare frigate to create a wide reaching air-defence umbrella for its task forces. The Turkish Navy is defining her require-

The photograph shows *Heybeliada* in the course of fitting out at Istanbul Naval shipyard in June 2010. *(Devrim Yaylalı)*

Table 2.4A.2: INDIGENOUS TURKISH NAVY SURFACE SHIP CONSTRUCTION

CLASS	MILGEM	NEW TYPE PATROL BOAT	COAST GUARD SEARCH AND RESCUE SHIP
Builder:	Istanbul Naval Shipyard	Dearsan Shipyard	RMK Shipyard (Koç Group)
First of Class Delivery:	2011	2010	2011
Number in Class:	12	16	4
Full Load Displacement:	2,000 tons	400 tons	1,700 tons
Principal Dimensions:	99m x 14m x 4m	56m x 9m x 3m	88m x 12m x 5m
Propulsion:	CODAG, c. 29 knots	Diesel, c. 25 knots	Diesel, c. 22 knots
Armament:	2 x quad Harpoon SSM	1 x twin 40mm Oto Melara Compact gun	1 x 40mm gun
	1 x 76mm Oto Melara Super Rapid gun	2 x STAMP weapons stations	2 x 12.7mm machine guns
	2 x twin fixed 324mm torpedo tubes	ASW mortar and depth charges	1 x light helicopter
	1 x RAM 21-cell CIWS		
	2 x STAMP weapons stations		
	1 s SH-60 Seahawk helicopter		
Crew:	c. 95	c. 35	c. 60

ments, with the Under-secretariat for Defence Industries defining the acquisition model. The TF-2000 programme will probably start when MILGEM production is handed over from the Istanbul Naval Shipyard to private shipbuilders. The current plans suggest four TF-2000 frigates will be commissioned in the 2018-20 timeframe.

COASTAL PATROL BOATS

Another important ongoing construction project is the New Type Patrol Boat project (NTPB). The Turkish Navy currently uses old minesweepers and aged patrol boats for security and ASW duties in and around harbours, bases and their approaches. Their planned replacements are the first warships to be designed and built by a private Turkish shipyard for the Turkish Navy. On 23 August 2007 a contract was signed between the Under-secretariat for Defence Industries and Dearsan Shipyard to build sixteen NTPBs for the Turkish Navy. Construction of the first boat, *AB-200*, with pennant number P-1200 started in May 2008. It was subsequently launched on 9 April 2010. AB is a Turkish abbreviation of *Avcı Botu* literally meaning 'Hunter Boat'. These boats will be built in four batches. The total value of the project is reported as €402m (US$500m), although it is not clear whether this includes all sub-systems.

The NTPBs are 55.8m long and have a beam of 8.9m. Their displacement is 400 tons. Main machinery will consist of two MTU 16V 4000 M90 diesels, each of which can produce 2,720KW or 3,700SHP. The design speed is 25 knots. The main armament of the new patrol boats will be one Oto Melara twin 40mm L70 Compact gun mount fitted in the 'A' position. The secondary armament comprises two STAMP remote stabilised weapon stations fitted with 12.7mm machine guns. For anti-submarine warfare the boat will be armed with an A/S mortar and depth charges. The A/S mortar and the remote-controlled guns are both produced by Aselsan.

Just as for the MILGEM programme, a high degree of local content is an important project aim. Even so, the amount of foreign content will be around 40 per cent of the total project value, including the main engines (from Germany's MTU), the ASW sonar (a Norwegian Simrad SP92 Mk II hull-mounted system) and the main gun (supplied by Italy's Oto Melara). One of the main elements of local content will be the combat management system. Havelsan, as a subcontractor to Dearsan shipyard, is responsible for the production of a scaled down version of the GENESIS system for the class, as well as for the associated system integration. Another Turkish company, Yaltes – in co-operation with Imtech – will produce the class's integrated platform management system.

COAST GUARD SEARCH AND RESCUE SHIPS

In looking at current surface-ship construction, reference should also be made to the Turkish Coast Guard's Search and Rescue (SAR) programme. The first SAR vessel – named *Dost* – was launched on 9 June 2010 by the RMK shipyard, part of the giant Koç conglomerate. The project will supply the coast guard with four ships, which will be the largest vessels operated by the force. Current vessels in its inventory cannot operate in Sea State 5 or above and cannot support helicopter operations: the new ships will rectify this. Based on the Italian *Sirio*, the class will be 88.4m long and 12.2m in beam on a displacement of 1,700 tons. Maximum speed is 22 knots, with a range of 3,000nm (5,500km) at 15 knots. Koç doubtless hope that RMK's involvement in this contract will create further opportunities when MILGEM production is passed to the private sector.

AIP-EQUIPPED SUBMARINES

With fourteen diesel-electric submarines in service, the Turkish Navy is the biggest operator of conventionally-powered submarines amongst both European and NATO countries. All boats are of German design, of which the six 'Ay' class (Type 209/1200) are the oldest currently in service. The first was delivered in 1976 and the newest in 1990. The remaining eight submarines are also of Type 209 design but have greater displacement. They were built in two batches, with all assembly taking place at the Gölcük naval shipyard from materials provided by HDW. The production run of the four submarines in the first batch started in 1989 and ended in 1998. These Type 209/1400 submarines are locally known as the *Preveze* class. The production of the second batch started in 2000 and ended in 2007. This batch is known as the *Gür* class. Although the two batches are not distinguishable externally, electronics, sensors and weapons feature significant differences.

Another German design has been selected as the fourth generation of Turkish submarines; the Type 214 AIP-equipped boat. On 2 July 2009, a contract worth c. €2.5bn (US$3.1bn) was signed between the Under-secretariat for Defence Industries and a

Current Turkish submarines are based entirely on the German Type 209 design, including eight of the Type 209/1400 variant shown here. All eight boats were built at the Gölcük facility, where the newly ordered Type 214 AIP-equipped class will also be assembled. *(Devrim Yaylalı & US Navy)*

consortium of Howaldtswerke-Deutsche Werft GmbH (HDW), Kiel – part of ThyssenKrupp Marine Systems – and MarineForce International LLP (MFI), London for the delivery of six material packages for the construction of Type 214 class submarines in Turkey. All the submarines will be built at Gölcük and there is an 80 per cent offset deal.

The signing of the contract marked the end of a long series of bureaucratic procedures that started in 2006. In spring 2006, the Under-secretariat for Defence Industries called for companies to summit technical information. In late 2006 a request for proposals (RFP) was published and – in December 2007 – three companies submitted their offers: HDW put forward the Type 214, Navantia offered the brand new S-80A and DCNS proposed their 'Scorpène' design with AIP. According to the technical specifications, the Turkish Navy wanted to have a proven and working AIP boat with eight torpedo tubes.

This specification effectively eliminated the French and Spanish contenders. Spain is the only country that has ordered S-80A submarines to date and the first boat is still being built and is not yet launched. S-80A was therefore a risk for the Turkish Navy, as it was an unproven design. As demonstrated by the controversy surrounding the first Type 214 ever build, the Greek *Papanikolis*, the first boat of a new design may suffer from problems that are difficult to cure. The DCNS boat, 'Scorpène', has enjoyed more export success than the S-80A, having been selected by Chile, Malaysia and India. However,

The Turkish Navy is supplemented by a powerful Coast Guard. This is a model of the first of four new SAR (search and rescue) ships, *Dost*. ((*Devrim Yaylalı*)

none of these boats have an integrated AIP system. Whilst both Malaysia and India have options to retrofit AIP by cutting their submarine in half and inserting the AIP module, DCNS was not able to demonstrate a 'Scorpène' submarine with a working AIP capability. In July 2008, the selection of Type 214 was announced by the Defence Industry Executive Committee. After that, contract negotiations commenced, eventually leading to the 2 July 2009 announcement. However, some contractual details are still being worked out at the present time.

The production of the Type 214 class will be the third batch of submarine production in Turkey, following on from the last three members of the 'Ay' class and the two *Preveze* class production runs. For all these previous boats, Turkish input was limited. However, in line with the emphasis on increasing the capabilities of the local defence sector, many Turkish

defence companies will supply their own systems for Type 214 production. For example:

- Havelsan will take part in the development of the command and control software of the submarines. Through its involvement with the GENESIS project, this company gained a lot of know-how in respect of combat systems for surface ships. With the Type 214 project they will also gain know-how in respect of software design and integration for submarine systems. In particular, the company will become integration and maintenance provider for the ISUS underwater command and control system supplied by Atlas Elektronik.
- Koç Savuma Sistemleri – another subsidiary of the Koç conglomerate – will develop a torpedo countermeasures system for self-defence.
- MILSOFT will supply Link11/22 data transfer software.
- TUBITAK will supply their underwater telephony system and self-noise and other signature measuring systems
- STM will gain know-how in submarine construction and system integration.

When the Type 214 class was chosen as the new submarine for the Turkish Navy, an obvious question was what to do with the old 'Ay' class boats. A number of modernisation plans have been circulating, including cutting the boats in two and inserting an AIP section, just as ThyssenKrupp Marine Systems planned for similar Greek submarines under the now abandoned Neptune II project. However, such an expensive upgrade programme did not make economic sense considering the remaining service life these old boats have left in them. In March 2010 a new modernisation S-348 project for the 'Ay' class

The NTPB project envisages the construction of sixteen locally-built new type patrol boats for security and ASW duties in and around harbours. They feature a sonar system based on commercial fish-finding sonar technology. First of class AB-200 was launched in April 2010. (*Devrim Yaylalı*)

therefore emerged. The oldest two boats – *Atılay* and *Saldıray* – will be decommissioned as soon as the first Type 214 submarines enter into the fleet. The periscope, ESM/ECM and communication systems of the remaining boats will be upgraded. In order to keep costs down, integration of a modern, purpose-built underwater command and control system is not planned in the project. These old boats will get a powerful punch though, as it is planned to modify four of the torpedo tubes for Mk48 ADCAP Mod 6 AT heavyweight torpedoes. The introduction of Mk48 torpedoes will make some software changes in the Signaal M8 weapons control system necessary, possibly providing further opportunities for Turkish industry.

Another project related to Turkey's underwater forces is a plan for the procurement of one submarine rescue ship (MOSHIP) and two rescue and towing ships (RATSHIP). The Under-secretariat for Defence Industries is expected to award a contract for these in the last quarter of 2010. The existing submarine rescue and salvage ships in the Turkish Navy were built in the 1950s and they are now reaching the end of their life-spans. It is important for the Turkish Navy to maintain an appropriate degree of salvage and recovery capability to support its large submarine force, so this project is being accorded a relatively high level of priority. Accordingly, on 15 June 2010 the defence industry executive committee (SSIK) decided to start contract negotiations with Istanbul Shipyard for these ships.

AMPHIBIOUS ROAD MAP

In 2006, the long-term amphibious ship acquisition goals of the Turkish Navy were set out by its then commander, Admiral Yener Karahanoğlu, as follows:

- One amphibious transport dock (LPD).
- Two tank landing ships (LST).
- Eight fast tank landing craft (LCT).
- Twenty-seven amphibious assault vehicles (AAV/AAAV).

In accordance with this road map, in 2007 the Under-secretariat for Defence Industries published an RFP for eight LCTs. From the four companies that bid, the ADIK shipyard was chosen. On June 2009, a contract was signed between the Under-secretariat and ADIK for the production of eight LCT-type ships. The exact value of the contract was not made public but it is estimated to be around €100m

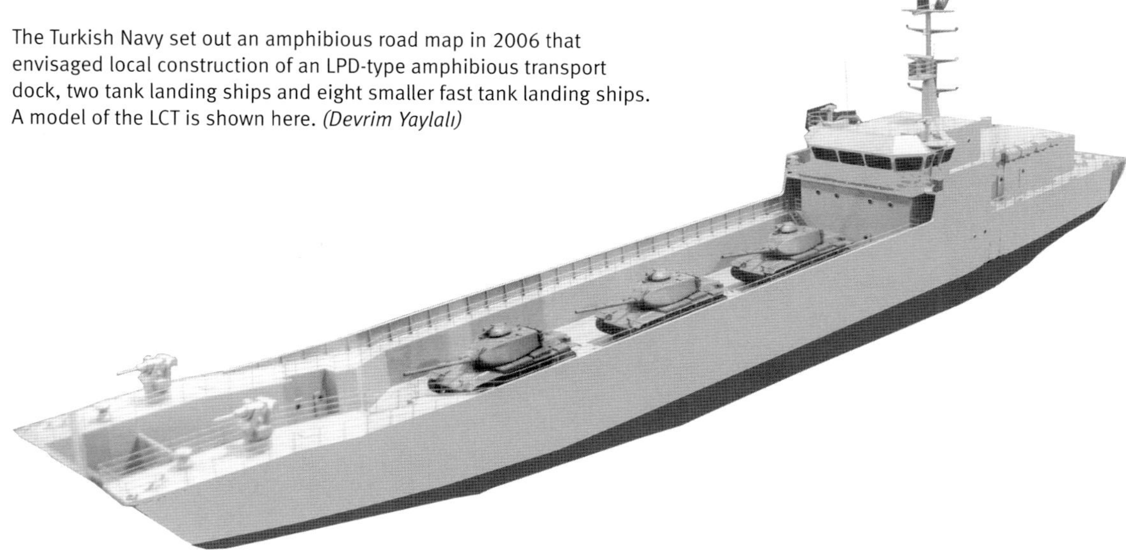

The Turkish Navy set out an amphibious road map in 2006 that envisaged local construction of an LPD-type amphibious transport dock, two tank landing ships and eight smaller fast tank landing ships. A model of the LCT is shown here. *(Devrim Yaylalı)*

(US$125m). On 29 January 2010, the construction of these ships officially commenced. According to the CEO of the Furtrans company that owns ADIK shipyard, the scheduled delivery date for the first LCT is August 2010. With a length of 79.9m, the LCT has a displacement of 1,150 tons and a cargo capacity of 320 tons. The design speed is 20 knots.

For the LSTs, the Under-secretariat for Defence Industries submitted an RFP in May 2008. On 6 January 2010, the ADIK shipyard was again declared as the winner of the bid and detailed contract negotiations with the company commenced. The proposed design looks very similar to *Osman Gazi* (NL-125) that is already in commission. However, the builder's model shows a side ramp amidships, indicating that the ship will be able to roll-on and roll-off vehicles at regular port facilities.

The most important project set out in the previously-mentioned roadmap is, of course, the acquisition of a LPD-type amphibious transport ship. According to the initial request for information (RFI), the landing dock ship will be required to be able to deploy a battalion-sized force of up to 1,000 troops and personnel, eight utility helicopters, three unmanned aerial vehicles, thirteen tanks and eighty-one armoured vehicles. The early estimates of the cost are around US$500m. This ship will be a force multiplier for the Turkish armed forces and the first in its kind in the Turkish Navy. Furthermore, it will be available for various domestic and international humanitarian missions. After the devastating earthquake in 1999, US amphibious ships were amongst the first foreign help that arrived in the striken area. The Turkish Navy learned many valuable lessons from that disaster, which also hit its main naval base at Gölcük very hard. With the issue of an RFP, the official acquisition process of the LPD has now started.

It is noteworthy that the initial RFI for the new ship was sent only to local shipyards registered in the Defence Industries Sectoral Strategy Document. However, none of these shipyards have the necessary know-how to design and build such a complex ship as a LPD. Therefore it is safe to say that British, Dutch, French, German, Italian, South Korean and Spanish shipyards that have the knowledge of designing and manufacturing big amphibious ships will be teaming up with these Turkish shipyards to assist with the project. Nonetheless, materialisation of the programme will doubtless involve further development of domestic capabilities, building on the advances in building an indigenous naval construction industry that have already been achieved.

Notes

Readers wanting to find out more about the Turkish Navy have only a limited number of English language sources available. The English language version of the navy's official website at http://www.dzkk.tsk.tr/english/HOMEPAGE.php. is a good starting-point, whilst the author's website and blog at www.turkishnavy.net/ and turkishnavy.blogspot.com/ respectively provide valuable – and often more up to date – information. The websites of the various shipbuilding and electronics companies named in this chapter might also prove to be of interest to the particularly diligent enthusiast.

ASTUTE CLASS SUBMARINES

A Quantum Leap in Capability for the 'Silent Service'

Author:
Richard Beedall

Astute is the first of an advanced new class of nuclear-powered attack submarines which will replace the *Swiftsure* and *Trafalgar* classes in the Royal Navy (RN) of the United Kingdom. Major technological advances have been incorporated into *Astute*, including reduced noise levels, an enhanced sonar suite, a 50 per cent greater weapon load, new intelligence-gathering capabilities and the ability to deploy Special Forces.

Originally intended as a relatively low-risk low-cost approach to providing a next generation SSN (Ship Submersible Nuclear), the *Astute* project has been plagued by serious design problems, delays and cost increases. However, *Astute* is now at sea, spending 2010 undergoing an intensive trials, testing and commissioning programme. The RN's Submarine Service is already delighted with the vastly improved capabilities that are being provided by its first new-build SSN since the last of the *Trafalgar* class (*Triumph*) in 1991. Defence Equipment and Support (DE&S) Director Submarines, Rear Admiral Simon Lister, describes

Astute arriving at Faslane for the first time in November 2009. She is the first of an advanced new class of nuclear-powered attack submarines that will replace the Royal Navy's existing *Swiftsure* and *Trafalgar* classes. (*Crown Copyright, by courtesy of BAE Systems*)

Astute as being 'a quantum leap in capability from the *Trafalgar* class'.

Astute is expected to enter operational service during 2011, about six years later than the originally planned date of June 2005.

ORIGIN OF THE *ASTUTE* CLASS

Most classes of warship can demonstrate a complex origin as requirements change and ideas evolve, but the story of the *Astute* class is particularly convoluted.

In the mid-1980s it was proposed that the *Trafalgar* class submarines then being built would be succeeded in the RN's shipbuilding programme by an all-new class. In 1987, Vickers Shipbuilding and Engineering Limited (VSEL) was awarded a contract by the UK's Ministry of Defence (MOD) to carry out design work for the 'W' class (sometimes called SSN-20), with the aim of ordering the first-of-class in 1990 for commissioning in 1997. However, with the end of the Cold War, no order for the expensive 'W' class was placed. Instead, in June 1991, it was decided to commence studies into a cheaper 'Batch 2 *Trafalgar* Class' (B2TC) submarine. In August 1991, VSEL was invited to develop a design based on the evolution, with minimum change, of the existing *Trafalgar* class.

On 14 July 1994 the MOD issued an invitation to tender for the building of three of the new BT2C submarines, with an option for one or two more.

Competitive bids were received in June 1995 from GEC and British Aerospace. GEC had never previously designed and built submarines but partially remedied this deficiency in the same month by purchasing VSEL. This became Marconi Marine (VSEL) – part of the company's GEC-Marconi division.

GEC-Marconi was formally identified as the MOD's preferred bidder for the B2TC submarines in December 1995 and 'no acceptable price, no contract' (NAPNOC) negotiations began. With construction of the *Vanguard* class Trident missile submarines winding down, GEC-Marconi badly needed new work for the former VSEL shipyard at Barrow-in-Furness, which it now owned. However, it was not until 17 March 1997 that the company was awarded a fixed price contract worth nearly £2bn for the design, build, and initial support of three submarines (Boats 1-3) to be called *Astute*, *Ambush* and *Artful*. The new submarines were now officially recognised as being of a new class – the *Astute* class – and it was planned that the first would enter service in June 2005. At that time, it was expected that five *Astute* boats would eventually be built to replace the five remaining *Swiftsure* class SSNs. The *Astute* class would then be succeeded in manufacture by an advanced new Future Attack Submarine (FASM), which would replace the seven *Trafalgar* class boats.

In 1999 British Aerospace purchased Marconi Electronic Systems (as GEC-Marconi had been renamed in 1998), thus becoming the prime contractor for construction of the new *Astute*s. The merged company called itself BAE Systems and has since undergone several re-organisations. Responsibility for the *Astute* submarine programme currently lies with BAE Systems Submarine Solutions, with its head office at Barrow-in-Furness. From a government perspective, the *Astute* project is currently managed by the Submarine Production Team in the MOD's Defence Equipment and Support (DE&S) organisation.

REQUIREMENTS AND CAPABILITY

During the Cold War the Royal Navy's nuclear-powered attack submarines – or 'fleet submarines' in RN parlance – had two primary roles: protecting the ballistic missile submarines that provided the UK's nuclear deterrent and conducting autonomous operations against enemy maritime forces. However, since the end of the Cold War (*c*.1991) they have proven to be extremely adaptable and well suited to other tasks, resulting in the *Naval Strategic Plan 2006* emphasising the need for a 'future underwater capability to contribute to maritime strike, ISR (Intelligence, Surveillance, and Reconnaissance), theatre entry and security.' Thus, despite their very high cost, SSNs have remained at the heart of the Royal Navy's plans and future force structure.

It is expected that the new *Astute* class will make a major maritime contribution to joint operations with other UK armed services, and with those of allied nations. This contribution may include covert delivery of Special Forces, surveillance, intelligence gathering, land attack with Tomahawk land-attack missiles (TLAM), and close support of amphibious task groups, as well as continuing to conduct more traditional roles such as protecting the *Vanguard* class submarines and anti-ship and anti-submarine operations. They will be capable of deployment as an integrated layer of defence within a task force or task group, or of independent operation for extended periods.

The *Astute* class submarines are thus required to perform a wide range of military tasks. These require a submarine platform that provides global reach, endurance, covertness, sustained high speed and the ability to conduct unsupported operations in hostile environments. The ability of the *Astute*s to meet these requirements is being measured using nine key

An unusual view of the Royal Navy *Trafalgar* class submarine *Tireless* sitting on the surface of the North Pole during exercises with the US Navy in April 2004. The boat was to lose two crew members to a tragic accident during a similar deployment some three years later. The *Astute* class was initially conceived as an improved version of this preceding design. *(US Navy)*

performance measures (KPM), all of which will apparently be met according to a National Audit Office report published in 2009:

- KPM 01: Weapon system effectiveness.
- KPM 02: Sonar performance.
- KPM 03: Hull strength (survivability).
- KPM 04: Top speed.
- KPM 05: Endurance.
- KPM 06: Acoustic signature.
- KPM 07: Complement.
- KPM 08: Land attack capability.
- KPM 09: Special Forces capability.

The definition of these high-level KPMs is classified and it is only possible to speculate on such matters as *Astute*'s top speed (KPM 04) and maximum diving depth (KPM 03).

DESIGNING *ASTUTE*

In origination, the design of the *Astute* class was closely related to that of the earlier *Trafalgar* Batch 1 boats. The intention was to install an updated version of the tactical weapon system already being developed for refit to the *Swiftsure* and *Trafalgar* submarines, utilise an enlarged hull to accommodate the Rolls-Royce Pressurised Water Reactor 2 (PWR2) that had been developed for the *Vanguard* class submarines and incorporate a few features from the recently-built *Upholder* class of diesel-electric submarines, such as their bow design. However, this 'pick and mix' approach initially resulted in a design which had some basic flaws, for example in regards to the trim of the submarine. As the technical problems were resolved and the new design evolved, the result began to have little in common with the *Trafalgar*'s – indeed about 75 per cent of the final *Astute* design is either new or has been re-qualified.

One of the most notable features of *Astute* (frequently referred to as Boat 1) is her size and weight compared to the previous *Trafalgar* class, which displace 5,200 tons submerged. Early versions of the *Astute* design were estimated at 6,800 tons submerged but this gradually grew to about 7,800 tons submerged in the final design. This displacement is similar to that of many Second World War cruisers.

At an early stage of the project a decision was made that the submarines would be built using fully modular construction techniques and this heavily influenced the *Astute* class design work. Prior to *Astute*, the standard method used in the UK to build submarines had been to assemble components inside the pressure hull after it had been completed: equipment was fed in through the hatches in a process that made the final fit-out very time-consuming. It was hoped that the use of the modular construction approach – which allowed the concurrent construction and fitting out of multiple modules – would cut *Astute* design time by 25 per cent and production time by 30 per cent compared to previous submarine projects (the smaller *Trafalgar* class had averaged six years to build). Although the modular construction of submarines had been proven by submarine builders in Sweden and Germany, the fact that it would be a new technique at Barrow-in-Furness (the sole remaining submarine yard in the UK by the mid-1990s) inevitably caused some controversy within BAE Systems and involved a calculated amount of risk.

Another key early decision was to employ the latest computer-aided design (CAD) methods for the *Astutes*' design and construction. It was hoped that this would allow concurrent engineering and enable the work of designers at several companies and at several sites to be fully integrated, reducing overall design time.

The cost savings anticipated by using the modular approach permitted a decision to make the *Astute* pressure hull much larger than the *Trafalgar* class – partly to help reduce the risks associated with using the new construction technique. The 10.7m diameter adopted was essentially determined by the space needed to accommodate a PWR2 reactor. Early B2TC design studies examined bulging the hull only around the reactor. However, it was found that this would be more complicated and costly than extending the widened diameter to the whole submarine and thus simplifying construction. Another benefit of the larger hull was that it created space for 50 per cent more weaponry.

The modular design of the hull allows it to be built in ring-like sections which are initially constructed and fitted out in a vertical orientation, with considerable advantages in terms of health and safety. Components can be assembled simultaneously and installed before the sections are welded together at the latest possible stage. The *Astute* design is actually broken down into nine hull sections and five main modules – the latter including a 178-ton Command Deck Module and the Main Propulsion Machinery Package. This has sophisticated 'raft' mountings to isolate it from shock, vibration and noise. Shock protection of varying levels is also provided to the nuclear reactor plant, as well as to the command deck, accommodation and the other modules. There is also a 65-ton Bridge Fin and more

than thirty mini-modules. After the hull modules have been finally welded together, the restricted access to the interior multiplies the time it takes to carry out further work.

Table 3.1.1 provides full technical details on the *Astute* design. The final design features significant improvements over the preceding *Trafalgar* class submarines, including:

- Reduced crew size.
- The latest, fully-integrated submarine combat system.

Two computer-generated images showing surface (1999) and underwater (1997) views of early versions of the *Astute* design. The actual boats display a number of detailed differences. *(BAE Systems)*

Astute on the surface. Stealth is a major consideration. Anti-sonar coatings are applied to all outboard equipment. The main body of the hull is covered by 39,000 acoustic tiles to mask the submarine's sonar signature. *(Crown Copyright, by courtesy of BAE Systems)*

- Significantly (50 per cent) increased weapons load – including Spearfish torpedoes, Sub-Harpoon surface-to-surface missiles (now out of RN service) and Tomahawk land-attack missiles.
- Two optronic periscopes with electronic displays to avoid hull-penetrating masts.
- External actuation for all control surfaces to reduce hull penetrations and simplify aft end construction.
- A digital control and information system that minimises costly cabling.
- Extensive improvements to avoid outdated equipment, improve operability and save cost.
- Reduced radiated noise. Anti-sonar coatings are applied to all outboard equipment. The main body of the hull is covered by 39,000 acoustic tiles to mask the submarine's sonar signature.

Crew numbers are intended to be the minimum possible consistent with maintaining operability and skill levels. Crews will certainly be smaller than the 130 of the *Trafalgar* class and the prime contractor was originally incentivised to keep total numbers down to a maximum of eighty-four, excluding trainees and sea-riders. The final crew size of *Astute* is slightly larger at ninety-eight, but that is still small enough to avoid the need for 'hot bunking', i.e. assigning more than one crew member to a bed.

Below: The *Astute* class are built using modular construction techniques, with rafts of components assembled simultaneously and installed before hull sections are welded together. This image shows the 178-ton Command Deck Module being shipped into the hull of *Artful* during February 2010. *(BAE Systems)*

Table 3.1.1.

HMS ASTUTE PRINCIPAL PARTICULARS

Building Information:

Keel Laid Down:	31 January 2001[1]
Launched:	8 June 2007[1]
First Voyage:	14 November 2009
Builders:	BAE Systems Submarine Solutions at its facility in Barrow-in-Furness, Cumbria.

Dimensions:

Displacement:	6,690 tons surface displacement, 7,800 tons dived displacement.
Overall Hull Dimensions:	97.0m x 11.3m x 10.0m

Weapons Systems:

Armament:	6 x bow 21in (533mm) torpedo tubes. Space for up to 38 missiles, torpedoes or equivalent. Typical weapons outfit includes:
	– Raytheon Tomahawk Block IV land-attack cruise missile. Internal navigation with GPS backup to 1,600km (900nm) at Mach 0.7
	– BAE Systems Spearfish heavyweight torpedo. Active/passive homing to 65km (35nm) at up to 80 knots. Depth to 900m
	– BAE Systems Stonefish seabed mine (two for one in lieu of torpedoes and missiles)
Countermeasures:	Thales Sensors outfit UAP(4) ESM system. Launchers for SCAD 101 and 102 decoys and SCAD 200 sonar jammers.
Principal Sensors:	Thales Underwater Systems 2076 integrated sonar suite. Surface search and navigation radar. Atlas DESO 25 echo sounder.
	2 x Thales Optronics CM010 non-hull-penetrating masts with colour TV and thermal imaging cameras.
Combat System:	BAE Systems Astute combat management system (ACMS). Communications include Links 11 and 16.

Propulsion Systems:

Machinery:	Nuclear-powered steam turbine. 1 x modified Rolls Royce PWR2 pressurised water reactor and 2 x Alstom geared turbines.
	Combination provides 27,500shp through one shaft with pump jet propulsion. 2 x MTU auxiliary diesels with retractable propeller.
Speed and Range:	Designed maximum speed is in excess of 30 knots. Endurance – effectively limited by provisions – is 90 days submerged.
Diving Depth:	Officially 'over 300m', probably about 600m.

Other Details:

Complement:	A typical crew comprises 98 personnel plus 3 trainees. Accommodation is provided for 109, including 12 officers.
Class:	Five boats out of a planned total of seven have been ordered and four officially named to date – *Astute*, *Ambush*, *Artful* and *Audacious*.

1 Keel laying was a ceremonial act and actual fabrication commenced in October 1999. Similarly, *Astute*'s actual launch took place a week after the 8 June naming ceremony. Formal delivery to the RN is scheduled during 2010. *Astute* is Yard No 1122 and her Pennant is S119.

Sonar 2076 Arrays

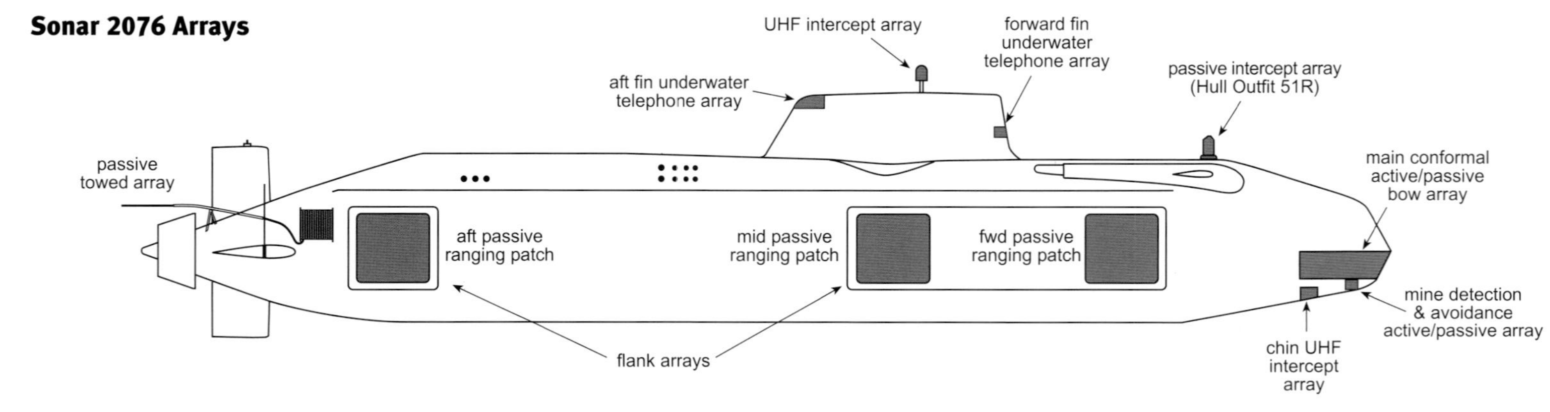

Plan and profile *Astute* (2009)
1:700 scale

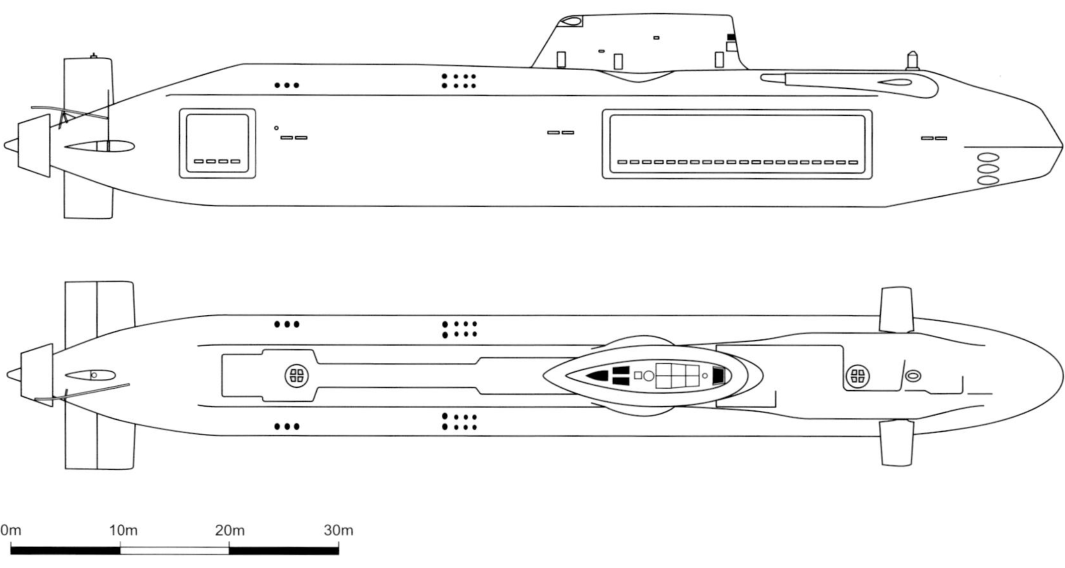

Inboard Profile

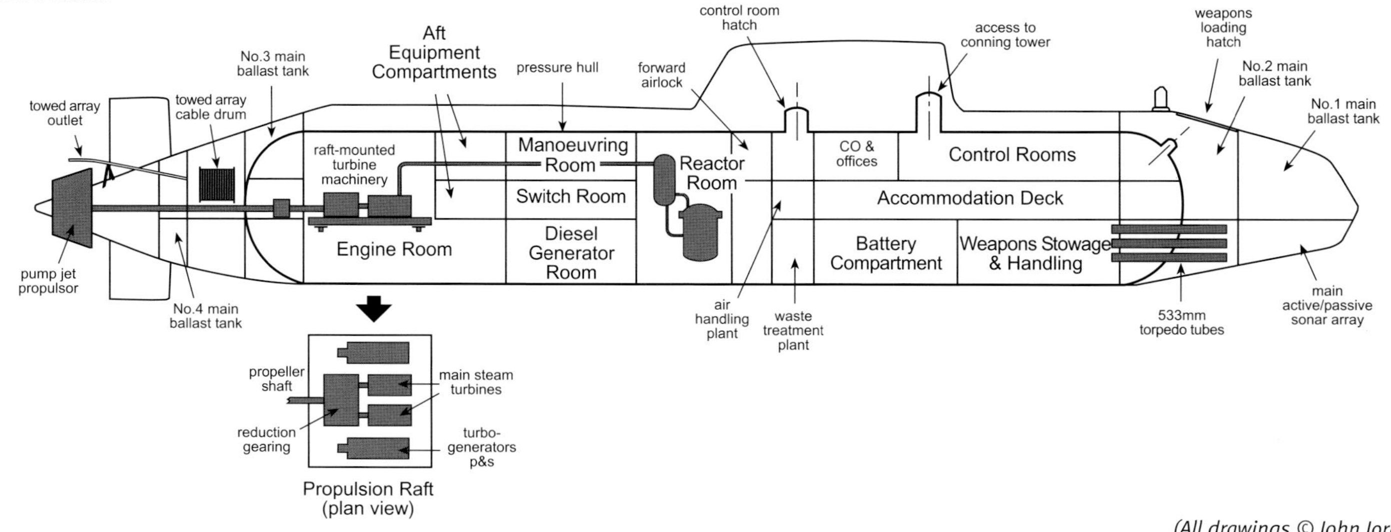

(All drawings © John Jordan, 2010)

Astute pictured during basin diving testing prior to commencement of full scale sea trials. Power is provided by a Rolls Royce PWR2 nuclear steam-raising plant, with twin Alstom turbines driving a single shaft to a pump-jet propulsor. *(BAE Systems)*

Senior rates accommodation onboard *Astute*. Crew size is low enough to avoid the need for 'hot bunking'. *(BAE Systems)*

The most important set of sensors fitted to the *Astute* class is the Sonar 2076 system. This comprises a range of arrays, with one of the large passive flank arrays with smaller square ranging arrays at each end pictured here. *(Thales UK)*

An image of the sensor head of a CM010 optronic mast equipped with Thales Sensors Outfit UAP (4) multifunction antennae. *(Thales UK)*

EQUIPMENT, WEAPONS AND SYSTEMS

Rolls-Royce Marine Power Operations Limited is the technical authority responsible for the design, manufacture and supply of the PWR2 nuclear steam-raising plant for all of the *Astute* boats. Major sub-contracted components include the PWR2 reactor high pressure vessel from Doosan Babcock, main coolant pumps from Weir and protection and control instrumentation from Ultra Electronics PMES. The reactor is designed to have a 25-year lifespan and *Astute* is fitted with a new long-life core (known as core H) which will allow her to circum-navigate the globe forty times. The core is expected to be able to power *Astute* for her whole service life, eliminating the need for costly reactor refuelling and associated long overhaul periods.

The other main items of machinery are two Alstom turbines, which drive a single shaft to Rolls-Royce pump jet propulsor that consists of moving rotor blades within a fixed duct. There are also two diesel alternators, one emergency drive motor and one auxiliary retractable propeller. CAE Electronics supplies the digital, integrated controls and instrumentation system for steering, diving, depth control and platform management. Rolls-Royce also provides secondary equipment such as Turbo Generators, whilst Wellman Defence supplies the fuel cell stacks for emergency electrical power.

Strachan and Henshaw (now owned by Babcock International) provide the air turbines, discharge air and hydraulic systems. They also manufacture the automated weapon handling and launch system.

Astute is the first RN submarine not to be fitted with a traditional periscope. Instead she is equipped with two CM010 optronic masts manufactured by Thales UK, with mast control units provided by MacTaggart Scott. These are non-hull-penetrating electro-optical devices which carry radio frequency, infra-red and optical (high-definition colour television quality) sensors. The masts send collected data to systems and consoles inside the submarine. With a reduced acoustic, visual, radar and thermal signature, the CM010 masts are highly suited to covert intelligence gathering.

The countermeasures suite fitted to *Astute* includes both decoys and electronic support measures (ESM). The ESM system is the Thales Sensors Outfit UAP(4), which has two multifunction antenna arrays mounted on the CM010 masts. *Astute* is also equipped with the Eddystone communications and electronic support measures (CESM)

The Astute Combat Management System being tested on the first of class. It is a development of the SMCS Submarine Command System originally designed for the *Vanguard* strategic missile submarines. *(BAE Systems)*

system. This was developed by DML in the UK and Argon ST in the USA; it provides advanced communications, signal intercept, recognition, direction-finding and monitoring capabilities.

EADS provides the external communications system (ECS) that enables *Astute* to communicate over all the frequency ranges used for tactical communications – transmitting voice, data and imagery. ECS is installed on the submarine's command deck module and is controlled by a special software package, allowing the system to be operated by a single person from a central workstation.

Undoubtedly the most important set of sensors fitted to *Astute* is Sonar 2076. This is a very advanced, fully integrated, passive/active search and attack sonar suite supplied by Thales UK. Outboard, the suite comprises large flank arrays with smaller square passive ranging arrays positioned at each end, plus an additional square installed aft. There is also a conformal passive/active bow array, a chin mine and obstacle avoidance array, and intercept arrays (one UHF intercept array under the chin, and – probably – one atop the fin). Small fore and aft domes on the

fin cover cylindrical underwater telephone arrays. Mounted on the deck forward is the intercept array transducer Hull Outfit 51R. This is fitted within a free-flooding, carbon fibre dome forward that closely resembles the prominent PARIS array fitted to many previous RN submarines. Outfit 51R is optimised to receive returns from active sonar transmissions from other warships. The 2076 suite also has a 1,200m-long fibre-optic towed array with a 400m cable: the towed array is reelable.

Inboard of *Astute* are all the associated processing cabinets and user consoles associated with Sonar 2076. Software is used to generate a sonar picture which can be displayed in the control room. *Astute* is currently fitted with the 2076 Stage 4 system but she will be upgraded with new hardware and software to the latest Stage 5 standard by 2011 – this will involve the replacement of old equipment with the latest commercial off-the-shelf components and the adoption of a more open architecture. Boat 4 (*Audacious*) will be fitted from build with 2076 Stage 5 and a new Thin Flank Array. The current flank array is the largest acoustic sensor fitted to any submarine in the

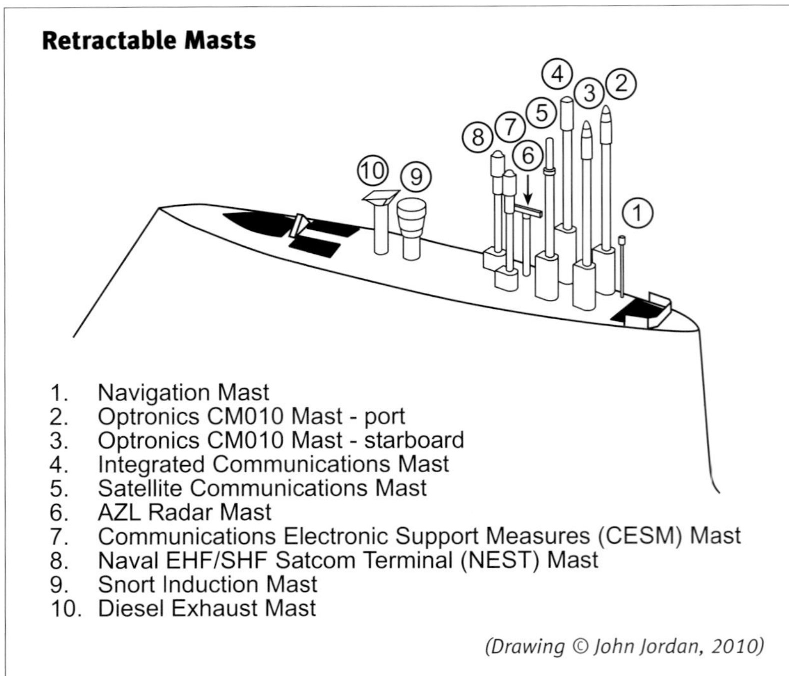

(Drawing © John Jordan, 2010)

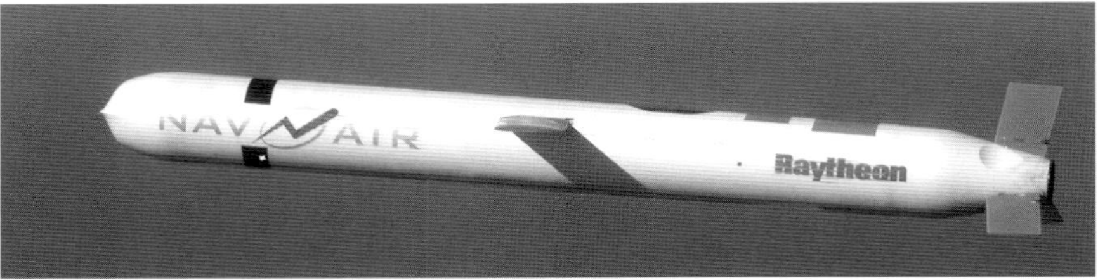

The *Astute* class has six 21in (533mm) torpedo tubes and capacity for thirty-eight weapons. Principal weapons are likely to be BAE Systems' Spearfish heavyweight torpedo and the Block IV version of Raytheon's Tomahawk land-attack missile. *(BAE Systems, US Navy)*

world, but it is both heavy and costly to fit. Improvements in acoustic materials technology allow a significant reduction in the weight of the array without losing performance, and also a simplification of the installation process. It is intended that the same technology will also be used to simplify the bow array fitted to Boat 5 onwards.

Astute is currently fitted with the Astute Combat Management System (ACMS). This has three subcomponents: an upgraded version of Submarine Command System (SMCS) originally designed for the *Vanguard* class submarines in the 1980s for tactical information and torpedo weapon control; a command support system that can show the recognised maritime picture; and a command workstation which can receive periscope and other video. The three systems are interfaced over an Ethernet network, with SCMS also connecting to the Sonar 2076 suite and other important systems using the fibre-optic-based Tactical Weapons Systems (TWS) Highway. The ACMS layout includes seven multi-function consoles – six on the tactical side of the control room and one on the sonar side. Each console includes two 18in (45.7cm) flat-screen displays, a keyboard and mouse.

The introduction of ACMS and Sonar 2076 Stage 5 will be a major step towards deploying the future Common Combat System (CCS) later this decade.

CCS is being developed by the *Astute* Innovative Combat System Rainbow Team led by BAE Systems Submarines Solutions; it also comprises Insyte, Thales, QinetiQ and SEA. It is expected that all *Astute*s will eventually be fitted with CCS.

In terms of weapons, *Astute* has six, 21in (533mm) torpedo tubes and capacity for thirty-eight full loads, a possible mix would be fourteen Tomahawk missiles and twenty-four Spearfish torpedoes. These can be substituted by equivalent load-outs, for example two Stonefish mines could be carried instead of one torpedo.

The only missile currently likely to be carried by *Astute* is the Block IV version of the Tomahawk land-attack missile, which is manufactured by the American company, Raytheon. The Royal Navy has purchased a tube-launched version of TLAM, which can strike at targets up to 1,600km away. Tomahawk targeting is not done through AMCS; instead a standalone missile control system equivalent to the US Navy's ATWCS is used. *Astute* also carries Spearfish heavyweight torpedoes manufactured by BAE Systems Underwater Systems. Each is powered by an open-cycle, bi-propellant gas turbine engine, which provides the weapon with a high sprint speed (up to 80 knots) and high endurance (at least 40km – and up to 65km has been speculated). The torpedo is provided with a copper wire command data link to

the launch platform but can also operate autonomously. It has an active/passive homing head and a directed energy warhead for use against both surface and deep-diving submarine targets. Whilst not officially confirmed, *Astute* might also carry a wire-guided uninhabited underwater vehicle (UUV) for use in visual and sonar intelligence roles, as well as for remote satellite communications.

Finally, *Astute* can be fitted with a dry deck shelter (DDS) aft of the fin structure. This is connected to the submarine's after hatch to permit free passage between the submarine and the DDS while the submarine is underwater. With the submarine still submerged, Royal Marines from the Special Boat Service can exit the DDS and ascend to the surface, bringing with them equipment and rubber rafts. Alternatively, they can mount a swimmer delivery vehicle and travel several kilometres underwater to their objective.

CONSTRUCTION

All of the *Astute* class submarines will be assembled in the Devonshire Dock Hall (DDH) at Barrow-in-Furness; this is a huge shipbuilding construction complex which covers an area of 25,000m. Originally built to accommodate the massive *Vanguard* class Trident missile submarines – which displace nearly 16,000 tons submerged – three or four *Astute*s can be worked on at once with room to spare. Major hull sections are built in the nearby New Assembly Shop before being moved by road the one kilometre to the DDH. Equipment and components for the submarines arrives at the DDH from subcontractors all over the UK, Europe and further afield. Delays and changing schedules have resulted in material and equipment being stored for years before it is finally fitted or used.

The first steel for Boat 1 (i.e. *Astute*) was cut in October 1999, although the keel (actually the first pressure hull unit) was not formally laid down at the DDH until 31 January 2001 in an act of purely ceremonial value. By early 2002 all of the major components and systems for *Astute* had been delivered by sub-contractors to the Barrow shipyard. However, during 2001 and 2002 shipyard workers found that the designs they were working to simply did not make sense, and that equipment would not fit together as it was supposed to. Unassembled materials rapidly accumulated at Barrow, whilst delays lengthened as the designers tried to resolve the rapidly multiplying issues.

BAE Systems was unable to disguise from the MOD the increasingly obvious fact that it was making slower progress in the detailed design and in the build-up of production than had been anticipated. On 9 July 2002, Mr Lewis Moonie, Armed Forces Minister, stated in answer to a Parliamentary Question that the first of class, *Astute*, had been due to enter service in June 2005, but was 'not now expected to enter service before late 2006, although this date has yet to be agreed with the contractor'. With all the problems, in November 2002 the MOD put the '*Astute* Second Buy' – an order expected to encompass three further boats at a cost of £1.7bn – on hold.

BAE Systems blamed the delays on 'engineering complexities' but this was overly simplistic. Part of the problem was the significant gap between the *Vanguard* class construction contract and the award of the *Astute* class deal, resulting in the loss of many experienced staff. Also, work on the new submarines was hampered by the diversion of management effort and skilled workers to meet a surge in orders – the Barrow-in-Furness shipyard winning in rapid succession contracts for the construction of two *Albion* class amphibious assault ships and two 'Wave' class fleet auxiliary tankers – as well as for the reactivation of four *Upholder* class conventionally-powered submarines for Canada. However, the fundamental

source of most of the delays was massive difficulties arising from the introduction of a computer-aided design tool. The system chosen was CADDS5, made by the American software company, PTC. Although this was a proven piece of software, *Astute* was the first UK submarine to be designed in a three-dimensional computer model and the adopted system was simply overwhelmed by the size and complexity of the task. Despite the best efforts of PTC to customise the product, it was just too slow and time consuming for designers to use for the production of 7,000 design drawings with over one million components, 160km of electrical cabling, and 23,000 pipes totalling more than 10km in length.

In the face of increasing dissatisfaction from the MOD over its performance, on 11 December 2002 BAE Systems publicly admitted that 'additional issues' had arisen and that it had 'become apparent that there are substantial schedule and cost implications'.

PROJECT RESTRUCTURING AND RECOVERY

The MOD was not prepared to protect BAE Systems fully from its failure to perform on the *Astute* project but it did acknowledge that the original contract had made cost-saving assumptions with regards to the use of computer-aided design techniques that had proven difficult to realise on a programme of great complexity. Throughout January and February 2003 the MOD negotiated with BAE Systems on the basis that the introduction of CAD required more time and effort than had originally been anticipated.

A hull section for an *Astute* class submarine being transported from the New Assembly Shop to the Devonshire Dock Hall at Barrow-in-Furness. The journey is approximately 1km. *(BAE Systems)*

Left: *Astute* under construction in December 2005. By this time problems with computer-assisted design technology were being resolved with the help of General Dynamics' Electric Boat division and the programme was heading back on track. *(BAE Systems)*

Agreement was reached on 19 February, with the MOD increasing funding by £430m, whilst BAE Systems contributed another £250m. An amendment to the Boat 1 contract was signed in December 2003, with Boat 1 production continuing under a revised target cost incentive fee arrangement. Production work on Boats 2 and 3 was essentially suspended until the design had matured sufficiently that a new price for these two boats could be agreed.

Apparently at the MOD's instigation, Mr Murray Easton – former head of BAE Naval Ships – returned from a short retirement to become MD of BAE Systems' Submarine division in June 2003, charged with sorting out the *Astute* project. A complete review of the *Astute* design began, with personnel from the US General Dynamics Electric Boat Division being brought in to reinforce the project team and allow them to benefit from Electric Boat's recent CAD experience with the *Seawolf* and *Virginia* class submarines for the US Navy. By April 2004, Electric Boat had thirteen staff at Barrow, and another fifty working on the project at Groton in the US. They provided design and production expertise; assisted with the development of computer-aided design (CAD) tools and their use in submarine design and production processes; created *Astute* class production drawings; and exchanged expertise on submarine construction techniques. The Americans continued to assist the project well into 2007, with the eventual value of the work undertaken being over US$200m.

On 24 November 2004 the then First Sea Lord Admiral, Sir Alan West, said of the *Astute* project, 'I think it is firmly back on track now … they have started to master the computer-assisted design, which was a much bigger issue than anyone thought it would be, and I am very impressed that they are getting to grips with it.' Other issues at the Barrow shipyard such as overhead costs, quality control, absenteeism and accident levels were also starting to show a positive trend and long lead items worth £70m for a fourth boat were quietly ordered.

By early 2007 the recovery of the project seemed solid, with the MOD noting that 'all the programme's revised anchor milestones continue to be met'. It was finally possible for the MOD and BAE Systems to

Right: Two images of *Astute* in the process of being rolled out of the Devonshire Dock Hall in Barrow-in-Furness prior to her naming ceremony on 8 June 2007. *(BAE Systems)*

reach agreement on the price of the second and third *Astute*s – this included a £580m increase on previous agreements to reflect inflation and the Government's acceptance of a share of the responsibility – along with BAE Systems – for the underestimate of the required effort and the consequent design delays. Even better, on 23 May 2007, the MOD announced a £200m contract for BAE Systems Submarine Solutions to begin preparing for construction of Boat 4 (*Audacious*) at Barrow-in-Furness in Cumbria. The boat was fully contracted for in the following year.

However, the National Audit Office kept a perspective on the situation a few months later when its *Major Projects Report 2009* revealed that the expected cost of the first three *Astute*s had risen from the original approved budget of £2,578m to £3,933m, and that the in-service date of *Astute* herself (defined as safe operation and start of operational work-up) had slipped from June 2005 to March 2010 – and the later date was not to be met.

It is currently expected that Boat 4 – which will be very similar to the first three – will cost as much as £1,589m to build. However BAE Systems Submarine Solutions and its suppliers have been working hard to identify modifications for Boats 5-7 that will help reduce costs. Consequently, it is anticipated that Boat 7 will cost at least 10 per cent less than *Audacious*.

COMPLETING *ASTUTE*

A major landmark in the life of *Astute* was her rollout from the Devonshire Dock Hall on 8 June 2007. She was then formally named by the Duchess of Cornwall in front of a crowd of approximately 10,000 people. As is traditional for submarine launches at Barrow-in-Furness, the naming ceremony was performed by using a bottle of beer brewed by the submarine's crew as opposed to the more traditional bottle of champagne!

A week later *Astute* was lowered on a shiplift in to the water. On completion of initial basin trials she returned to the Devonshire Dock Hall for final outfitting, which included the installation of the reactor core. At this stage it was planned that she would be delivered by November 2009, and BAE Systems was publicly hoping for August 2009. But during 2008 several programme and technical prob-

Astute pictured at sea for the first time in November 2009 during her voyage from Barrow-in-Furness to her new home port of Faslane. *(BAE Systems)*

lems arose – in particular serious damage to the vessel's propulsion system was accidentally caused by staff inexperienced in the testing and commissioning of nuclear submarines. The additional delay increased to nearly a year after a small fire broke out in the conning tower (fin) on 18 April. Nevertheless, in July 2008 *Astute* passed a major milestone on her programme – the successful fuelling of her reactor core and she entered the final stages of the testing and commissioning of her reactor, propulsion and ships systems.

Under the command of Commander A L Coles, on 14 November 2009 *Astute* finally slipped her moorings and departed Barrow-in-Furness for six days of basic sea trials before arriving for the first time at her home port of Faslane on the River Clyde in Dunbartonshire. After a couple of months of defect resolution alongside at Faslane, *Astute* was given clearance to go back to sea for further sea trials, sailing on 16 February 2010 and returning on 26 February. A major milestone was reached on 18 February when she conducted her inaugural dive in open waters in the Scottish Exercise Areas, safe-guarded by the Type 23 frigate HMS *Montrose*. Afterwards the Commanding Officer signalled that 'the submarine has handled exceptionally well, and, with a few exceptions has stood up to the rigours of the sea trials very well'. It had been planned that *Astute* would be delivered and commissioned during April, but this was delayed to the summer because of technical problems rather more numerous and serious than the signal indicated.

In May 2010 *Astute* conducted her first deep dive (the depth is classified, but probably 600m) and full power trial. During full power testing, she reached her maximum speed (again classified – but believed to be in excess of 30 knots). Further extensive testing and training was then conducted under the guidance of a team of Flag Officer Sea Training's (FOST) submarine safety experts before she commenced a short maintenance period in June 2010 to resolve outstanding technical issues.

A final package of sea trials is scheduled before *Astute* will be delivered by BAE Systems Submarine Solutions to the Ministry of Defence, and formally commissioned in to the Royal Navy. HMS *Astute* (now officially 'Her Majesty's Ship') is then scheduled to carry out trials to test her war-fighting capability before sailing to America to carry out procedural test firings of her Tomahawk missile and Spearfish torpedo weapon systems. Full operating capability should be declared in early 2011 following operational workup and agreement with BAE Systems on any outstanding requirements, defects or deficiencies.

THE FUTURE

In May 2001 the MOD effectively cancelled the increasingly unaffordable FASM project, deciding instead to order additional *Astute*s to replace the *Trafalgar* class. Speculation that at least nine *Astute*s might be built proved ill-founded as defence cuts continued to reduce the Royal Navy's SSN force. Indeed when the last of the *Swiftsure* class (*Sceptre*) retires in December 2010, the only nuclear-powered attack submarines left in RN service will be the six remaining *Trafalgar* class boats plus *Astute* herself, with the latter still undergoing her operational work-up

The Defence Industrial Strategy published in 2004 targeted a new submarine order every twenty-two months to ensure vital skills and capabilities were not lost to BAE and its supply chain. By 2005 the expectation was that eight *Astute*s would be built, but senior officials then increasingly indicated that this was a 'funding permitting' target. The MOD's 2007 Equipment Plan allowed for seven boats and this is likely to be the final total unless the Strategic Defence and Security Review being undertaken by the UK's new Conservative-Liberal Democrat coalition government decides differently when it reports in late 2010. Possibly only six *Astute*s would be built but for the need to sustain the UK's capability to build submarines until the construction of the first of the Trident armed 'Successor' submarines – *Vanguard* class replacements – planned to commence around the end of the decade.

In March 2008 the MOD removed £139m from the *Astute* Project for the financial years 2009/10 to 2012/13. This deferment of expenditure has resulted in delays to the delivery of Boats 2-4 by about nine months and also to the build start dates and to the

Astute surfaces after her first open-water dive on 18 February 2010 whilst undertaking trials in the Scottish Exercise Areas. *(BAE Systems)*

Astute and the new Type 45 destroyer *Dauntless* pictured in company whilst undergoing trials off the Scottish coast. *(BAE Systems)*

Table 3.1.2: ASTUTE SSN CLASS LIST

BOAT	NAME	PENNANT	ORDERED	LAID DOWN	ROLLED-OUT	COMMISSIONED	IN SERVICE	STATUS (JUNE 2010)
1.	*Astute*	S119	17 March 1997	31 January 2001	8 June 2007	[Summer 2010]	[2011]	Sea Trials
2.	*Ambush*	S120	17 March 1997	22 October 2003	[Summer 2010]	–	[2012]	Testing and Commissioning
3.	*Artful*	S121	17 March 1997	11 March 2005	[2012]	–	[2014]	Under construction
4.	*Audacious*	S122	23 May 2007	24 March 2009	–	–	[2016]	Under construction
5.	*[Agamemnon]*	S123	25 March 2010	[2010]	–	–	[2018]	Initial fabrication
6.	*[Anson]*	S124	[2012]	–	–	–	[2020]	Reactor ordered
7.	*[Ajax]*	S125	–	–	–	–	[2022]	Planned

Ambush (right) and *Artful* (left) pictured under construction in BAE Systems' giant Devonshire Dock Hall in Barrow-in-Furness during the first half of 2010. *(BAE Systems)*

procurement of long lead items for Boats 5-7. As a consequence of this short-term economy, *Astute* project costs for seven boats will actually grow by £539m and BAE Systems Submarine Solutions has slowed the overall rate of construction for the class to roughly one every two years. The cost of the *Astute* project, including the build of the first four boats, is expected to be over £5.5bn and the final total price of the seven boats is likely to be about £10bn.

On 25 March 2010, the government announced that it had a made a contractual commitment with BAE Systems to proceed with the initial build of *Astute* Boat 5 and had also authorised the long lead procurement activities (in particular the ordering of the reactor) associated with Boat 6, at a total cost of over £300m.

By June 2010, the second of class, *Ambush*, was essentially complete and she was undergoing testing work in preparation for a roll-out from the DDH during the summer of 2010. The command deck module had been shipped in to Boat 3, *Artful*, welding of the hull sections was nearly complete and the fin had been fitted. Outfitting of *Artful* will continue prior to the 2012 roll-out now planned under the latest schedule. The first sections of *Audacious* have been moved to the DDH and fabrication work has started in the nearby New Assembly Shop on Boat 5.

The names of Boats 5-7 are not yet officially announced, but leaks indicate that they will be called *Agamemnon*, *Anson* and *Ajax*. Please see Table 3.1.2 for further details.

CONCLUSION

It seems likely that only seven *Astute*s will be built to replace the twelve nuclear-powered attack submarines that were in Royal Navy service as recently as 2004. However, *Astute* is undoubtedly a very capable submarine. Based on unclassified information, the US Navy's *Seawolf* (SSN-21) class probably remains unsurpassed. However, *Astute* may be able to equal – or even occasionally exceed – the capabilities of the US Navy's lower cost follow-on, the *Virginia* (SSN-774) class, for example in terms of the versatility of her mast sensors.

Astute's advanced systems, in particular the Sonar 2076 suite, would seem to make her far more capable than the best SSNs currently in service with the Russian (Project 0971A, 'Akula II'), French (*Améthyste* class) and Chinese (Type 093 'Shang' class) navies. For example the flank sonars fitted to *Astute* are far superior to equivalent French systems in terms of channels, number of beams and tracking distances.

Given her extraordinary versatility, combined with a patrol endurance of three months, *Astute* provides the UK government with a nearly unique military capability. In a crisis she can sit discreetly off a coast gathering intelligence and then – if necessary – conduct devastating precision attacks on enemy land and sea targets. Unfortunately the *Astute* Project has been badly affected by cost increases. Each *Astute* submarine will now cost the UK tax payer about £1.4bn (approximately US$2.1bn), rather than the £850m originally estimated. However, this is still less than the c.US$2.7bn of the broadly comparable *Virginia*.

For 2011, the 'Silent Service' is quietly looking forward to deploying its first new attack submarine for two decades and utilising the new and enhanced capabilities that *Astute* will provide.

Notes

1. Information on the *Astute* Project is quite hard to find – a lot of the information in the public domain is a repetition from very old sources, or even speculation. This would seem surprising given the value and importance of the project, but there are undoubtedly national security considerations and suppliers are therefore reluctant to release information. Another aspect would seem to be the limited export opportunities which give suppliers little incentive to promote the project and their own involvement.

2. BAE Systems Submarine Solutions does not have its own website. A limited amount of information can be found at www.baesystems.com/Businesses/SubmarineSolutions/

3. The MOD has re-organised its procurement arm and responsibility for the *Astute* project now lies with the Submarine Production Team at DE&S. A small amount of information can be found at: www.mod.uk/ DefenceInternet/MicroSite/DES/OurTeams/Submarines Teams/SubmarineProductionTeam.htm

4. The Royal Navy has embraced the Public Relations opportunity presented by *Astute* to a limited extent. Information and news on the class can therefore be found on their official website at www.royalnavy.mod.uk/oper ations-and-support/submarine-service/future-submarines/

5. A primary source of information on the *Astute* Project is the *Ministry of Defence: Major Projects Report* published annually by the National Audit Office. Their website is at www.nao.org.uk/

6. The assistance of Chris Nelson and Neil Lauderdale of BAE Systems and Kathryn Bell from Thales UK is acknowledged with gratitude.

A stern view of *Astute* during trials in February 2010. The Royal Navy's 'Silent Service' is quietly looking forward to deploying its first new attack submarine for two decades in 2011. *(BAE Systems)*

Author:
Mrityunjoy Mazumdar

3.2 SIGNIFICANT SHIPS

DELHI CLASS DESTROYERS

An Overview of India's Project 15, Project 15A and Project 15B Series

The commissioning of *Delhi* – the lead ship of the Indian Navy's three-ship Project 15 *Delhi* class destroyers – on 15 November 1997 was a watershed moment for the Indian Navy. The event marked the coming of age for both India's naval shipbuilding industry and the navy's in-house design organisation, the Directorate of Naval Design (DND). *Delhi* was followed by *Mysore* in June 1999 and *Mumbai* in January 2001. At the time, the *Delhi* class destroyers were the largest and most complex warships designed and built in India. Not only that, they were also the first ever gas-turbine propelled warships to be designed indigenously. Building upon previous Indian designs such as the Project 16 *Godavari* frigates, the destroyers are particularly noteworthy in their combination of Western and Russian design philosophies, as well as the integration of a diverse mix of Western, Russian and indigenous combat systems, hull machinery and equipment. Table 3.2.1 gives overall design details.

In service, these ships have turned out to be highly successful weapon platforms, with excellent seakeeping performance. In addition, they have served very well as goodwill ambassadors for the Indian Navy in numerous flag-showing visits, exercises with other navies and operational deployments. When *Delhi*, bristling with a formidable array of weapons and sensors, showed up at Malaysia's Langkawi International Maritime Exhibition shortly after commissioning in December 1997, she certainly garnered a lot of attention.

The Project 15 design has subsequently formed the basis for two follow-on classes using the same hull form: the three-ship Project 15A *Kolkata* class and the soon to be ordered Project 15B, four units of which have been sanctioned to date. These additional ships are a significant improvement on the *Delhi* class, incorporating extensive stealth features as well as vastly improved weapon and sensor packages. The first of the Project 15A destroyers should enter service in 2012, by which time construction of the following Project 15B series should have commenced. The Project 15B type will feature progressive advances over the Project 15A in terms of automation, weapons, and sensors. Please refer to Table 3.2.2 for a general comparison of the three classes.

PROJECT 15 ORIGINS

The Project 15 destroyer programme was originally conceived in the early 1980s as a gas-turbine powered follow-on to the Project 16 *Godavari* ('G') class frigates. The new ships were also intended to incorporate an improved weapon and sensor package. The indigenous Project 16 frigates, originally displacing around 3,600 tons, started assembly in the late 1970s after previous licence-built construction of the British broad-beam *Leander* design. The 'G' class ships were notable in being the first warships anywhere to feature a combat system with a combination of Western and Russian weapons and sensors integrated into a hull of Western origins, as well as embarking two Sea King helicopters on a frigate-sized platform.

Initial concept studies commenced in July 1980. The relevant DND team came up with a conceptual design that was slightly larger than the 'G' class, displacing around 4,000 tons. Over the next four years, the navy deliberated over various weapons and gas turbine options. At the time, three gas-turbine solutions were considered: the American General Electric (GE) LM2500; the British Rolls Royce SM-1 series; and engines from the erstwhile Soviet Union's Zorya Mashproekt concern in Ukraine. The Indian Navy already had considerable experience of the last-mentioned company's products aboard a variety of platforms. Consideration was also given to both Western and Russian-origin weapon and sensor packages. In particular, French Exocet missiles and Italian Oto Breda guns – such as the popular 76mm and larger 127mm calibre weapons – were studied. Eventually, around mid-1983, the Soviets offered a

A close up view of India's second Project 15 destroyer *Mysore*. When completed, the class were the largest and most complex warships built by India. (*Captain S K Sharma, Indian Navy*)

'large' and modern weapons package along with the Zorya M-36E gas turbine power plant, featuring DT-59 reversible gas turbines. This became the preferred option.

At this stage, it was realised that the 4,000-ton conceptual frigate-sized design was simply not large enough to accommodate the equipment that the Soviet Union had offered and that a much larger platform would be needed. In September 1983, the Indian government approved a plan to seek foreign assistance for re-designing the frigates. Consequently, the design evolved into a larger destroyer-sized ship, displacing around 6,300 tons. Upon approval of this design, various contractual negotiations were concluded over the following year.

DESIGN WORK COMMENCES

A project design team headed by Commander (later Rear Admiral) N P Gupta commenced basic design work on the Project 15 ships – that is to say, on the hull form definition, hull structure, internal arrangements, weapons layout and overall configuration – in mid-1984. Concurrently, data for weapons package integration from the Soviet design bureaux involved in the programme, notably the Severnoye Design Bureau (SDB) and the then RosVooroZhenie (RVZ) arms export agency, started flowing in. In Soviet times, all design data from various weapon and sensor vendors was channelled through a single window – in this case, a team of surface design specialists. Some Soviet designers were also deputed to work alongside their Indian counterparts at the DND offices in New Delhi. The general arrangement design was completed sometime in late 1985.

The Project 15 design represented a quantum leap over anything the DND had attempted previously. To begin with, it was the first time gas-turbine propulsion had been incorporated into an Indian-built warship: previous experience had been entirely with steam turbines. In addition, the weapons package was more advanced than anything the Indian Navy had attempted to integrate before. The biggest challenge, however, was the hull form design for a ship displacing over 6,000 tons as opposed to the less than 4,000 tons of the 'G' class. At the time, access to modern design software was practically non-existent. Therefore, the vast majority of calculations – on stability, hull form hydrodynamics and the like – had to be completed manually on the basis of data from similar-sized ships. Without much previous data to draw upon and lacking designers who had been posted to other duties, Commander Gupta and his team of relatively inexperienced naval architects had to stretch themselves to the limits in coming up with the hull form design. In his words, much time was spent in introspection. Whilst some help was derived from studying the Soviet-built Project 61 'Kashin' class, modified versions of which were then entering Indian service, no usable design data on these ships was provided by the Russians.

Model tests on the hull form were carried out at SSPA in Sweden over a period of six months from mid-1985. Results suggested that the ship would have excellent sea-keeping characteristics: a conclusion confirmed directly to then naval chief Admiral R H Tahiliani when he visited SSPA's laboratories. However, given that this was the first time the DND had attempted a hull form design of this size and, considering also the Soviet origin of much equip-

Above: The Project 15 destroyer was conceived as a gas-turbine powered follow-on to the Project 16 *Godavari* ('G') class frigates, which had a significant impact on the P-15 design. Here *Godavari* is pictured in the Arabian Sea during 2008. *(Canadian Navy)*

Right: The Indian Navy's 'Kashin II' class destroyer *Ranjit*. These Russian-built ships were another key influence on the Project 15 design. *(US Navy)*

ment, it was considered desirable to revalidate the model tests at the Krylov Institute in St Petersburg, Russia. When identical results were achieved, the DND designers felt vindicated and confidence levels grew. Given the lack of experience and data to draw on, it is quite remarkable that the original calculations were bang on target the first time.

It is important to note that the platform design was entirely Indian, even though there were conceptual similarities to contemporary Soviet designs, most notably the 'Kashins' and the more modern Project 956 *Sovremenny* class. Given SDB's role as weapons and sensor integrator, arrangements for these systems tended to be modelled after SDB designs.

CONSTRUCTION AT MAZAGON DOCK LTD

Shipbuilder Mazagon Dock Ltd (MDL) received an order for the three Project 15 ships in March 1986. The expectation was that the lead ship would be constructed in a period of about six years and that all deliveries would be completed between 1993/4 and 1996. Estimated project costs were Rs 882 crores (Rs 8.2bn or c. US$700m). Production commenced in 1987. The keel for *Delhi* – then Yard 715 – was laid down on 14 November 1987. She was launched on 1 February 1991. The keel for the next ship, Yard 725, was laid down the next day – 2 February 1991 – and she was launched on 4 June 1993 as *Mysore*. The keel for the third ship, Yard 735, was laid down on 14 December 1992. She was launched on 20 March 1995 as *Bombay*. She was renamed *Mumbai* following the city's official name change.

Construction of the hull and installation of the main machinery proceeded largely to plan. However, the breakdown of the centralised Soviet supply system after Communism's collapse resulted in non-delivery of weapons equipment. Significant elements of the weapons package had to be renegotiated. For example, the planned suite of Moskit (NATO: SS-N-22 Sunburn) supersonic surface-to-surface missiles was changed to the Uran system with the KH-35/3M24E (NATO: SS-N-25 Switchblade) missile. The surface-to-air missile system was also revised. As

The Indian Navy's third and final Project 15 *Delhi* class destroyer, *Mumbai*, pictured on exercises during September 2007. She was launched as *Bombay* on 20 March 1995, but renamed following that city's name change. An Indian Navy Sea Harrier FRS51 is seen passing overhead. *(Captain S K Sharma, Indian Navy)*

a result, the DND had to devise major design changes, resulting in re-working of large sections of the ships and inevitable delays. All in all, DND and MDL had to implement over thirty design changes before the ships were ready for trials.

Typically, the contract for the first of a series of ships is agreed on a cost-plus basis, with the remainder on fixed-price contracts. However, given the impact of the prevailing situation in Russia, as well as other cost escalations, the navy concluded new cost-plus contracts with MDL in November 1992. These included revised delivery dates of 1996-1999, i.e. a construction period of nine years. In the event, the lead ship was completed after ten years, with subsequent ships taking around eight years. As of 1995, the

Left: *Delhi* on the point of being launched from the Mazagon Dock Ltd's facility at Mumbai on 1 February 1991. Difficulties in obtaining equipment from the former Soviet Union after the collapse of Communism meant that she was not commissioned until November 1997. *(Mazagon Dock Ltd)*

cost estimates had risen upwards to Rs 2,137.1 crores.

At the time of their construction, *Delhi* and her sisters were easily the most complex warships built in India. More than 30,000 production drawings were required for their construction. Approximately 530km of cabling and well over 500 types of major equipment connected fifty-three different systems. Admiral Gupta recalls how, upon his return to DND in 1993, he found himself immersed in dealing with the aftermath of the fall of the Soviet Union and the breakdown in its supply system. Negotiations had to be restarted both with the Russians and with emerging regional entities. Several problems encountered in the final fitting out stages – the setting to work phase – had to be locally resolved as the

Below: *Delhi* departing Portsmouth Harbour in June 2009. The class features a handsome, flush-decked profile that bristles with weapons and sensors. *(Conrad Waters)*

An aerial view of *Mysore* taken at the end of India's 2006 fleet review. The large stacks for the gas turbine intakes and exhausts are offset from the centreline. *(Mrityunjoy Mazumdar)*

Russians generally insisted that resolving these issues were not a part of their contractual obligations.

GENERAL DESIGN FEATURES

At around 6,700 tons full load displacement, and with an overall length of 163.2m, the three Project 15 destroyers are the largest surface combatants in the Indian Navy. To put their size in perspective, the *Delhi*s are some 10m longer than the British Royal Navy's Type 45 *Daring* class destroyers.

In general appearance, this handsome yet ferocious-looking class displays an interesting mix of Russian and Western design philosophies – a mix of modernised 'Kashin' with India's Project 16 *Godavari*. The fore section of the ship is strongly reminiscent of the 'Kashin' type with its pronounced sheer line, sharp or piercing bow and flared hull, which were adopted because they offered excellent sea-keeping properties. As one proceeds aft, the impact of the Project 16 becomes evident in the large double hangar arrangement. Influences from the Russian *Sovremenny* and *Udaloy* type destroyers can also be seen. There are some visible differences between the various ships. For example, *Delhi* also has two missile blast deflectors originally sized for the Moskit, whereas, the two follow-on ships have a slightly different arrangement in this area. *Mumbai* features an alternative close-range anti-missile armament.

The ships bristle with weapons and sensors.

Weapons are concentrated on the foredeck, exceptions being the AK-630M close-in weapons system (CIWS) cluster mounted amidships – as in the 'Kashin' – and the aft 3S-90 launcher for surface-to-air missiles that is mounted atop the hangar. A quintuple torpedo launcher is mounted behind the forward stack. There are two masts and two large stacks for the gas turbine intakes and exhausts, the latter being offset from the centreline in correlation with the engine rooms. A large hangar structure for two helicopters with the flying control position in the middle is another prominent feature. The cambered helicopter deck has a surface area of 500m². The quarterdeck has small windows and cutouts on the transom on either side. The deck below the flight deck has a number of fairleads, bollards, a warping capstan, towing hooks as well as gear for towed torpedo decoys. *Mysore* may still retain her original centre cutout for a variable-depth sonar (VDS).

The all-welded hull uses high quality 'B' steel for structural strength. Hull form – adopting generally fine lines – is characterised by flare and a high sheer line, with 'V' shaped forward sections and a sharp turn at the bilges. There is a long cutup to the transom, as well as a sharp turn at the stern. Length to beam ratio is over 9:1. This hull form, as well as twin stabilisers and twin bilge keels provides good manoeuvrability and sea-keeping: the platform's seaworthiness and robust construction has been

proven many times. For example, *Delhi* was unavoidably caught in severe storm conditions in the South China Sea in mid-1999. Waves as high as 25m broke over the ship and a 30m-tall following wave crashed onto the aft portion. The ship withstood these severe impacts without damage to the main or primary structures such as the flight deck – only the hangar doors suffered minor damage. With the ship having survived this sort of pounding from the seas in Sea State 10, the designers felt justifiably proud of their work. Admiral Gupta indicates that all the commanding officers of the 'D' class ships have commented on how well their ships handle compared to other Indian surface combatants.

PROPULSION SYSTEM

The class has a COGAG propulsion system. The Ukrainian Zorya M-36E (E for Export) gas turbine plant with four DT-59 reversible gas turbines produces over 64,000 hp. The reversible gas turbines are unlike their Western counterparts such as the LM2500, allowing the use of fixed pitch propellers. The shafting is of Ukrainian origin. The gas turbines are grouped in two pairs, each pair driving one five-bladed fixed-pitch propeller through a RG-54 gearbox. The engines pairs are offset longitudinally into forward and aft engine rooms.

The DT-59 turbines belong to the UGT-16000 family produced by Zorya Mashproekt and entered

Aerial views of *Mysore* (D60) and *Mumbai* (D62) taken in February 2006. Both show the Project 15 class's balanced outfit of anti-air, anti-submarine and anti-surface weaponry to good effect. Note also detailed differences, most notably *Mumbai*'s retention of two pairs of AK630M Gatling guns as opposed to the AK630M/Barak PDMS combination on *Mysore*. (Mrityunjoy Mazumdar)

service in 1980. In cold temperatures, each produces 21,500hp but power output drops to around 15,000–16,000hp in tropical conditions. A three shaft design, it consists of a two-spool gas generator (comprising the compressor, combustion chamber, and gas generator turbines), a freely spinning power turbine with a unique flow reversing mechanism, associated inlet and exhaust sections, an attached lube oil system, a fuel system, electrically operated devices for starting, a pneumatically-controlled auxiliary gear system and the 'Buran' microprocessor based automated control and monitoring system supplied by Avrora. The power turbine has a concentric blade arrangement such that the small upper blades and large lower blades have opposing flow directions.

The flow reversing mechanism consists of a U-shaped screen which normally directs the high-energy exhaust gas flow from the gas generator turbine to the larger lower blades for forward motion but directs airflow to the small upper blades for reverse thrust. The flow distribution gear can reverse flow and vice versa in around twelve seconds. Reverse operations are possible in conditions ranging from idle up to a maximum of 50 per cent of rated power, which appears to be the thrust ceiling for reversing operations. A 'stop shaft' operation is performed by directing airflow through both sets of blades.

According to Zorya literature, these turbines can be started up in around three minutes. Acceleration from idle to rated power mode takes 300 seconds, whereas deceleration from rated power to idle takes around a minute. It takes around two minutes to fully reverse the gas turbine.

Electrical power is provided by four Russian-made 1250E gas turbine generators each rated at 1,250KW. There are two in each engine room. There is also a 500KW diesel alternator generator for use in emergencies.

A detailed view of *Delhi*'s forward superstructure. Two quad KT-184 launchers for Uran surface-to-surface missiles are positioned in front of a prominent blast deflector, which was originally designed for the more powerful Moskit. They are controlled by a Garpun Bal fire-control radar immediately atop the bridge. Other sensors pictured include the T-91E fire-control radar for the AK-100 gun and a rectangular Fregat MAE search radar for the surface-to-air missile system. *(Conrad Waters)*

Another view of *Delhi*'s forward superstructure, showing the rear of the Fregat MAE array to the front of the mast and Ellora electronic warfare equipment, including the ESM antenna atop the mast and two sets of jammers above and below the mast-mounted 3R-90 illuminator. 3R-90 illuminators are used to direct the Kashmir surface-to-air missiles. *(Conrad Waters)*

WEAPONS AND SENSORS

The Project 15 destroyers are designed as general-purpose surface combatants. Their main roles include anti-surface warfare, anti-air warfare against aircraft and cruise missiles and anti-submarine warfare (ASW), as well as providing command, control and communications (C3), electronic warfare and other fleet support capabilities. When embarking up to two Sea King helicopters, extended anti-surface, anti-submarine and electronic support missions are possible. Key weapons packages are summarised below:

Anti-Surface Warfare: Primary weapons comprise a battery of sixteen KH-35E Uran surface-to-surface missiles (SSMs) with the Garpun Bal (NATO: Plank Shave) fire-control radar. There is also a 100mm AK-100 gun with a T-91E (NATO: Kite Screech) fire-control radar.

Anti-Air Warfare: Ships are fitted with the medium-range Kashmir (NATO: SA-N-7 Gadfly) surface-to-air (SAM) missile system, with two single-arm 3S-90 launchers, six 3R-90 (NATO: Front Dome) fire-control illuminators and two M-22E telesights for electro-optical control. Up to forty-eight missiles are carried. The Kashmir system works in conjunction with the Fregat MAE (NATO: Half Plate) 3D and Thales LW-08 2D search radars for receiving targeting data.

Close-in defence against airborne targets, sea-skimming cruise missiles and surface targets is handled by a combination of two AK630M guns and the Israeli Barak point-defence missile system (PDMS). This comprises thirty-two missiles, with fire-control provided by two Elta EL/M-2221 radars. One ship, *Mumbai*, is still fitted with four

---

Table 3.2.1.

DELHI PRINCIPAL PARTICULARS

Building Information:

Keel Laid:	14 November 1987
Launched:	1 February 1991
Delivered:	15 November 1997
Builders:	Mazagon Dock Ltd, Mumbai, India.

Dimensions:

Displacement:	6,700 tons full load displacement.
Hull Dimensions:	163.2m x 17.4m x 6.5m

Weapons Systems:

Missiles:	2 x single S3-90 launchers for 48 Kashmir/Shtil (SA-N-7 Gadfly) surface-to-air missiles. 4 x 8-cell Barak 1 PDMS.
	4 x quad KT-184 launchers for 16 KH-35E Uran (SS-N-25 Switchblade) surface-to-surface missiles.
Guns:	1 x 100m AK-100 gun. 2 x AK-630M guns as part of CIWS.
Torpedoes/ASW:	1 x quintuple PTA-53-15 533mm torpedo mounting. 2 x 12-tube RBU-6000 A/S rocket launchers.
Aircraft:	2 x AgustaWestland Sea King MK42B helicopters or equivalent.
Countermeasures:	Ellora electronic warfare suite. 2 x PK2 decoy launchers. TOTED torpedo decoy system.
Principal Sensors:	1 x RAWL-02 (Thales Nederland LW-08) 2D long-range search. 1 x Garpun Bal (Plank Shave) F/C radar for SSM system.
	1 x Fregat MAE (Half Plate) 3D target-designation radar and 6 x 3R-90 (Front Dome) illuminators for SAM system.
	1 x T-91E (Kite Screech) gunnery fire-control radar. 2 x EL/M-2221 F/C radars for CIWS/PDMS.
	Surface search and navigation radars. APSOH hull-mounted sonar and HUMVAD variable-depth sonar[1]
Combat System:	Indian Navy 'in house' combat management system. No data network.

Propulsion Systems:

Machinery:	COGAG. Zorya Mashproekt M-36E plant with four DT-59 reversible gas turbines.
	Plant provides in excess of 64,000shp in tropical conditions through two shafts.
Speed and Range:	Designed maximum speed 32 knots. Range is 5,000 nautical miles at 18 knots.

Other Details:

Complement:	A typical crew comprises c. 350 personnel, including c. 40 officers.
Class:	Three ships have been commissioned: *Delhi* (D61), *Mysore* (D60) on 2 June 1999 and *Mumbai* (D62) on 22 January 2001.

1 Latter now possibly replaced by ATAS.

AK-630M gun mounts and two MR-123 Vympel (NATO: Bass Tilt) directors.

Anti-Submarine Warfare: There are two RBU-6000 A/S rocket launchers and a quintuple 533mm PTA-53-15 torpedo launcher, the latter mounted amidships. The RBU-6000 fires RGB-60 rocket projectiles that are reportedly very effective against underwater targets. Both rocket and torpedo launchers are controlled by the Purga ASW fire-control system, which uses target data provided by the hull-mounted sonar and the VDS or towed-array sonar.

Helicopters are used for long-range ASW, with control through a locally-developed Link 2 UHF/VHF datalink.

Electronic Warfare and Countermeasures: The destroyers have a powerful electronic warfare suite. Originally equipped with the indigenous Ajanta system designed by Bangalore's Bharat Electronics (BEL), they have since been retrofitted with the company's state-of-the-art Ellora system. Ellora provides both electronic support measures (ESM) and electronic countermeasures (ECM) functions,

including active jamming to allow multiple threats to be handled simultaneously. This system is claimed to be more advanced than the SLQ-32 system used in current US frigates and destroyers. Identification friend or foe (IFF) equipment is fitted to the radars.

Two Russian PK-2 countermeasures systems, each with one 140mm ZIF-121 decoy launcher capable of firing fifteen rounds per minute in automatic mode and a fire-control system are fitted for self-protection against anti-surface missiles. The launchers fire chaff, IR and pyrotechnic rounds for confusion and distraction. TOTED towed torpedo noisemakers are

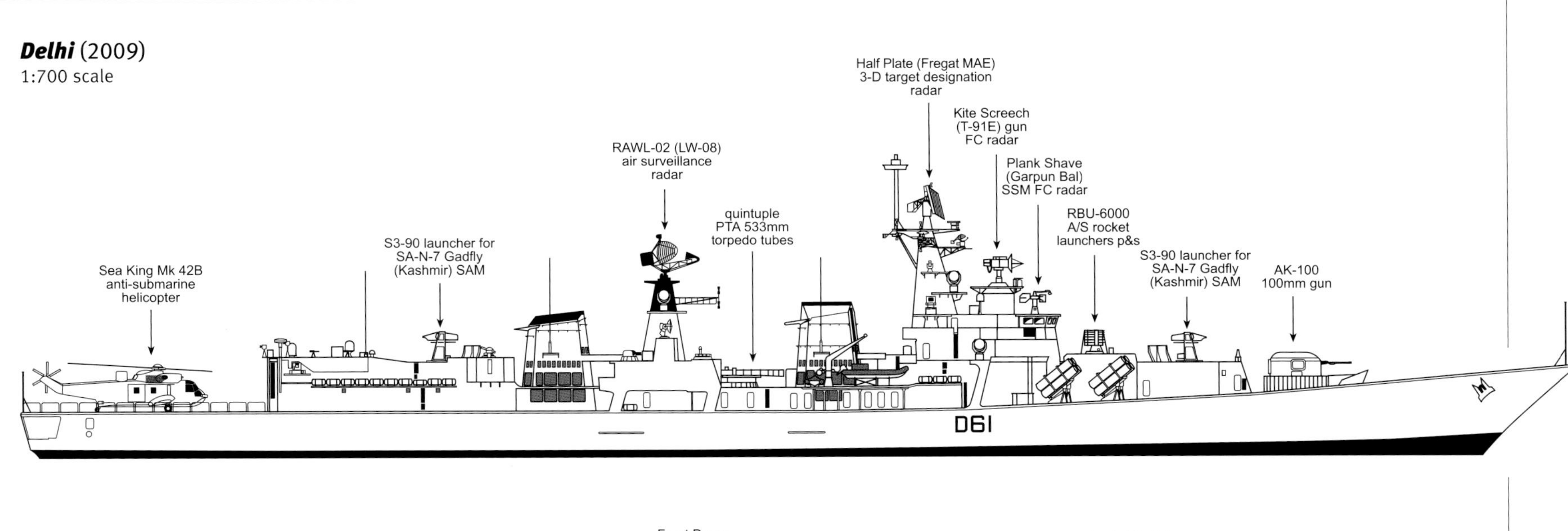

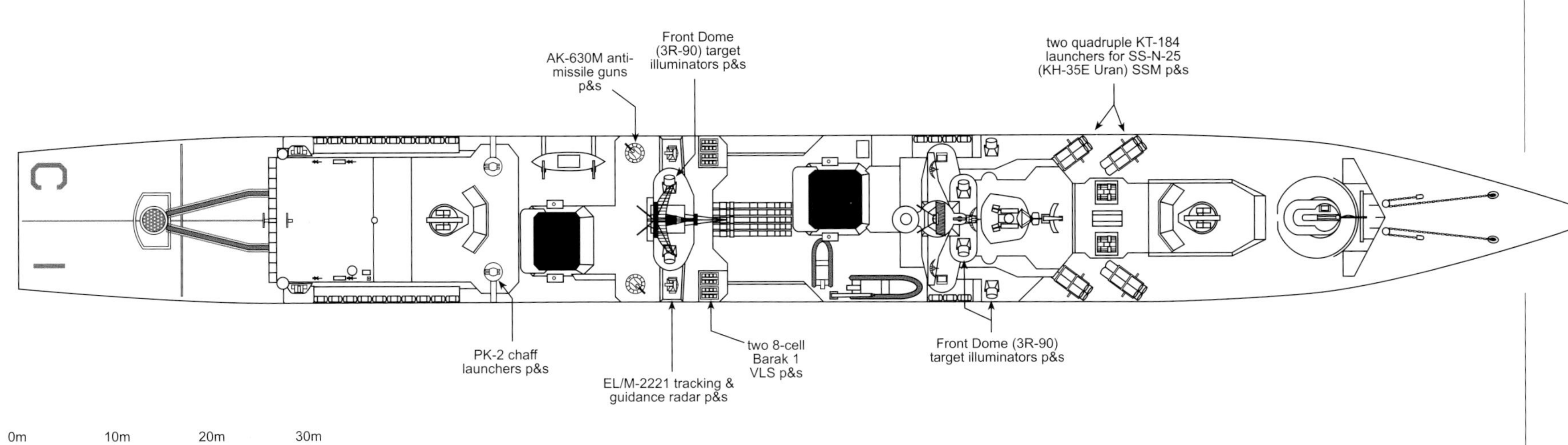

(Drawings © John Jordan, 2010)

Above: *Delhi* firing a RBU 6000 ASW rocket launcher during a practice anti-submarine engagement. The RGB-60 rocket projectile is reported to be very effective against underwater targets. *(Captain S K Sharma, Indian Navy)*

employed for defence against submarine launched torpedo attack.

A more detailed description of the most significant weapons and sensors follows:

AK-100 gun & T-91E fire-control radar: The main gun is an Arsenal-designed AK-100 gun mount with a single water-cooled 100/70 gun barrel and prominent Kondensor electro-optical sight. The steel turret is unmanned and reported to weigh about 49 tons. This gun fires three types of high explosive as well as an inert training round. As installed on *Delhi*, the gun's firing arc is about 240 degrees while elevation is -10 degrees to +85 degrees. Rate of fire is adjustable from single shots to bursts at 30-60rpm. Range against surface targets is around

Left: The RAWL-02 (LW-08) 2D long-range search radar on board *Delhi*. This is essentially a licence-built version of the Thales Nederland system. *(Conrad Waters)*

20km, with 8km possible against air targets.

This gun works in conjunction with an Ametist-built T-91E fire-control radar that is pedestal mounted atop the bridge. The T-91E radar is an element of the MR-145 fire-control system. The radar has a circular antenna and a central V-shaped antenna feed with two bands (centimetric and millimetric) to improve detection performance against low flying and waterborne targets operating amid sea clutter or ECM conditions. The transmitter, receiver, turning and stabilisation gear is mounted behind the antenna.

Uran SSMs & Garpun Bal fire-control radar: The principal surface strike system comprises four KT-184 quad launchers equipped with KH-35E Uran (3M24E) anti-ship missiles, a Garpun-Bal-E radar and a ZR-60UE fire-control system. The system is capable of salvo firing at an interval of two to three seconds against up to six targets at a time. It can be operational in under two minutes from a cold start.

The Uran missiles – built by the Tactical Missiles Corporation (formerly Zvezda) – are 4.4m long with a diameter of 0.4m and weigh 620kg including booster. They are fitted with a 145kg blast fragmentation warhead. Broadly similar in concept to the US Harpoon, they fly at subsonic speeds – Mach 0.8 –

The sonar systems deployed in the Project 15 class have changed as sonar technology has advanced. This is indicated by the different stern arrangements of *Delhi* (above) and *Mysore* (below). *(Conrad Waters & Mrityunjoy Mazumdar)*

Delhi's starboard CIWS complex. An EL/M-2221 fire-control radar is located on a platform between two eight-cell Barak 1 point-defence missile clusters and an AK630M Gatling-type gun. *(Conrad Waters)*

and at low altitudes of 10-15m, descending to 4m and possibly as low as 1.5m in the terminal phase. Launch range is 5-130km. Targeting data can be supplied both from the launching platform or other platforms fitted with suitable data links. The missile is fitted with a nose mounted ARGS-35 active radar seeker with a maximum range of 22.2km for target selection and terminal guidance. The seeker scans 90 degrees in azimuth and +10 degrees to -20 degrees in elevation. It is switched on some 24km from the target, after which it can be commanded to select specific-sized targets.

The Uran missiles are initially controlled by the Garpun-Bal fire-control radar, mounted atop the bridge. Unlike many fire-control and search radars, it combines active and passive channels using a single rectangular parabolic antenna. In the active target-designation mode, it operates in the I/J-bands (US X-band) and can handle up to 150 targets at ranges of between 35-45km. The passive channel operates in ESM mode, searching for pulse and continuous wave signals, identifying the bearing of hostile emitters from a built-in classification library of up to a thousand signatures. The maximum range of the passive channel is over 100km depending on frequency and radar ducting conditions. The radar is also believed to provide warnings about 'own-ship' detection by an adversary's radars.

Kashmir SAM and Fregat MAE search radar: The main air-defence weapon is the semi-active radar-homing 9M38M1 Kashmir SAM. The complete system includes two launchers, six 3R-90 Orekh illu-minators, four M-22E telesights, a 3D Fregat MAE search radar for targeting information and a fire-control system with processors and displays.

Each launcher complex comprises a 3S-90 single arm trainable launcher and an automated magazine with two twelve-cell drum magazines below decks. Missile load-out is forty-eight rounds. The launchers have a 330-degree firing arc and an elevation range of +10 to +80 degrees. They can be trained at speeds of 84 degrees/second in azimuth and 46 degrees/second in elevation. Rate of fire is claimed to be one missile per launcher every twelve seconds. Typically, two missiles are fired at each target according to Russian practice to increase kill proba-bilities. The reaction time is said to be between sixteen to nineteen seconds when the ship is on alert or three minutes from cold start.

The Kashmir missile, also known as Shtil and Uragan, is a navalised version of the land-based Buk SAM. Each missile is 5.6m long, weighs 690kg and carries a relatively large 70kg warhead which is trig-gered by a radar proximity fuse. The semi-active homing radar head, autopilot equipment, power source and a warhead are located in the forward compartment of the missile. A dual-mode solid-propellant rocket motor provides the missile with a maximum speed of around Mach 3. Engagement range is between 3km and 40km, while engagement altitude is from 30m to 25km. Precise figures are unclear but it is considered that published figures are not reflective of achievable ranges, which may only be limited by the range of illuminators. Manufacturer's literature also suggests that crossing target aircraft can be engaged at ranges of up to 18km, while missiles can be targeted at up to 6km. The double-round kill probability of kill ratio against aircraft varies from 0.81 to 0.96; against missiles it is between 0.43 and 0.86. Missiles may be capable of limited engagements against surface targets.

The six 3R-90 (also known as the MR-90) Orekh illuminators permit engagements against up to six targets. Two are located on the fore mast, two on a platform one level below the bride and two on the main mast aft. Each illuminator uses a different frequency and provides one channel of fire. The system is reportedly capable of controlling three designators simultaneously against one high-threat target. There are also four M-22E TV cameras mounted atop the bridge and hangar sides for tracking missiles during radar silence or in severe ECM conditions.

Target acquisition data comes from the Half Plate Fregat MAE radar, as well as the LW-08/ RAWL-02 2D radar set. It is not clear what version of the former is installed. Depending on the exact radar type and frequency, instrumented range is anywhere from 150km to 300km, with an altitude of up to 30km. The antenna rotates at 15rpm with a maximum scan rate of four seconds. It is fitted with IFF equipment atop the canted antenna.

LW-08/RAWL-02 Mk 1, Mk 2 radar: This is a D band (US L band) 2D radar providing long-range air and surface situational data. It is used for cueing the Fregat MAE and Garpun Bal radars to generate a more precise targeting solution. The Indian Navy has good experience of this system on a large number of ships. It is manufactured by BEL (with certain modi-fications) under licence from Thales Nederland.

AK-630M and Barak close-in defence systems: The class was originally fitted with four AK-630M gun mounts mounted amidships and two mast-mounted MR-123 Vympel directors for close-in defence against aircraft and missiles. This fit has since been altered on the *Delhi* and *Mysore*, which have received two eight-cell Barak 1 vertical launch units, for a total of thirty-two Barak missiles, in place of the two forward AK-630M mountings. The two Vympel directors were also replaced by two EL/M-2221 directors mounted atop a newly constructed plat-form. This combination has proven to be effective against subsonic cruise missiles such as the P-20/21/22 Styx family.

Mumbai currently retains its original CIWS suite, with one MR-123 Vympel system controlling two AK-630M gun mounts on either beam. The AK-630M has a six-barrelled AO-18 Gatling-type gun, with 2,000 ready-to-fire rounds within the gun mount. Rate of fire is 1,500-5,000 rpm. In practice, the gun is said to fire 400-round bursts with a short cooling interval between bursts. The MR-123 director uses H/I (US X) band radar along with a TV camera and a laser rangefinder. Engagement ranges are up to 4,000m using the radar, increasing to 5,000m using the electro-optical system. After a target has been acquired and designated by an operator, the system goes into an automatic mode. There is a back-up optical control post with a Kolonka sighting station.

The Barak 1 system retrofitted to the other ships is a short-range, all-weather, quick-reaction missile system with command line of sight guidance for countering supersonic sea skimmers. Each missile has a length of 2.2m and a body diameter of 0.2m. The wingspan of the cruciform control surfaces is 0.7m. The missile weighs 98kg, including a 22kg blast frag-mentation warhead. A proximity fuse with both IR and electronic sensors is fitted. Reaction time, presumably under 'hot' conditions' is said to be three seconds. Max speed is Mach 2 and the missile is capable of performing 25G manoeuvres. Minimum effective range is 500m and maximum range is around 10km. The missile is said to be able to inter-cept sea skimmers flying at a height of 2m above sea level up to a maximum altitude of 5,500m.

The EL/M-2221 fire-control radar was developed as part of the Barak 1 system. A mono-pulse, dual-band, Pulse-Doppler radar, it uses a composite Cassegrain antenna and a travelling-wave tube trans-mitter. Electro-optical and infra-red systems are also fitted as backup for operations in heavy ECM condi-

tions. Elta claims the radar can acquire missiles at 15km, fighter-sized objects at 30km and surface targets up to radar horizon. It can guide Barak missiles in single or salvo firings and can also be used for gun direction against airborne and surface targets.

APSOH, HUMVAD, HUMSA & ATAS sonar systems: Targeting data for anti-submarine weapons is obtained from a hull-mounted sonar in a fixed dome, along with a VDS or a towed array sonar depending on the ship. The first two ships were fitted with an APSOH hull mounted sonar and a HUMVAD VDS while *Mysore* has the improved HUMSA and a towed array system known as ATAS, now also seemingly retrofitted to *Delhi*. It is not clear if the latter is a Thales or a locally developed unit.

The Advanced Panoramic Sonar Hull-mounted (APSOH) is a medium-range, solid-state, dual-frequency sonar system designed for performing active ranging, passive listening and auto tracking of targets and classification. It was developed under the direction of then Commodore A J Paulraj, an engineer in the Indian Navy's electrical branch. Derived from the British Royal Navy's Graseby 184 solid state sonar, it features much improved signal processing algorithms and a host of other improvements to suit local operating conditions in high salinity waters. On its first trial aboard the *Leander* type frigate *Himgiri*, it achieved detection ranges of 16km. This sonar served as the basis for future ship sonar developments in India. In production, it is known as the HUS001 by Bharat Electronics. Depending on the transmission mode, maximum range could be in excess of 30km. The system, which employs both semi-automatic active tracking and fully automatic passive tracking, feeds digital data to the ASW fire-control system.

The Hull Mounted Variable Depth (HUMVAD) VDS is a variant of APSOH with additional electronics and transducers for variable depth. It entered service in 1983. To save development time, HUMVAD retained the same towing winches, towing cable and tow cable fairing as the British vari-

Mysore conducting a replenishment exercise in company with the fleet tanker *Aditya* and the US destroyer *Chafee*. The Indian ship's complex mix of weapons and sensors contrasts with the 'cleaner' image of the US design. *(Mrityunjoy Mazumdar)*

able-depth sonar 199 fitted in the first Indian-built *Leander* class frigate, *Nilgiri*. The HUMVAD units fitted to the *Delhi* and *Mysore* in the 1990s may have a different towed body than the UK's VDS 199, possibly the Indal 15-750.

The Hull Mounted Sonar Advanced (HUMSA) was designed in the 1990s: the HUS003 type fitted to *Mysore* is an enhanced version. This family of medium range active-cum-passive dual band sonars, optimised for both shallow and deep-water operations, has proved itself in the highly variable tropical waters. HUMSA's advanced signal processing techniques are responsible for its superior performance. The sonar uses multiple transmission modes for short- and long-range surveillance. It also provides

Delhi entering Portsmouth Harbour in June 2009 as flagship of the first task group deployed by the Indian Navy to the Atlantic Ocean. *(Conrad Waters)*

selective sector illumination to minimise interference in case of multi-ship operation.

Having received targeting information from sonars, underwater targets are prosecuted with embarked helicopters at longer ranges or with A/S rockets and torpedoes at shorter ranges. Twin RBU-6000 A/S rocket launchers are mounted on the forecastle, whilst the amidships mounted PTA-53-15 quintuple 533mm torpedo tube launcher is capable of firing heavyweight torpedoes of primarily Russian origin. RBU 6000 is a twelve-tube launcher, each tube being 212mm in diameter. It is capable of salvo and single-shot firing of RGB-60 depth rocket bombs with a 25kg warhead up to ranges of 1,000m. The Purga fire-control system – used to control both the RBU and the torpedo tubes – can engage three targets simultaneously.

COMBAT MANAGEMENT SYSTEM (CMS)

Details of the Project 15 class's CMS are somewhat limited. The Indian Navy's 'in house' R&D centre, the Weapons Electronics Systems Engineering Establishment (WESEE) – along with partners Bharat Electronics – was responsible for integrating the various Russian and Western sensors and equipment. Combining Russian and Western practices, the Indians have followed the Russian practice of using redundant sensors for each weapon system but also combine information so that a unified tactical picture is available, as in Western fleets. It is understood that the CMS uses LINUX operating systems.

The ship is fitted with a Russian Computerised Action Information Organisation (CAIO) for the Russian-origin weapons, with horizontal and vertical displays. There are some Indian-built displays, as well as Dutch and Israeli equipment. WESEE provided the necessary interface units between the Russian and non-Russian equipment. The various weapons systems have local operating panels.

DAMAGE CONTROL AND SURVIVABILITY

Staff requirements for the Project 15 ships were revised in the light of lessons learned from the Falklands War of April 1982 so these ships have enhanced survivability features. They are able to operate in a nuclear, biological and chemical (NBC) environment, although the damage control system is not as advanced as in the latest ships. The Ship Installed Radiac System – SIRS 4012 – gives warning against nuclear radiation only. A chemical agent warning system was to have been installed but, in the event, did not materialise before the ships were commissioned. This may well have been rectified subsequently. For NBC operations, the class is zoned into gastight citadels.

Fire protection is provided by a variety of fire-extinguishing systems including a fire main system for supplying large volumes of sea water at a pressure of 8-10 bar; a halon gas drench system supplemented by water spray/aqueous film-forming foam system for the main and auxiliary machinery rooms. The halon system has since been replaced by the FM200 fire protection agent and possibly the similar NAF S125. A topside wash-down countermeasures system is also fitted. Fresh-water hose reels are distributed around the ship In the event of battle damage, a redundant emergency control post located in the main mast provides essential steering and control functions.

OPERATIONS

Delhi and her sisters have taken part in just about every major Indian Navy exercise and deployment, as well as in several international defence exhibitions and reviews. In this last capacity, *Mysore* became only the second Indian warship to visit the United States when participating in the 2000 International Naval Review in New York. They have served well as goodwill ambassadors for the navy in these flag-flying missions,

More significantly, the class has assisted humanitarian missions off Sri Lanka, Lebanon and elsewhere. In July 2006, *Mumbai*, as a part of Task Force 54 comprising the Project 16A frigates *Brahmaputra* and *Betwa* and the tanker *Shakti*, was in the Mediterranean when tasked with assisting the evacuation of Indian citizens during the Israel-Lebanon conflict in Operation 'Sukoon'. Other high-profile missions include the 1999 Operation 'Parakam', when *Delhi* and *Mysore* were deployed off Pakistan's coast during the tense stand-off between the two nations. Ten years later, a task group lead by Admiral Surinder Pal Singh Cheema in *Delhi* and including the Project 16A frigates *Beas* and *Brahmaputra* and the tanker *Aditya* completed the Indian Navy's first ever European/Atlantic Ocean deployment. Most recently, the ships have been active in anti-piracy operations off the Horn of Africa.

The launch of *Chennai* at Mazagon Dock Ltd on 1 April 2010. A pontoon-assisted method has been developed for recent launches to permit a higher launch weight than previously. *(Mrityunjoy Mazumdar)*

PROJECT 15A *KOLKATA* CLASS

These three, follow-on destroyers use the same hull form and propulsion as the *Delhi* but incorporate vastly improved signature management – so-called 'stealth' – features. The biggest visual difference is a sloped superstructure and generally uncluttered topside arrangement. They are also characterised by greater use of locally-built equipment, including licence-built weapons or improved derivatives. Initially, the new ships were intended to use a largely Russian-derived weapon and sensor package. However, this approach changed relatively early on in the programme's life as new Israeli weapons systems became available. Displacement will be slightly greater than the *Delhi* class at c. 6,800 tons.

Government approval for the destroyers' construction was received in May 2000. MDL received orders in FY2001/02, with construction scheduled to commence in October 2002. However, work on the first ship did not start until first plate cutting on 12 March 2003, followed by keel laying on 27 September 2003. The delay was largely due to non-availability of D-40S shipbuilding steel from Russia. The second ship, Yard 12702, was laid down on 25 October 2005, followed by the final unit, Yard 12703, on 21 February 2006. Yard 12701 was launched as *Kolkata* on 30 March 2006, followed by Yard 12702 as *Kochi* on 18 September 2009 and Yard 12703 as *Chennai* on 1 April 2010. The last two ships were launched using a 'pontoon-assisted launching' method which enabled MDL to achieve a launch weight of 4,060 tons or almost 60 per cent of the planned displacement of 6,700-6,800 tons. By comparison, *Kolkata* was launched with a weight of about 40 per cent of final displacement. Owing to unfavourable tidal conditions, MDL will utilise this launch method for future construction going forward. Planned commissioning dates are early 2012 for *Kolkata*, late 2012 for *Kochi* and August 2013 for *Chennai*.

While construction has been much smoother than for the *Delhi* class, there have been delays on account of the previously-mentioned weapons system changes, as well as due to supply chain issues. For example, propellers and shafting had to be ordered from Russia's Baltisky Zavod after non-receipt of similar items from a supplier in the Ukraine. Locally, there was a difficult learning curve for Indian vendors, who were not used to working to stringent quality requirements especially as it pertains to noise, vibration, electro-magnetic and radar signatures for shipboard equipment and machinery on these stealthy warships. On the upside, the local supply chain has now gained relevant experience which will pay dividends for future programmes, further increasing indigenous content. Sources suggest that Indian content on the Project 15A ships is no more than 60 per cent in terms of labour-connected inputs; the figure is much less in terms of raw materials and equipment.

Principal armament includes a single 76mm Oto Melara gun, sixteen BrahMos SSMs in two eight-cell complexes and forty-eight Barak 8 long-range SAMs in two 24-cell clusters forward and aft atop the hangar. The last-mentioned are active seeker-equipped missiles with a reported 70km range and are directed by the ships' principal radar, the Elta EL/M-2248 MF-STAR multifunction phased array. The MF-STAR is a brand new E/F band (US S) band multifunction radar with four fixed antenna faces much like the SPY-1 radar of the Aegis system. It is designed to perform simultaneous surface and air search operations while supporting engagements by multiple anti-aircraft, anti-missile and surface-attack shipboard weapons. The radar can automatically establish tracks of high-flying targets at ranges beyond 250km and at low-flying targets, at ranges above 25km. Installation of the radar-missile combination in *Kolkata* is expected to commence sometime in 2010, with India's Defence Research & Development Organisation (DRDO) being the nodal agency for integrating the radar-missile combination. The BrahMos missiles are likely to be supported by the Garpun Bal found on the *Delhi* class, whilst the latest variant of the tried and trusted LW-08 2D volume search radar will also be fitted.

Interestingly, the staff requirements specified a return to four AK-630M mountings for close-in defence: a departure from the proven AK-630M and Barak 1 combination. The anti-submarine system is largely indigenous in origin. An IAC Mod 0 fire-control system controls twin IRL (Indigenous Rocket Launchers) – an improvement over the

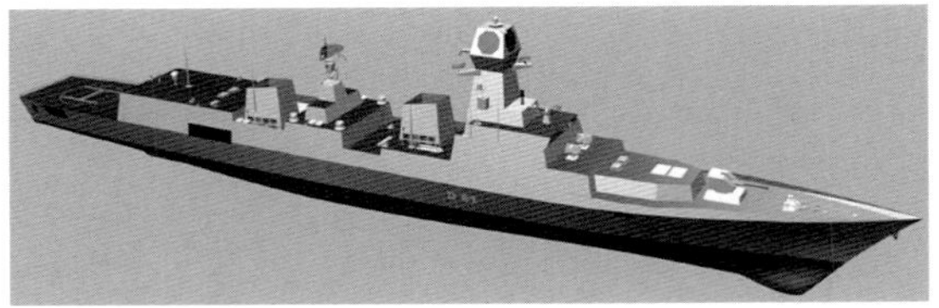

A graphic of the Project 15A destroyer design. Note the prominent MF-STAR multifunction radar atop the forward mast. *(Indian Navy)*

Russian RBU-6000 – and two transversely-mounted twin ITTL (Indigenous Twin Tube Launcher) 533mm torpedo tubes. A bow-mounted HUMSA-NG sonar – for which Atlas Elektronik supplied the dome and possibly the directing gear – was specified to reduce self-noise. The ships were also originally designed to ship a locally-developed NAGIN towed array but it is understood this selection has yet to be confirmed.

The ships' combat action information system – CAIO-15A – is very largely integrated by the Navy's WESEE and Bharat Electronics, with input from various weapons suppliers. These ships are also equipped with a comprehensive AISDN-15A fibre-optic network, with many multifunction consoles to

access, monitor and control shipboard weapons and equipment. This – as well as the class's Composite Communications System Mk 2 – is a major advancement over the capabilities of the *Delhi* class.

Countermeasures are provided by the Ellora electronic warfare system found on the *Delhi* class, supplemented by locally-developed Kavach decoy launchers and a Mareech towed anti-torpedo decoy system. The class will also have comprehensive NBC protection in the form of a total atmospheric control system maintaining positive air pressure within the ship at all times. Double bulkheads will ensure airlocks during ingress and egress. As in the *Delhi* class, a redundant Emergency Control Post located in the main mast provides back-up steering and control functions. Survivability is also enhanced by the attention to stealth already referenced, which also encompasses measures to reduce infrared emissions from the gas turbines similar to those used in the Project 17 *Shivalik* class frigates.

The Zorya M-36E COGAG propulsion plant is essentially identical to that fitted in *Delhi* and her sisters, whilst provision for electrical generation is also similar. No integrated platform management system (IPMS) is incorporated. This omission is

Table 3.2.2: INDIAN NAVY DESTROYER COMPARISONS – PROJECT 15, PROJECT 15A AND PROJECT 15B SHIPS

CLASS	PROJECT 15 *DELHI*	PROJECT 15A *KOLKATA*	PROJECT 15B
Builder:	Mazagon Docks Ltd	Mazagon Docks Ltd	Mazagon Docks Ltd
First of Class Delivery:	1997	2012	Post-2015
Number in Class:	3	3	4
Full Load Displacement:	6,700 tons	6,800 tons	6,800 tons+
Principal Dimensions:	163.2m x 17.4m x 6.5m	163.2m x 17.4m x 6.8m	163.2m x 17.4m x 6.8m
Propulsion:	COGAG, M-36E Plant, 32 knots	COGAG, M-36E Plant, 32 knots	COGAG, M-36E Plant, 32 knots
	No IPMS	No IPMS	IPMS
Armament:	1 x 100mm AK-100 gun	1 x 76mm Oto Melara gun	1 x 127mm Oto Melara gun
	2 x 3S-90 launchers for Kashmir SAM	2 x 24-cell VLS for Barak 8 SAM	Barak ER SAM
	4 x quad KT-184 launchers for Uran SSM	2 x eight-cell VLS for BrahMos SSM	BrahMos SSM
	4 x eight-cell Barak PDMS, 2 x AK-630M guns	4 x AK-630M guns	AK-630M likely
	1 x quintuple PTA A/S torpedo mounting	2 x ITTL fixed A/S tubes	2 x ITTL fixed A/S tubes likely
	2 x 12-tube RBU-6000 A/S launchers	2 x 12-tube IRL A/S launchers	2 x 12-tube IRL A/S launchers likely
	2 x helicopters	2 x helicopters	2 x helicopters
Primary Sensors:	1 x RAWL-02 long range search	1 x RAWL-02 long range search	SMART-L derivative likely
	1 x Fregat MAE 3D, 6 x MR-90 F/C (SAM)	Elta EL/M-2248 MF-STAR	Elta EL/M-2248 MF-STAR
	1 x Garpun Bal F/C (SSM)	1 x Garpun Bal F/C (SSM)	Fire control for SSM
	Fire control for gun/CIWS	Fire control for gun/CIWS	Fire control for gun/CIWS
	APOSH and ATAS sonar	HUMSA NG and NAGIN sonar	
CMS:	Indigenous CMS. No data network	CMS-15A, AISDN-15A data network	CMS-15B, AISDN-15B data network
Crew:	c. 350	c. 310	c. 300

partly rectified by provision of an auxiliary control system through a collaboration between Italy's Avio and Bharat Heavy Electricals Ltd (BHEL) for both 'hotel' and key damage control functions. Very spacious modular accommodation spaces are provided for the crew, including a few cabins for female officers.

While the Project 15A design was largely completed by the surface ship group of the Indian Navy's in house design directorate, Mazagon Docks' own designers are responsible for much detailed integration work related to, for example, the vertical launch missile systems, the multi-function radar and the bow-mounted sonar. There have been many new systems to integrate and – in the absence of modular construction processes – outfitting has proved laborious and time-consuming. As of mid-2010, *Kolkata* was about 60 per cent complete with sea trials targeted for the end of 2011.

According to MDL, the estimated cost of each of the Project 15A destroyers, excluding ammunition and helicopters, should not exceed Rs 3,500 crores (US$750m at current exchange rates). However, actual figures will not be confirmed until the first of class has been completed.

PROJECT 15B CLASS

Four additional destroyers, the Project 15B class, were approved by India's Defence Acquisition Council in February 2009. At the time of writing, a contract award was imminent. The class will be a further improvement over the Project 15A ships in terms of weapons, sensors, communications, shipboard automation and, possibly, the propulsion system. However, details are only slowly emerging.

Armament will encompass a 127mm Oto Melara main gun licence-built by BHEL. Missiles will include the 100km, extended range version of Barak 8 – suggesting continued reliance on MF-STAR as the principal radar – whilst Brahmos-2 hypersonic as well as Nirbhay cruise missiles seem probable. The LW-08 radar will most likely be replaced by a derivative of the Thales SMART L.

The new class was originally designed to be fitted with GE LM2500 gas turbines but this decision is in doubt following a debacle relating to the supply of similar equipment for the Project 17 class during 2009. GE failed to obtain proper approval – a Technical Assistance Agreement – from the US State Department to install a commercial product on a military vessel and commissioning was delayed whilst

An interesting April 2010 view of Mazagon Dock Ltd in Mumbai, where all the Project 15 destroyers have been built. The first Project 15A ship, *Kolkata*, can be seen fitting out in dry dock to the right of the picture. In the centre foreground is a Project 17 frigate, with *Kochi* behind. The newly-launched *Chennai* is in the process of being berthed next to her sister. (*Mrityunjoy Mazumdar*)

an essentially bureaucratic problem was resolved. Predictably, the upset caused a minor crisis in India's DND and a re-examination of Zorya alternatives. However, having successfully commissioned the first Project 17 ship, *Shivalik*, it appears that confidence in GE's ability to support Indian naval programmes is rising again. An IPMS system seems certain to be incorporated regardless of the choice of gas turbines.

Notional timelines citing a four-year build time for the lead ship may prove unrealistic, although the intention to deliver the ships at a rate of one per year should be achievable. Some form of modular construction is to be utilised but this is dependent on completion of MDL's modernisation project, which is currently a good two years away.

CONCLUSION

India's trio of home-built P-15 multi-role guided-missile destroyers are significant warships. They successfully combined Western and Russian design philosophies to support a powerful weapons and sensor package. At the time, they were the biggest surface combatants to emerge from Asia with the exception of Japan. Since then, these ships have

served as the basis for two follow-on classes – the Project 15A and Project 15B – with vastly enhanced capabilities and a level of technological sophistication that is on a par with contemporary Western warships. These ships, along with others designed by the Indian Navy, have placed India on the map as a competent shipbuilding nation well able to produce world-class warships within limited means.

Notes

1. Those interested in further information on the development of the Indian Navy can find great insights into India's Directorate of Naval Design (DND) and warship projects in the official Indian Navy trilogy by the late Vice Admiral G N Hiranandani. The books are:

Transition to Triumph, The Indian Navy 1965-1975, (New Delhi, Lancer Publishers, 2000).
Transition to Eminence, The Indian Navy 1975-1990, (New Delhi, Lancer Publishers, 2005).
Transition to Guardianship, The Indian Navy 1991-2000 (New Delhi, Lancer Publishers, 2010).

2. Chapter 2.3A, pages 75-85 of the *Seaforth World Naval Review 2010* contains a full overview of recent Indian Navy developments and programmes.

Author:
Conrad Waters

FRIDTJOF NANSEN CLASS FRIGATES

Norway's Ticket to the Aegis Club

One of the most significant naval developments of the post-war era occurred on 22 January 1983. On this date, the first USN Aegis-equipped cruiser, *Ticonderoga* (CG-47), was commissioned at Pascagoula, Mississippi. Combining cutting-edge radar technology with an unprecedented degree of weapons-system integration, Aegis represented a long-awaited solution to the threat of saturation attack from advanced jet aircraft and anti-surface missiles. It therefore provided an effective means of making surface ships far less vulnerable than hitherto. However, for the first twenty years after *Ticonderoga*'s delivery, the Aegis club was an exclusive one. US caution over the release of such an advanced and capable system to all but its closest allies was one reason for this. However, the fact that Aegis' size and complexity meant that it could only be installed in large, costly surface escorts was probably the key limiting factor. The deployment of Norway's *Fridtjof Nansen* class frigates therefore marks a new chapter in the system's evolution, demonstrating its application to smaller navies operating only modestly-sized vessels. The fruit of successful collaboration between the Spanish shipbuilder Navantia, the US defence

contractor Lockheed Martin and the Norwegian defence ministry, *Fridtjof Nansen* and her four sister-ships are amongst the most capable ships of their type in the world. They also provide a step change in capability for the *Kongelig Norske Marine*.

CLASS ORIGINS

Positioned on the northern flank of the NATO alliance adjacent to the Soviet-era naval bases bordering the Barents Sea, Norway occupied an important strategic position during the Cold War. The result was substantial investment in naval capabilities, both to counter Russian submarines attempting to access the Atlantic Ocean and also to protect the lengthy Norwegian coastline against amphibious assault. The core component of the Royal Norwegian Navy's surface forces during the later years of this stand-off was the five *Oslo* class frigates. All were commissioned during 1966-7. Derived from the USN's *Dealey* class destroyer escorts and partly financed with American cash, they were relatively small ships displacing less than 2,000 tonnes in full load condition. Principally designed for anti-submarine operations in conjunction with other NATO forces in the Norwegian Sea, the class was approaching the end of its design life as the Cold War drew to a close. The replacement frigate programme established in the early 1990s consequently developed against a backdrop of marked change in the

international environment. However, the proximity of Russia's Northern Fleet and its still-potent submarine flotillas remained a major influence.

Whilst, therefore, the Royal Norwegian Navy specified a multi-purpose design when launching a competition for design and construction of up to six new frigates in 1997, anti-submarine warfare was still the primary role envisaged for the class. The project attracted a substantial amount of interest from European and North American firms. A short-list of three bidders was selected from these contenders during 1998. The finalists were (i) Germany's Blohm & Voss – subsequently part of Thyssen Krupp Marine Systems – offering a variant of the popular MEKO 200 type, (ii) the local NorEskort consortium – initially comprising Kvaerner, Umoe and Kongsberg – with an entirely new frigate design and (iii) Spain's Bazán – now Navantia.[1] The last-mentioned offered two variants of its F-100 type frigate, one equipped with BAE Systems' Surface Ship Command System (SSCS) and one featuring Lockheed Martin's SPY-1F variant of the Aegis weapon system.

The selection of a successful bid hinged on a complex mix of technical, industrial and financial considerations. There was inevitably considerable political support for a solution that maximised indigenous involvement. However, the NorEskort team's proposal was fatally compromised when Kvaerner

A view of *Fridtjof Nansen* arriving in Norwegian waters. Along with her four sister-ships she provides a step change in the Royal Norwegian Navy's capability. (*Conrad Waters*)

announced that it was to exit its shipbuilding activities whilst the short-listed bids were still under consideration. Reports at the time suggested that Blohm & Voss made an attractive proposal but that Norway saw significant attractions in the enhanced surveillance and self-defence capabilities provided by Aegis. Ultimately, this latter argument won the day and Bazán was informed in May 1999 that its Lockheed Martin variant was the preferred way forward. Subsequent lengthy negotiations to agree an acceptable contract price were not concluded until the following year. On 23 June 2000, a 220bn Spanish peseta (c. US$1.25bn at then current exchange rates) contract for five frigates was finally signed with the shipyard under a total project initially valued at 14bn Norwegian kroner (c. US$1.5bn). The programme was the most expensive to date concluded by the Norwegian Ministry of Defence.

CONTRACT AND CONSTRUCTION

The contract awarded to Bazán saw the Spanish company taking the lead role as the programme's prime contractor, with Lockheed Martin acting as subcontractor for the integrated weapons system (Aegis). However, Norwegian industry was also allocated a significant share of the project. For example, former NordEskort member Kongsberg worked with Lockheed Martin to provide many elements of the combat system, most notably its anti-submarine and anti-surface warfare sub-systems. In addition, Norwegian shipyards constructed major parts of the ships' constituent blocks and were initially tasked with final assembly of the last two frigates.

The significant degree of production-sharing envisaged from the early days of the project was facilitated by the integrated modular construction methodologies pioneered by Bazán. These allowed fabrication to be broken down into a large number of constituent sub-assemblies or 'intermediate products' from which larger sub-blocks and ultimately blocks were assembled. The concept permitted a material part of the construction process to be contracted to facilities not previously involved in the construction of surface escort vessels. It also accelerated overall building time due to the simultaneous completion of structural, outfitting and painting tasks. A key element in the success of this process was the effective sharing of information through use of the 'in house' *Necora* ERP (enterprise resource planning) software system to co-ordinate areas such as the purchase and assignment of construction materials. Each frigate was ultimately assembled on the slipway from twenty-four major blocks. Thereafter, completion was split into six separate final outfitting zones defined by the joining of different blocks on the slipway and grouped by geographical and functional criteria. The later ships of the class were c. 80 per cent complete at launch.

The work-sharing agreement reached with Norwegian industry was based on a pre-defined allocation of blocks between Bazán and the Mjellem & Karlsen shipyard in Bergen. In essence, the Bergen facility was responsible for constructing the bow and stern blocks. The central hull and superstructure were to be fabricated in Spain. Additionally, Mjellem & Karlsen was tasked with the assembly, launch and final outfitting of the last two members of the class. The flexibility inherent in the Spanish company's production methodologies were soon put to the test

An aerial view of *Fridtjof Nansen* taken in June 2008. Norway's selection of the design was driven by the advantages offered by the Aegis weapon system. The AN/SPY-1 multi-function radar associated with Norway's variant of the system is fitted in the prominent octagonal tower. *(Navantia)*

Fridtjof Nansen on the slipway at Navantia's Ferrol shipyard, with bow module 110 being fitted into place. Each ship was assembled from twenty-four major blocks constructed in both Spain and Norway. *(Navantia)*

after its Norwegian partner went into insolvency in August 2002. Subsequent discussions saw Norway's BMV and Kleven Floro yards step up to assume Mjellem & Karlsen's former responsibilities for block construction. A further contract amendment negotiated towards the end of 2004 saw additional block fabrication for Vessels 4 and 5 transferred to the Norwegian companies in compensation for the concentration of all final assembly work in Spain. The fact that these changes were accommodated with only modest delays to the overall build process is a good indication of the strength of the overall project management framework.

Fabrication of first-of-class *Fridtjof Nansen* commenced on 18 December 2001 with initial steel cutting.[2] Keel-laying at the Ferrol naval shipyard in north-west Spain followed on 9 April 2003. Subsequently, the amount of pre-outfitting inherent in the integrated construction process allowed rapid progress to be achieved, with launch taking place on 3 June 2004. Sea trials commenced in October 2005 and the ship was commissioned into the Royal Norwegian Navy on 5 April 2006 at Ferrol. The ship arrived in Norwegian waters towards the end of spring in the same year. Construction of follow-on ships has taken place at roughly annual intervals, with delivery of final class member *Thor Heyerdahl* currently projected towards the end of 2010.

OVERALL DESIGN: ANTECEDENTS AND FEATURES

The *Fridtjof Nansen* class is essentially a scaled-down version of the *Álvaro de Bazán* (F-100) type Aegis-equipped frigate. First ordered in 1997, four units of this type were delivered to the *Armada Española* between 2002 and 2006. In addition, Navantia is currently completing a slightly improved fifth member of the class at Ferrol. The ships marked a major step forward for Spanish naval construction in so far as they were the first class of major surface ship to be constructed to a purely national design. The

The launch of *Fridtjof Nansen* at Ferrol on 3 June 2004. Substantial use of integrated modular construction techniques mean the frigate was substantially complete at launch. *(Navantia)*

Table 3.3.1: *ÁLVARO DE BAZÁN* AND *FRIDTJOF NANSEN* CLASS COMPARISON

CLASS	F100 *ÁLVARO DE BAZÁN*	*FRIDTJOF NANSEN*
Builder:	Navantia, Ferrol	Navantia, Ferrol
Country:	Spain	Norway
First of Class Delivered:	September 2002	April 2006
Number in Class:	5 (+3 *Hobart* class for Australia)	5
Full Load Displacement:	5,900 tons	5,200 tons
Principal Dimensions:	146.7m x 18.6m x 4.9m (7.2m maximum)	133.2m x 16.8m x 4.9m (7.6m maximum)
Propulsion:	CODOG, 28 knots maximum	CODAG, 27 knots maximum
Armament:	Aegis weapons system	Aegis weapons system
	AN/SPY-1D multi-function radar	AN/SPY-1F multi-function radar
	2 x fire-control illuminators	2 x fire-control illuminators
	6 x eight-cell Mk41 vertical launch modules	1 x eight-cell Mk 41 vertical launch module
	Standard SM-2MR and ESSM surface-to-air missiles	ESSM surface-to-air missiles
	2 x quad Harpoon surface-to-surface missiles	2 x quad NSM surface-to-surface missiles
	1 x Mk45 127mm gun	1 x 76mm Oto Melara Super Rapid gun
	2 x twin fixed 324mm torpedo tubes	2 x twin fixed 324mm torpedo tubes
	1 x SH-60B Seahawk helicopter	1 x NFH-90 helicopter
Crew:	c. 210 (space for c. 235)	c. 120 (space for c. 145)

Álvaro de Bazán departing Portsmouth in September 2009. The *Nansen* class are essentially scaled-down versions of the Spanish ship. *(Conrad Waters)*

class was also notable in successfully incorporating Aegis and its AN/SPY-1D fixed arrays in the c. 6,000-tonne hull of what is effectively a small anti-air warfare destroyer.[3] The F-100 design therefore proved the feasibility of fitting Aegis into a moderately-sized vessel and, as a result, opened up the possibility of its adoption by smaller fleets. However, it was the commissioning of *Fridtjof Nansen* that took this process to its ultimate conclusion in actually delivering a small, Aegis-equipped escort into operational service.

Displacing just over 5,200 tonnes in full load condition, the *Nansen* class are notably lighter and smaller than their Spanish counterparts. Perhaps even more significantly, they have a considerably lower acquisition cost and are operated by a much smaller and, consequently, cheaper crew. Key factors behind these differences are the Norwegian Navy's selection of the new compact SPY-1F 'budget' version of Aegis, as well as restricting anti-air weaponry to the short range RIM-162 Evolved Sea Sparrow Missile (ESSM). This compares with the Standard SM-2/ESSM combination used in the Spanish ships. The more compact nature of the Norwegian choice is reflected in the limitation of the space-consuming Mk 41 vertical launch system (VLS) to just one eight-cell module (with space and weight reserved for an additional eight cells) compared with the F-100's six-module design. Whilst the inevitable result of this approach is a materially less effective air-defence capability, this makes sense when considering the *Nansen* class's primary anti-submarine role.

Fridtjof Nansen and her sisters incorporate many other differences in detail compared with their Spanish predecessors. These include a modified propulsion system and considerable use of indigenously-sourced weapons and electronics. In spite of this, the two classes share a distinct familial resemblance, not least through a common approach to the use of stealth technology. The hull form – derived from work carried out by Bazán in the 1980s – is also based on that used in the F-100 design, albeit ice-strengthening has been incorporated under DnV (Det Norske Veritas Foundation) classification 1A1 ICE-C to take account of the class's likely deployment in Arctic waters. Other evidence of 'Arcticisation' includes fully enclosed bridge wings, the provision of electrically-heated windows in exposed positions and extensive use of de-icing and anti-icing systems in decks and air intakes. The class

Fridtjof Nansen and *Roald Amundsen* operating in company. The class features a number of modifications to equip them for comfortable operation in the Arctic, most notably fully-enclosed bridge wings. *(Navantia)*

are equally capable of operating in a tropical climate.

Table 3.3.1 provides a detailed comparison of the F-100 and *Fridtjof Nansen* designs.

WEAPONRY AND COMBAT SYSTEMS

The heart of the *Fridtjof Nansen* class' combat potential is inevitably provided by the Aegis weapon system. Named after the Greek God Zeus' shield, Aegis is commonly associated with the distinctive octagonal AN/SPY-1 fixed arrays that form a key part of its air-defence capabilities. However, it is important to appreciate that Aegis is a much broader, integrated weapons system that is effective across anti-air, anti-submarine and anti-surface missions. This range of capabilities explains Norway's selection of Aegis for general-purpose escorts with a primary anti-submarine warfare role. Command and control functions are built around interlinked weapons control and command and

decision computer systems, into which the SPY-1 arrays, ESSM and other key sensors and weapons are integrated.[4] In the Norwegian frigates, the anti-submarine and anti-surface components of the wider system are provided by Kongsberg Defence and Aerospace under contract to Lockheed Martin. The latter manufactures and integrates the core weapons control and the command and decision elements of Aegis, as well as the AN/SPY-1 radar.

Although *Nansen* and her sisters are equipped with the lightweight SPY-1F version of the AN/SPY-1 multifunction radar series, the fundamentals of this technology are broadly similar across all Aegis-equipped ships. The series originates from a US government contract for Aegis' development signed with the RCA electronics group in 1969. Designed to combat the threat of saturation attack by aircraft or missiles, AN/SPY-1 is an example of an electronically scanned or 'phased' array. These use electronics

rather than mechanics to form and direct their radar beams. In comparison with traditional mechanical radars, the additional flexibility inherent in electronic scanning allows one multipurpose system to identify, track and target large numbers of possible contacts virtually simultaneously over a considerable geographical area. When combined with a sophisticated, rapid-reaction command and control system such as that forming Aegis' core, the probability of a successful saturation attack is significantly reduced.

The major difference between SPY-1F and its predecessors is its physical dimensions. Each of the four fixed phased-array antennae (arranged to give 360-degree coverage) are 8ft (2.4m) in diameter. This compares with the 12ft (3.7m) diameter of earlier radars in the series. The reduced dimensions are reflected in a much reduced number of individual radar elements. Each array has just 1,856 compared with 4,350 in the previous versions. This means that SPY-1F has considerably reduced power – and hence less surveillance range – than the SPY-1D variant fitted in larger destroyers. However, its lighter weight means that it is placed higher in the ship, providing some compensation.

It is reported that SPY-1F has been optimised for enhanced performance in the littoral and against anti-surface missiles. This makes sense in a Norwegian context given the geographical peculiarities of the country's fjords, as well as the danger of attack from submarine-launched 'pop up' missiles inherent in ASW operations. However, it is worth noting that Aegis' broader surveillance capabilities are also of considerable value to Norway's armed forces given that ensuring the safety of the nation's extensive natural resources in the Norwegian and adjacent seas is a key defence priority.

As for all versions of the AN/SPY-1 series, SPY-1F operates in the 2,000-4,000 MHz frequency E/F bands (USN S-band). This provides a compromise between the greater surveillance range obtainable from lower frequency systems and the enhanced tracking abilities of radars operating in higher frequency bands. The United Kingdom's Sampson radar operates at a similar frequency. In anti-air engagements, SPY-1F works in conjunction with semi-active ESSM (quad-packed in each of the eight Mk 41 missile cells) and two TIS (Target Illumination System) missile illuminators. The last-mentioned are a more modern variant of the USN's established AN/SPG-62 system developed by Lockheed Martin and Kongsberg. The multi-func-

Above: A close-up of the eight-cell Mk41 VLS on *Helge Ingstad*. Sufficient space and weight has been reserved for at least one further eight-cell module. *(Conrad Waters)*

A view from the bows of *Helge Ingstad* showing the 76mm gun, forward TIS illuminator and SPY-1F radar tower, as well as surface-search and navigation arrays. *(Conrad Waters)*

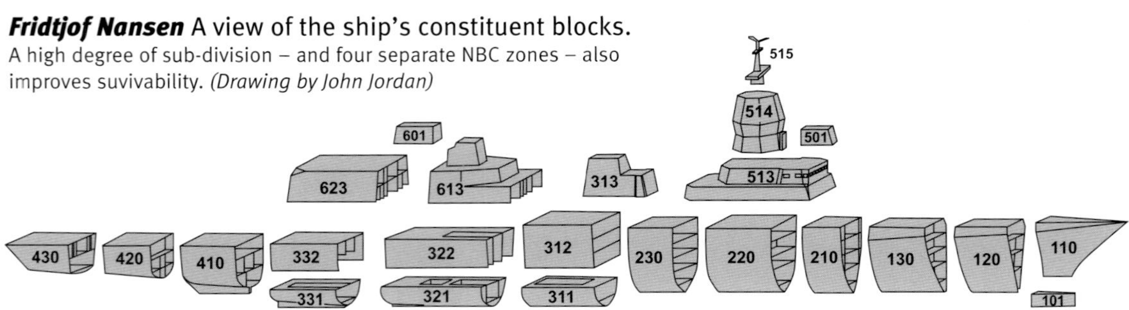

Fridtjof Nansen A view of the ship's constituent blocks. A high degree of sub-division – and four separate NBC zones – also improves suvivability. *(Drawing by John Jordan)*

The heart of the *Nansen* class's combat capability is provided by the Aegis weapon system. The class is fitted with the lightweight AN/SPY-1F version of the system, which features smaller radar arrays. Two of the four fixed 8ft (2.4m) diameter panels can be seen in this image of *Helge Ingstad*. *(Conrad Waters)*

tion radar is used for overall surveillance and to track likely targets prior to an engagement commencing, whilst also directing missiles on an impact trajectory by means of a commandable autopilot once action has been initiated. The TIS illuminators are 'slaved' to the main system and take over the engagement in its final seconds. The time-limited nature of the illuminators' role means that several engagements can be carried out simultaneously up to ESSM's reported maximum range of more than 50km.

The effectiveness of ESSM in ensuring local air defence means that the *Nansen* class are not fitted with a specific close-in weapons system (CIWS) as a backup. However, this option was considered in the original design and there is sufficient space and weight for one to be installed should the need arise.

In addition, the Oto Melara 76mm/62 Super Rapid medium-calibre gun fitted forward of the Mk41 launcher can be used in the CIWS capacity in addition to its anti-surface role. A Sagem Vigy 20 electro-optical sensor system is fitted for fire-control purposes. The frigates' main surface strike capability will be comprised of two quadruple Kongsberg NSM (Naval Strike Missile) anti-ship missiles that are also intended to form the principal armament of the *Skjold* class fast attack craft. Featuring composite materials to reduce radar cross-section, the NSM benefits from terrain-following capabilities to improve its effectiveness in a littoral environment and has a range in excess of 100nm (185km). A contract valued at 2.7bn Norwegian kroner (c.US$500m) was signed for series production of the missile in June 2007. Installation in the *Nansen*s is planned from 2012. Kongsberg also produce the Sea Protector remote weapons system that is fitted to the frigates to combat asymmetric threats.

Key anti-submarine sensors are a Thales Spherion MRS 2000 hull-mounted sonar and a Combined Active/Passive Towed Array Sonar (CAPTAS) Mk 2 V1 manufactured by the same company. Along with anti-surface systems, these are integrated into Aegis by means of Kongsberg's Multi-Sensor Integrated Fire Control (MSIFC) system. MSIFC is reportedly derived from technology contained in France's SENIT 2000 – used in the *Skjold* class – and the MSI-90U combat system found in the *Ula* and Type 212A submarines. A similar system has also been specified for South Korea's KDX-III destroyers. Shipboard ASW weaponry comprises two fixed twin 324mm torpedo launchers equipped with BAE Systems' Stingray lightweight anti-submarine torpedoes. The Mod 1 version of this weapon was ordered under a £99m (c.US$150m) contract announced in February 2009.

Fridtjof Nansen and her sisters represent a major

advance over previous Royal Norwegian Navy escorts in being designed to operate and sustain a shipborne anti-submarine helicopter. The European NH90 helicopter was selected to fulfil this function as long ago as 2001. Six of the type's NFH sea control variants were contracted at that time as part of a fourteen strong order that also included eight additional aircraft for the Coast Guard. The helicopters deployed on the class will be operated by a Royal Norwegian Air Force detachment of approximately ten personnel. They will be equipped with Thales FLASH dipping sonar and ENR surveillance radar, as well as with Stingray torpedoes. Unfortunately the broader NH90 project has suffered significant development delays and, as a result, the frigates have commenced their initial deployments without an aircraft embarked. Nevertheless, the addition of a helicopter will provide a major enhancement in core anti-submarine capability once delivered.

COUNTERMEASURES AND SURVIVABILITY

The *Nansen* class's weaponry is supplemented by a comprehensive range of electronic warfare systems and other countermeasures, as well as by extensive survivability features. Electronic countermeasures are built around the widely-used ES-3701 tactical radar electronic support measures and surveillance system from ITT Corporation. This is designed to detect, identify and locate hostile ship, aircraft and missile signals so that appropriate defensive measures can be implemented. It is reported to be particularly effective in performing in littoral waters, where the electronic spectrum is likely to be more crowded. 'Soft kill' capabilities are provided by two twelve-barrelled Terma DL-12 decoy launchers. These are located to port and starboard aft of the bridge and can dispense infrared, radar and acoustic decoys. The latter include British company QinetiQ's new LOKI torpedo countermeasures solution, for which the Royal Norwegian Navy was the first customer.

Ship survivability encompasses both stealth measures and steps to improve damage-resistance. Whilst details of the former are inevitably restricted, the class is similar to other modern European escorts in being specifically designed to minimise radar cross-section. In a similar fashion, close attention has also been paid to reducing acoustic, electronic and infrared signature. Specific information on damage-resistance is also limited, although reports suggest the hull is sub-divided into as many as thirteen

An EADS NFH-90 helicopter in French Navy colours. The type has also been ordered for the Royal Norwegian Air Force and will start to serve onboard the frigates from 2011. *(EADS)*

Fridtjof Nansen on manoeuvres. Ship survivability encompasses the incorporation of significant stealth measures as well as physical protection. *(Navantia)*

Thor Heyerdahl during final fitting-out at Ferrol in July 2009. Considerable attention has been paid to providing effective damage control features. *(Conrad Waters)*

watertight compartments. There are four separate NBC (nuclear, biological and chemical) damage control zones, each protected by blast and fragment resistant bulkheads. An element of physical protection is also incorporated into more critical areas of the design through use of steel armour plates. Shock resistance is in accordance with established NATO standards, whilst a retractable electric bow thruster can provide auxiliary propulsion if the main machinery plant is damaged.

OTHER KEY DESIGN FEATURES

The core propulsion system is provided by a combined diesel and gas (CODAG) arrangement. Two Navantia Bravo 12V diesels each provide

Below: *Fridtjof Nansen* pictured at speed during the Operation 'Atalanta' deployment off Somalia. A CODAG propulsion arrangement provides a top speed of 27 knots from two shaft lines, whilst split rudders aid manoeuvrability. *(Royal Norwegian Navy)*

A bird's-eye view of the third member of the class, *Otto Sverdrup*, at sea. Although displacement is around three times that of the preceding *Oslo* class, crew size is broadly similar. *(Navantia)*

Fridtjof Nansen towards the conclusion of her delivery voyage to Norway in 2006. Delivery was preceded by two sets of sea trials – builder's sea trials (BST) and sea acceptance trials (SAT). *(Navantia)*

4.5MW of power for a cruising speed of around 18 knots. A single 21.5MW GE LM 2500 gas turbine can be coupled through a cross-connected gearbox for a maximum sprint speed of 27 knots. It is claimed that the class is able to accelerate from cruising to sprint speed in around forty-five seconds, with stopping distance being in the order of four boat lengths. Endurance is c. 4,500 miles (7,242km). There are two shaft lines fitted with controllable pitch propellers, whilst a split rudder function – as well as the bow thruster – ensures good manoeuvrability at all speeds. The forward engine room contains the single gas turbine and two 1MW diesel generators, with a separate gearbox

compartment dividing this from the aft main engine room and the two diesel engines. A further pair of diesel generators is located in the next compartment aft. The arrangement provides a reasonable level of redundancy in case of action damage, albeit the single gearbox is a potential weakness. It is also interesting that the Norwegians have selected a comparatively noisy propulsion system for a modern ASW escort compared with, for example, the quieter combined diesel-electric and gas (CODLAG) arrangement found in the British Type 23 frigates.

The propulsion plant is operated from a machinery control room by an integrated platform management system (IPMS) of Navantia design. This is based on the Windows operating system but uses bespoke software developed by the group's own technicians. Technology used on the bridge has more of a Norwegian flavour: provision of the navigation system was another significant sub-contract allocated to Kongsberg.

In common with other modern warships, *Nansen* and her sisters are also equipped with sophisticated communications facilities, including both civilian and military satellite communications. These arrangements have been integrated through a control system provided by the German Aeromaritime group. NATO Links 11 and 16 are currently

Table 3.3.2.

FRIDTJOF NANSEN PRINCIPAL PARTICULARS

Building Information:

Fabrication Commenced:	18 December 2001
Launched:	3 June 2004
Delivered:	5 April 2006
Builders:	Navantia at its facility in Ferrol, Galicia.

Dimensions:

Displacement:	4,600 tons standard displacement, 5,200 tons full load displacement.
Overall Hull Dimensions:	133.2m x 16.8m x 4.9m (7.6m maximum). Length between perpendiculars is 121.4m.

Weapons Systems:

Missiles:	1 x Mk41 eight-cell VLS module for a total of 32 quad packed Evolved Sea Sparrow (ESSM) surface-to-air missiles.
	Provision for 2 x quad Kongsberg NSM surface-to-surface missiles.
Guns:	1 x 76mm Oto Melara Super Rapid. Sea Protector remote weapons system.
Torpedoes:	2 x twin fixed 324mm A/S torpedo tubes.
Aircraft:	Provision for 1 x NFH-90 helicopter.
Countermeasures:	ES-3701 electronic support measures (ESM) system. 2 x Terma DL-20 decoy launchers.
Principal Sensors:	1 x AN/SPY-1F multifunction radar (four fixed arrays). 2 x TIS fire-control illuminators. Surface-search and navigation radars.
	1 x Thales Spherion MRS 2000 hull-mounted sonar. Thales CAPTAS Mk2 V1 towed-array.
Combat System:	Lockheed Martin Aegis weapons system with Kongsberg anti-submarine and anti-surface modules.
	Communications include Links 11 and 16 with provision for Link 22.

Propulsion Systems:

Machinery:	CODAG. 1 x GE LM2500 gas turbine rated at 21.5MW. 2 x Navantia Bravo 12V diesels rated at 9MW.
	Combination provides in excess of 40,000shp through two shafts. A retractable bow thruster can provide auxiliary propulsion.
Speed and Range:	Designed maximum speed 27 knots. Range is 4,500 nautical miles at 18 knots.

Other Details:

Complement:	A typical crew comprises c. 120 personnel, including c. 50 officers. Accommodation is provided for c. 145.
Class:	Five ships have been ordered: *Fridtjof Nansen* (F310), *Roald Amundsen* (F311), *Otto Sverdrup* (F312), *Helge Ingstad* (F313) and *Thor Heyerdahl* (F314)

supported, whilst it is planned to add Link 22 at a later date. When combined with Aegis, this allows considerable interoperability with USN task groups. Another of Aeromaritime's responsibilities was design of the overall IFF (Identification Friend or Foe) interface. This incorporates the standard USN AN/UPX-37 interrogator and AN/APX-117 transponder and is automated with the Aegis weapons system.

Whilst enhanced military capabilities have clearly been a key requirement of the new warships, considerable attention has also been paid to improving crew efficiency through the provision of improved facilities. For example, the need to improve habitability

standards was a significant influence on the new design, as Norway's previous frigates were notoriously cramped. Although the *Nansen*s weigh in at around three times the displacement of the preceding *Oslo* class, the crew of c. 120 personnel – including the helicopter detachment – is broadly similar. Complement includes approximately fifty officers, thirty-five non commissioned officers and thirty-five enlisted sailors, whilst there are also berths for a further twenty-six personnel. These can be used, for example, to house command staff during overseas deployments or to assist with humanitarian operations. The availability of extensive medical facilities provides further flexibility in this regard.

Accommodation has been designed to facilitate the embarkation of up to 20 per cent female crew, whether of commissioned or enlisted rank.

TRIALS AND ENTRY INTO SERVICE

Although first-of-class *Fridtjof Nansen* was commissioned as long ago as April 2006, the protracted and complex process of bringing a modern warship into front-line service means that it is only in the current decade that the class will start to make its mark on operations. Following structural completion and outfitting, the normal practice has been for each ship to embark on two sets of sea trials – builder's sea trials (BST) and sea acceptance trials (SAT) – before

Otto Sverdrup (2008)
1:700 scale

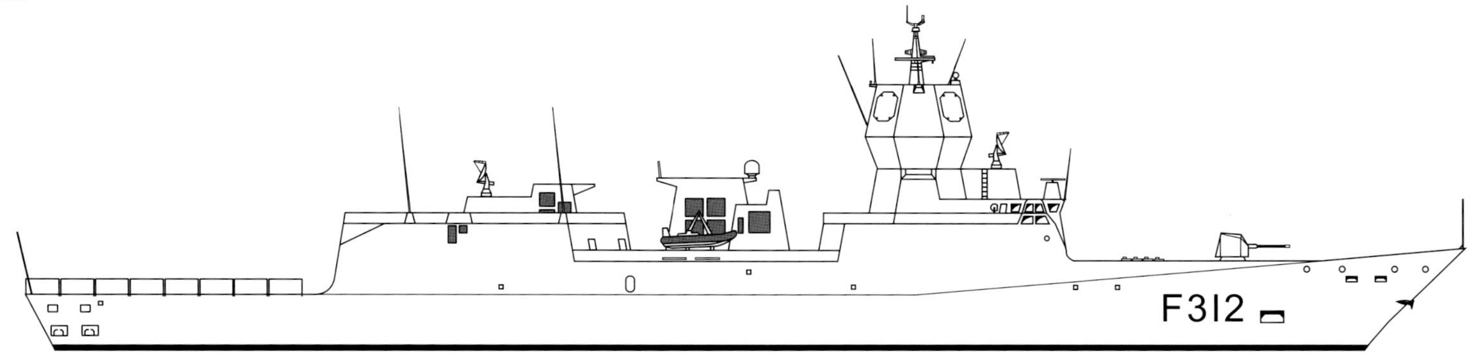

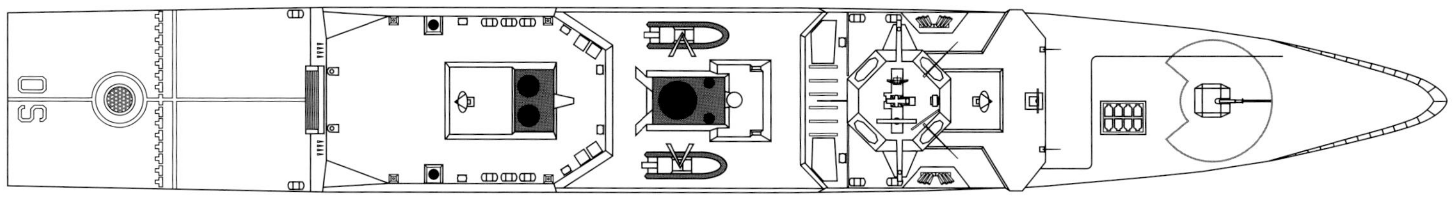

(Drawings © John Jordan, 2010)

Another image of *Fridtjof Nansen* and *Roald Amundsen* in company. The new frigates are based at Norway's principal naval facility near Bergen and have an important role in defending the country's 'High North'. *(Navantia)*

Otto Sverdrup departing Portsmouth in September 2009 as part of a NATO squadron. Ability to operate in conjunction with Norway's allies is a key requirement. *(Conrad Waters)*

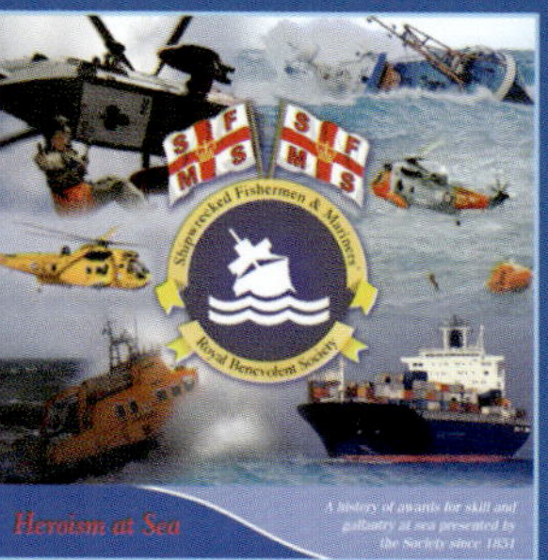

Fridtjof Nansen pictured shortly after commissioning in 2006. Over four years have passed since delivery, but it is only now that the class is entering full operational service. *(Navantia)*

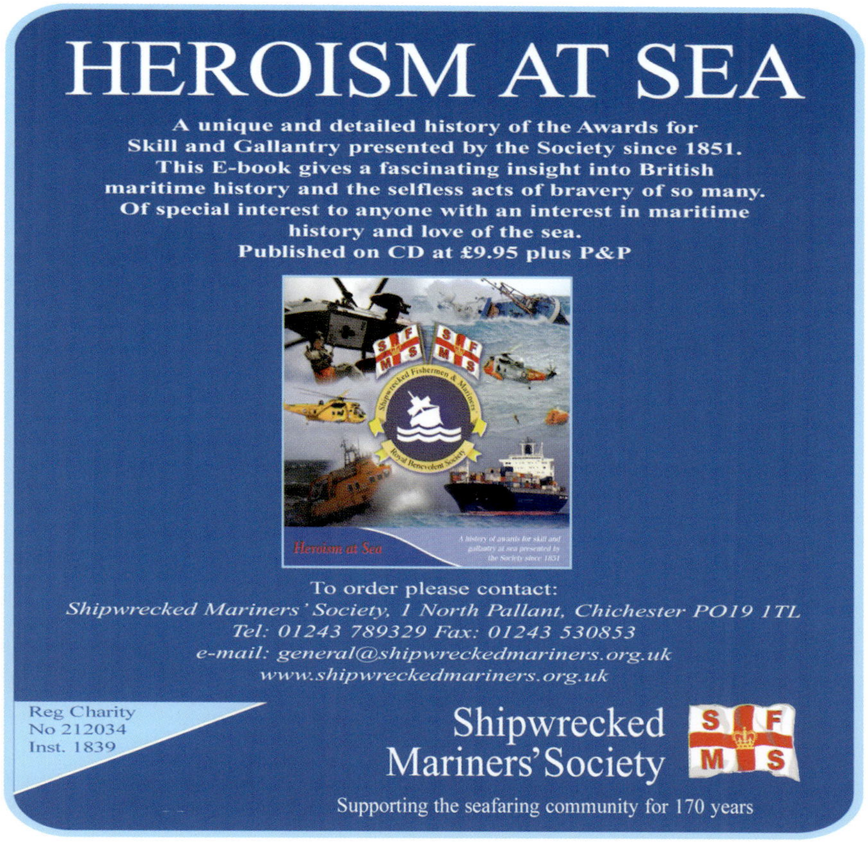

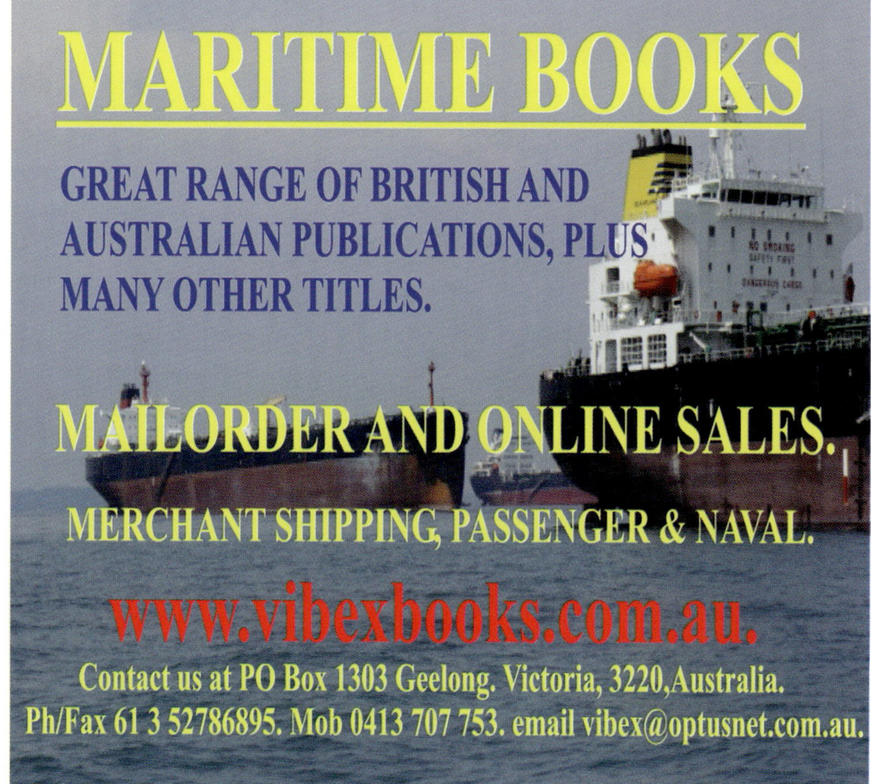

A view of the machinery control room of *Helge Ingstad*. Operation is by means of an integrated platform management system (IPMS) of Navantia design. *(Conrad Waters)*

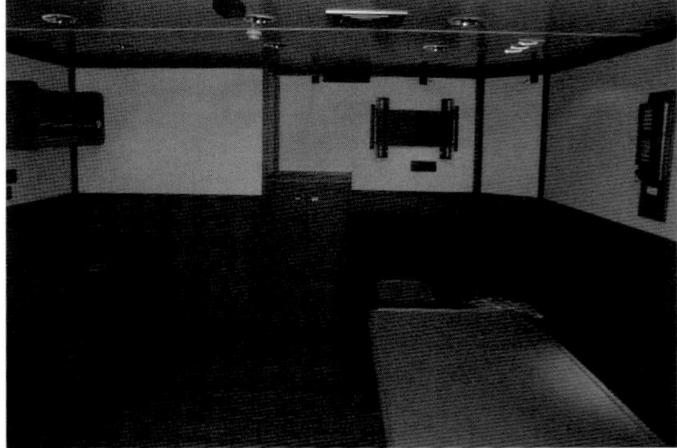

The commanding officer's quarters on *Helge Ingstad*. Overall levels of accommodation are far superior to those provided in the preceding *Oslo* class frigates. *(Conrad Waters)*

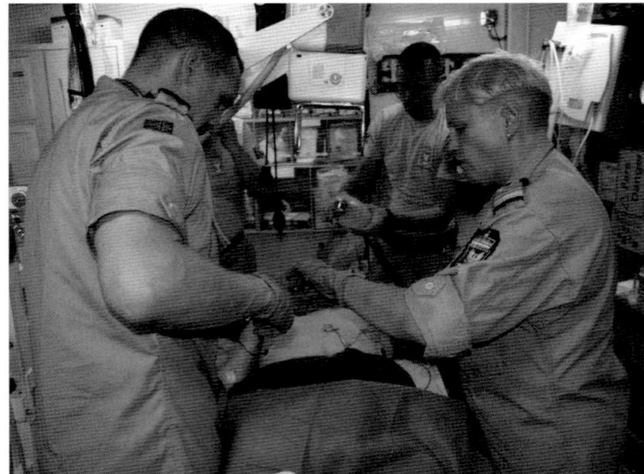

Fridtjof Nansen's medical facilities are pictured here in use during the frigate's deployment on the European Union's Operation 'Atalanta' off Somalia. These provide further flexibility during humanitarian missions. *(Royal Norwegian Navy)*

delivery to the Royal Norwegian Navy. Thereafter, the frigates have remained under builder's warranty for one year (two years in the case of *Nansen* herself) to allow any emerging defects to be resolved. Reports in the Norwegian and Spanish press shortly after *Nansen*'s delivery suggested issues with both rust and more general quality control that threatened to ignite a major controversy.[5] However, these issues were quickly downplayed by the Norwegian Defence Logistics Organisation and appear to have been satisfactorily resolved within the established warranty framework.

Given the fundamental importance of Aegis to the class's overall design, successful first-of-class trials of the weapon system were particularly crucial. These were carried out off the coast of California in June 2007 as part of the USN's Combat System Ship Qualification Trials (CSSQT) process. *Fridtjof Nansen* joined the USN's DDG-51 *Arleigh Burke* class destroyer *Gridley* (DDG-101) and Spain's F-100 class destroyer *Méndez Núñez* in these exercises in what was the first tri-nation CSSQT. The trials demonstrated the full potential of the SPY-1/ESSM pairing, with the Norwegian frigate successfully detecting and tracking targets in a range of air-defence scenarios and scoring hits with all six ESSMs that were fired. This included engagements against both supersonic high-diving targets and multiple sea-skimming threats.

The new frigates are being based at Norway's principal naval facility at Haakonsvern near Bergen as they commission. Their principal mission is the defence of Norwegian maritime interests in both littoral waters and the wider exclusive economic zone. The latter encompasses substantial natural resources ranging from oil and gas to fisheries. The renewed importance of securing effective surveillance and 'presence' capabilities in these waters has been emphasised in Norway's 'Capable Force' strategic concept first published in 2009, which places particular emphasis on the Arctic Ocean and its surrounds in the 'High North'.[6] The *Nansen* class are ideally suited for these activities given the enhanced endurance and habitability provided by their spacious hull, as well as the extensive surveillance capacity inherent in Aegis. In littoral waters, they are most likely to operate in support of the new *Skjold* class fast attack craft, which are now also starting to enter operational service.

Although the national defence role therefore remains paramount, it was always envisaged that *Nansen* and her sisters would participate in overseas operations in support of NATO and other international alliances. The potential inherent in the class was demonstrated at an early stage when second-of-class *Roald Amundsen* participated in the *Harry S Truman* (CVN-75) battle group work-up off the eastern seaboard of the United States in spring 2009. However, the class's first operational assignment commenced on 1 August 2009 when *Fridtjof Nansen* sailed from Norway to take part in the EU NAVFOR Somalia's Operation 'Atalanta' anti-piracy mission off the Horn of Africa. An active six-month deployment saw the frigate escorting ships of the UN World Food Programme, protecting vulnerable merchant ships and deterring and disrupting regional piracy. Whilst delays with the NH-90 programme meant that the ship sailed without a helicopter, the upgraded rigid inflatable boats (RIBs) that were embarked provided some compensation through their effective interception and boarding capabilities. During one of these operations on 11 November 2009, the boats were involved in a brief firefight with a group of dhows in an incident that might well have marked the Royal Norwegian Navy's first combat action since the end of the Second World War.

CONCLUSIONS

The *Fridtjof Nansen* class project represents a substantial investment for a country of something less than five million people. The programme was originally costed at 14bn Norwegian kroner in 2000. However, agreed adjustments for inflation and improvements to the specification have taken this figure to 19bn Norwegian kroner (US$3.2bn at current exchange rates) as of mid-2010. When additional equipment not specifically designated for the class – principally the NFH-90 helicopters and NSM surface-to-surface missiles are taken into account – the overall price rises to c. 25bn Norwegian kroner (US$4.2bn). It is therefore not surprising that the wisdom of this investment, as well as the costs involved in sustaining operation of the class, have been the matter of considerable debate.

In the event, many of the concerns initially expressed about the programme – relating to the choice of contractor, the ships' total cost and their relevance in the post-Cold War environment – have proved to be groundless. Although there was initially some disquiet – particularly from supporters of indigenous construction – about Navantia's credentials for being awarded the project given its limited previous experience of delivering major export contracts, the company has evidently risen to the challenge. Construction has been completed to budget and with only a modest level of delay, whilst the relevant offsets for Norwegian industry were achieved significantly ahead of schedule. Delivery of the class has certainly boosted Navantia's credibility as a major international ship-builder. This is most clearly demonstrated by its subsequent success in gaining lead roles in the Australian *Hobart* class destroyer and *Canberra* class amphibious assault ship contracts.

So far as cost is concerned, the *Nansen*s appear to represent good value for money. Effective international pricing comparisons between different warships are always difficult to achieve given the significant amount of variables involved. However, the class provides a well-balanced range of capabilities at a considerably lower unit price than the US$1bn and more attributed to the recent generation of specialised European air-defence escorts. The Norwegian ships are also less expensive than the French ASW variant of the FREMM multi-mission frigates now under construction, which arguably forms a much better comparison. It is also interesting to note that unit cost is broadly similar to the price tag attached to the initial members of both variants of the USN's littoral combat ship, which lack multi-function radar and rely on supplemental mission modules for their main capabilities. It is, perhaps, not surprising therefore that some voices in the US military have suggested that the *Nansen* class should

Fridtjof Nansen participated in the European Union Naval Force Somalia's Operation 'Atalanta' between August 2009 and January 2010. This successful deployment demonstrated the class's ability to conduct sustained international operations. *(EU NAVFOR Somalia)*

be considered as a potential alternative for the 'low end' of the USN's escort fleet.

Finally, it would also seem that *Fridtjof Nansen* and her sisters represent a sensible purchase for the Norwegian armed forces. When first ordered, the relevance of such sophisticated ships – and particularly their anti-submarine warfare emphasis – was questioned given the collapse of Soviet power in the aftermath of the Cold War. However, the successor Russian Federation has now returned to its historical role as an important influence on the Arctic and its surrounds in the High North and it is therefore

prudent for Norway to have the means to safeguard its own extensive interests in the region. The *Nansen*s are eminently well suited for this purpose, as they permit the deployment of cutting-edge surveillance, command and control and communications systems for extended periods. Equally, their anti-submarine capabilities, as well as the defensive shield provided by Aegis, make the class especially well-suited for countering the submarine forces that form the heart of Russia's Northern Fleet. At the same time, the new frigates are large and flexible enough to support Norway's allies in a broad range of out-of-area operations, making them a valuable asset at a time when numbers of surface escorts available to the traditional Western fleets are shrinking.

In conclusion, the *Fridtjof Nansen* class provide Norway with a valuable enhancement to its maritime capabilities through membership of the Aegis 'club' at a cost-effective price. It is worth noting that this allows access to the c. US$80bn of research and development expenditure already invested in the system, as well as access to the extensive operational experience of the c. 100 warships that have now been fitted with Aegis. Navantia's success in incorporating this technology in a frigate-sized hull is a significant achievement and one that has already been noted elsewhere, most notably in South Korea with its plans for KDX-IIA Aegis-equipped frigates. In its selection of the *Fridtjof Nansen* class, the Royal Norwegian Navy has acquired advanced and capable ships that should serve their nation well for many years.[7]

Notes

1. Tracing its origins to the network of arsenals constructed to support the Spanish Navy, Empresa Nacional Bazán was formed in the aftermath of the Spanish Civil War. It was subject to a short-lived merger with Spain's merchant shipyards to create Izar between 2000 and 2005. A further restructuring subsequently saw the enlarged group's military assets spun off to create the newly formed Navantia. Employing c. 5,500 workers and with a turnover of around €1.5bn in 2008, Navantia is one of Europe's largest shipbuilding groups. Principal facilities are in the Bay of Cadiz, at Cartagena and around the Fene-Ferrol complex in Galicia. The group is 100 per cent owned by the state controlled holding company SEPI (Sociedad Estatal de Participaciones Industriales).

2. The *Fridtjof Nansen* class are named after famous Norwegian explorers. **Fridtjof Nansen** (1861-1930) himself was both a significant Arctic explorer and a diplomat. He won the Nobel Peace Prize for his humanitarian work in the

aftermath of the First World War. The other ships are named after:

Roald Amundsen (1872-1928): Leader of the first Antarctic expedition to reach the South Pole in advance of Scott's ill-fated journey.

Otto Sverdrup (1854-1930): A notable Arctic explorer.

Helge Ingstad (1899-2001): An explorer and writer. He was responsible for proving that Vikings had settled in North America some 500 years before Christopher Columbus' discovery of the continent.

Thor Heyerdahl (1914-2002): Most famous for leadership of the *Kon-Tiki* voyage.

3. For a description of the F-100 design and its place amongst the new generation of sophisticated air-defence vessels, please refer to the author's 'Modern European Air Defence Escorts: Different Solutions to a Common Problem', *Warship 2010* (London, Anova Books), pp 140-55.

4. A good overview of Aegis is provided under 'Aegis

(Weapons System Mk7)' in Norman Friedman's *The Naval Institute's Guide to World Naval Systems* – Fifth Edition (Annapolis, MD, Naval Institute Press, 2006), pp 104-7.

5. Further information on views expressed in the Norwegian and Spanish press at the time can be fond by searching under *Fridtjof Nansen* on the widely-respected *Defense Industry Daily* website at www.defenseindustrydaily.com.

6. Please refer to *Capable Force: Strategic Concept for the Norwegian Armed Forces* (Oslo, Norwegian Ministry of Defence, 2009).

7. This chapter has inevitably relied heavily on contemporary press releases and news reports. In addition, the assistance of Captain (N) Nils Andreas Stensønes, Royal Norwegian Navy, Programme Manager New Frigates, and Miguel Rodriguez Lorenzo, Naval Engineer and Navantia's Head of the Norwegian Frigate Programme is gratefully acknowledged.

Author:
Scott Truver

3.4 SIGNIFICANT SHIPS

USS INDEPENDENCE (LCS-2)

Littoral Combat Ship – The 'Wow!' Factor

There's a 'Wow!' factor that cannot be denied when you see the USN's littoral combat ship *Independence* (LCS-2) for the first time, up close and personal … as in: 'Wow! This ship is a lot bigger than I thought!' Even more startling is that the ship looks like it's straight out of a Star Trek movie, prompting some wags to dub it the USN's 'Klingon Imperial Cruiser'. With its sleek, knife-like bow, twin 'out-riggers' and dramatically sloping sides, there has been nothing like it in the USN's inventory: until now.

Independence is a predominantly aluminium, high-speed (sprint speeds are in excess of 45 knots) trimaran surface warship built by a team led by General Dynamics Bath Iron Works (GD BIW) in Bath, Maine. Austal USA in Mobile, Alabama, is the building yard. The GD LCS team also includes GD's Advanced Information Systems (GDAIS) division, BAE Systems, L3 Communications, Northrop Grumman and Maritime Applied Physics Corporation. The LCS-2 design is based on the high-speed commercial trimaran *Benchijigua Express* built by Austal in Henderson, Australia, and operated by the Fred Olsen Express service based in the Canary Islands. LCS-2 joined the US fleet in January 2010. A second GD ship, *Coronado* (LCS-4), is under construction for a mid-2012 delivery.[1]

Independence's 'half-sister', *Freedom* (LCS-1) built by a team led by Lockheed Martin, is a semi-planing steel-monohull design with aluminium superstructure.[2] LCS-1 and LCS-2 were the first US warships designed and engineered under the new American Bureau of Shipping Naval Vessel Rules. As of mid-2010, both were locked into a 'winner takes all' down-select competition for the future littoral combat ship fleet.

USN plans call for fifty-five ships of the LCS class – upwards of fifty-three units of the successful variant in the 2010 down-select plus two 'orphans' of the unsuccessful variant – to provide much-needed tailored-mission capabilities at the lower end of the planned 313-ship navy.

LCS MISSIONS AND TASKS

At the LCS-2 commissioning in January 2010, the US Chief of Naval Operations, Admiral Gary Roughead, noted: 'LCS will have the capability … to secure the littoral regions upon which communities rely for food, transportation and for their well-being and to protect critical chokepoints in the global supply chain, to launch unmanned air, underwater and surface vehicles that will keep our trade at sea and our men and women ashore safe from harm.'

The LCS requirements are for a fast, agile, tailored-mission ship designed to defeat 'anti-access' threats in the shallow, coastal littorals, including fast surface craft, quiet diesel and advanced air-independent-propulsion submarines, and mines.[3] In addition to 'organic' weapons systems, the LCS features an interchangeable 'plug-and-fight' modular design that allows the ship to be reconfigured to meet specific mission requirements. Three mission packages were being integrated in the summer 2010: mine countermeasures (MCM); surface warfare (SUW); and anti-submarine warfare (ASW). The first MCM mission module was delivered September 2007; SUW and ASW modules were delivered in July and September 2008, respectively. The programme of record calls for twenty-four MCM, twenty-four SUW and sixteen ASW modules to be acquired.

Other missions are contemplated, including maritime interception operations, support for special operations (SpecOps) forces ashore, naval surface fire support, intra-theatre logistics lift, regional partnership-building and peacetime engagement, humanitarian assistance and disaster response, and intelligence/surveillance/reconnaissance (ISR).

Independence (LCS-2) whilst on trials. With an appearance akin to a Star Trek spacecraft, she has been nicknamed the USN's 'Klingon Imperial Cruiser' by some commentators. *(US Navy)*

Images of the *Freedom* (LCS-1) and *Independence* (LCS-2) variants of the USN's new littoral combat ship (LCS) type. As of mid-2010, both were locked into a 'winner takes all' down-select competition for the future littoral combat ship fleet. *(Lockheed Martin & US Navy)*

According to published accounts about the 2009 LCS concept of operations (ConOps), a key issue that remains to be fleshed out is where – in the United States or in countries overseas – to locate the mission modules and associated aircraft.[4] For now, MCM modules will be deployed in areas where USN minesweepers are stationed, including San Diego, Japan and in the Arabian Gulf. For other mission packages, 'the demand signal for cruiser-destroyer ships is used'.

The programme has also been sold on the ability to swap-out/swap-in mission packages quickly, with some identifying a turnaround of just twenty-four hours. Under this concept, an LCS configured for one tailored-mission area can be reconfigured rapidly to another to meet emerging requirements. That said, changing mission packages takes considerable time and effort. 'A mission package change-out is a complex, challenging and expensive evolution', the LCS ConOps underscores. 'It involves moving scores of tons of equipment, potentially a helicopter with a new aviation detachment, ammunition, and new mission package crews to a distant port, changing the MPs, and then retrograding the previous MP and crew back to their respective home facilities.' Sceptics are unconvinced. For example, the US Governmental Accountability Office (GAO) in early 2010 concluded: 'If the Navy cannot implement its concepts as envisioned, it may face operational limitations, have to reengineer its operational concepts, or have to alter the ship design. Many of the concepts will remain unproven until 2013 or later, when the Navy will have committed to building almost half the class.'[5]

The 2009 ConOps outlines a broad variety of LCS tasks, from humanitarian and disaster-relief missions and small-scale operations to confront 'irregular challenges' such as piracy to supporting large-scale combat. 'It may operate as part of a carrier strike group, an amphibious ready group, or work independently or jointly with smaller action groups,' the ConOps states. Operating with other warships such as destroyers or cruisers, the LCS 'will deliver modular, focused-mission capabilities to "kick in the door" and provide an even greater range of response options'.

The USN believes that speed and agility will be critical for efficient and effective conduct of the littoral missions. The LCS must be capable of operating at low speeds for littoral mission operations, transit at economical speeds, and high-speed sprints that might be needed to avoid or prosecute a small boat or submarine threat, conduct intercept operations over the horizon, or for SpecOps insertion or extraction missions. The ConOps explains that the ships are to be 'capable of extended deployments under challenging environmental conditions' and are expected to deploy up to eighteen months using multiple core and mission-package 'Blue' and 'Gold' crews. Each minimally-manned LCS is expected to operate with a core crew of only forty

LCS Mission Modules and Packages

Mission Module (MM): Mission System + Support Equipment
Mission Package (MP): Mission Module + Mission Module Crew + Manned and Unmanned Aircraft

'hybrid' sailors. A detachment of fifteen focused-mission sailors will operate the mine countermeasure and anti-submarine mission packages, while the SUW package requires only twelve. Another

twenty or so sailors comprise the air detachment to support helicopters and unmanned aerial vehicles (UAVs), adding up to a total of about seventy-five sailors.

Independence (LCS-2) pictured on builder's sea trials during July 2009. The LCS requirement is for a fast, agile, tailored-mission ship designed to defeat 'anti-access' threats in shallow, coastal, littorals. *(Austal Ships)*

Three images of *Independence* (LCS-2) taken during initial builder's trials in July 2009. The USN's concept of operations for the Littoral Combat Ship requires a flexible vessel capable of undertaking a wide variery of tasks. *(US Navy)*

THE NAVAL CLUB

Well placed in the heart of Mayfair, the Naval Club is the only London Club providing a Naval and Maritime environment where all those interested in the sea can feel at home.

- It is NOT necessary to have been a Naval Officer to become a Member. We welcome all those with an interest in maritime affairs and the sea in general.
- The Club is open 7 days a week throughout the year for accommodation and offers special reduced week end break rates.
- Private function and conference rooms are available.
- Ladies are welcome, both as Members and as guests.

For more information contact:
Commander John Prichard, Royal Navy, Chief Executive,
on 020 7493 7672, Fax: 020 7355 2644,
email: cdr@navalclub.co.uk
or visit our website at www.navalclub.co.uk

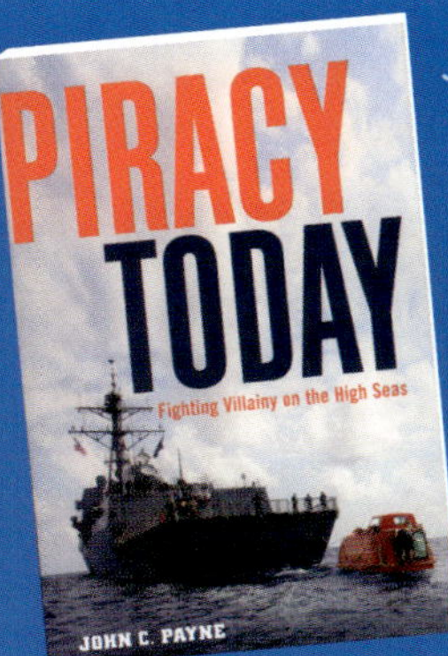

John C Payne

PIRACY TODAY

Fighting Villainy on the High Seas

In recent years, piracy at sea has become as much of a peril as terrorism on land or in the sky. Modern piracy is far removed from the romance of the pirate in popular culture. It is a billion-dollar business that takes advantage of inadequate international law, lax enforcement and under-crewed ships. Heavily armed gangs have been emboldened by successes in being paid off with six-figure ransoms. As the cost of cargo thefts and insurance premiums rises, so does the physical danger to mariners worldwide.

In this eye-opening account, which details hundreds of recent incidents, respected author and seaman John C Payne brings decades of experience to bear on looking at what is being done – and what more can be done – to tackle this global menace to sailors, and what precautions you can take with your own yacht.

"A comprehensive survey ... Piracy Today will help travelers and businessmen chart a safe course"
Wall Street Journal

"Timely, authoritative, well-written and downright scary ..."
Ian Scott, *former Director of the World Bank*

Illustrated Sheridan hardback, £19.95 + £2.05 p&p

SEAFARER BOOKS *Storytellers of the sea*
102 Redwald Road • Rendlesham • Suffolk IP12 2TE
☎ 01394 420789 fax 01394 461314
www.seafarerbooks.com • info@seafarerbooks.com

LCS PROGRAMME RECAP

In May 2004, the USN announced the selection of two teams headed by Lockheed Martin and General Dynamics each to carry out system design and options for the detail design and construction of two first-generation 'Flight 0' modular LCS 'sea frame' ships – i.e., the basic hull, propulsion, electrical and combat systems without mission modules. The LCS 'sea frame' can be thought of as a very fast naval 'truck' that can be configured for a broad spectrum of tasks. Under the original vision, the Lockheed and the GD teams would produce several fully operational Flight 0 ships of each design. The USN initially figured on building four Flight 0 ships and nine second-generation Flight 1 ships, along with the development and acquisition of various mission modules.

Lockheed Martin received a contract for the first ship, *Freedom*, during 2004. The keel was laid in June 2005 at the Marinette Marine shipyard in Wisconsin, and the ship was launched in September 2006. LCS-1 was delivered to the USN in September 2008 and was commissioned on 8 November 2008. On 16 February 2010, *Freedom* left the Naval Station Mayport, Florida, for its maiden deployment, two years ahead of what would have been a 'business as usual' fleet introduction. Among other tasks, its crew conducted operations against drug trafficking off the coast of Central America, seizing more than five tons of cocaine, capturing two 'go-fast' craft and taking nine suspected smugglers into custody. On 23 April 2010, LCS-1 arrived at its homeport of San Diego, California.

General Dynamics was awarded the contract for LCS-2 in October 2005, and the ship's keel was laid in January 2006 at the Austal USA shipyard. LCS-2 was launched in April 2008 and christened a few months later in October. The ship completed the builder's sea trials in October 2009 and was deliv-

Table 3.22.1.
USS INDEPENDENCE PRINCIPAL PARTICULARS

Building Information:

Keel Laid:	19 January 2006
Launched:	26 April 2008
Commissioned:	16 January 2010
Builders:	General Dynamics Bath Iron Works, Bath, Maine – systems integrator and prime contractor.
	Austal USA, Mobile, Alabama – shipbuilder.

Dimensions:

Displacement:	2,176 tons light displacement, 2,784 tons full load displacement.
Hull Dimensions:	127.1m x 31.6m x 4.5m.

Weapons Systems:

Missiles:	1 x SeaRAM CIWS.
Guns:	1 x 57mm Mk 100, 4 x 12.7mm machine guns.
Aircraft:	2 x MH-60R/S Seahawk or up to 8 x MQ-8 Fire Scout VTUAVs (typical load: 1 x MH-60R/S Seahawk and 3 x MQ-8 Fire Scout).
Countermeasures:	ES-3601 electronic support measures (ESM) system, 4 x SRBOC decoy launchers. NULKA active radar decoy system.
Principal Sensors:	1 x Saab Sea Giraffe 3D air- and surface-search radar, 1 x navigation array.
Combat System:	Northrop Grumman Integrated Combat Management System.
	Open architecture arrangement interfacing with interchangeable mission modules.
	Integrated communications suite includes Links 11, 16 and CEC.

Propulsion Systems:

Machinery:	2 x GE LM2500 gas turbines, 2 x MTU 20V 8000 M90 diesels powering 2 x Wärtsilä LJ-160E and 2 x Wärtsilä LJ-160E waterjets.
	1 x retractable bow-mounted azimuth thruster
Speed and Range:	Designed maximum speed is in excess of 45 knots. Range is 4,300 nautical miles at 18 knots.

Other Details:

Complement:	A typical crew comprises 40 core personnel, including 8 officers, supplemented by c. 35 mission-related personnel.
Class:	One additional ship, *Coronado* (LCS-4), is under construction.

Note: Other weapons and sensors are included in specific mission modules.

ered to the USN in December 2009. Following completion of acceptance trials in November, Rear Admiral James Murdoch, USN's LCS programme manager, noted, 'Independence performed extremely well … conducted two outstanding days at sea. We look forward to delivering this critical asset to the fleet.' Independence was commissioned on 16 January 2010.

Lockheed Martin was also to build LCS-3 to commission in 2009. A contract was awarded in June 2006 and construction was to begin in early 2007. However, because of dramatically increased costs and schedule delays, the USN ordered Lockheed Martin

to stop work on LCS-3 in January 2007. Three months later, the USN terminated the contract for LCS-3. In December 2006, the USN awarded General Dynamics a contract to build LCS-4, then named *Liberty*. Citing cost increases and schedule impacts, in October 2007 the USN terminated the contract for this ship as well.

By then, the cost of the programme had become contentious, leading to a US Congress-imposed cost cap of US$480m per ship.[6] Much was made of the USN-industry teams missing an earlier target of US$220m per unit. However, that figure was for the *fifth* ship in series production and calculated in

constant FY2005 dollars. Nevertheless, the end-cost estimate for LCS-1 grew from US$215.5m in the FY2005 budget to US$537m in the FY2009 budget, whilst estimated end-cost for LCS-2 had increased from US$213.7m to US$575m over the same time. When costs for outfitting, post delivery and the final system design/mission systems and ship integration team are included, the US Congressional Budget Office estimates that the first two littoral combat ships will cost approximately US$700m each.

Subsequently, in April 2008, the USN issued a new request for proposals to the two companies for three littoral combat ships. In March 2009, the Navy

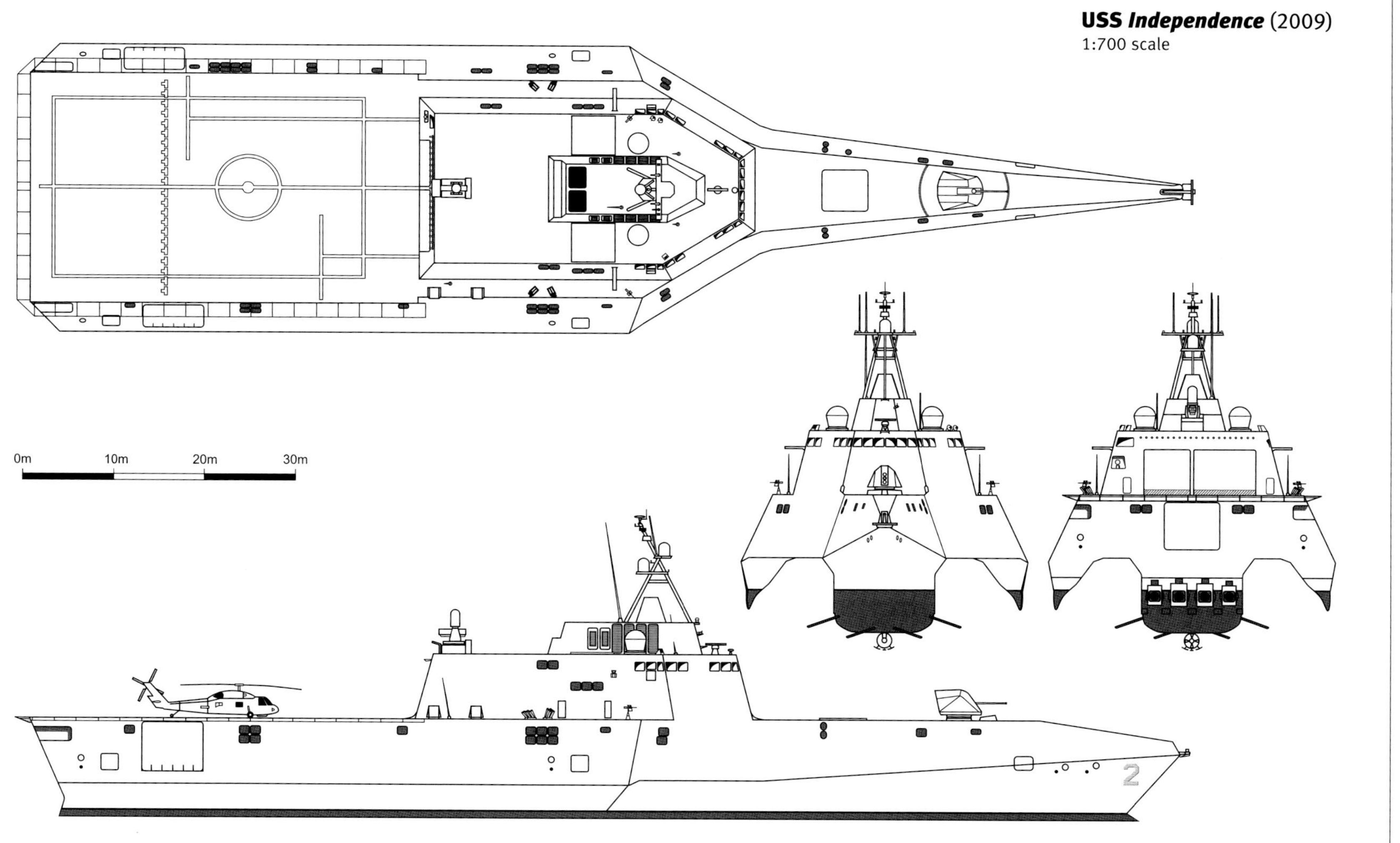

(Drawings © John Jordan, 2010)

Independence (LCS-2) under construction at Austal USA's facility at Mobile, Alabama. General Dynamics was awarded the contract for LCS-2 in October 2005, and the ship's keel was laid in January 2006. *(US Navy)*

Independence (LCS-2) was launched in April 2008. This photograph was taken during the intricate rolling out and launch process at the Austal USA's Mobile, Alabama, shipyard. *(Austal Ships)*

awarded Lockheed Martin a contract for the third LCS, *Fort Worth*. As of the early summer of 2010, this ship was on track for delivery in 2012. Navy projections peg the ship's cost at c. US$549m. The contract for *Coronado* was awarded to GD in April 2009, and the ship's keel was laid the following December. Under construction at Austal USA's Modular Manufacturing Facility (MMF), it is scheduled for delivery in 2012. Navy estimates project that LCS4 will cost approximately US$548m.

Two more ships – LCS-5 and LCS-6 – were to be procured in FY2010, but contract awards are currently pending yet another change in the acquisition strategy.

The Navy revamped the LCS programme in the autumn of 2009 to have a 'down-select' to a single design, with price being a principal, if not the primary, factor in the head-to-head competition. A decision was expected in mid-summer 2010. As the US Congressional Research Service's naval analyst Ronald O'Rourke explained:[7]

> The winner of the down select would be awarded a [fixed price] contract to build ten LCSs over the five-year period FY2010-FY2014, at a rate of two ships per year. The Navy would then hold a second competition – open to all bidders other than the shipyard building the ten LCSs in FY2010-FY2014 – to select a second shipyard to build up to five additional LCSs to the same design in FY2012-FY2014 (one ship in FY2012, and two ships per year in FY2013-FY2014). These two shipyards would then compete for contracts to build LCSs procured in FY2015 and subsequent years.

This proved to be controversial and catalysed US Senators Jeff Sessions and Richard Shelby and Representative Jo Bonner of the Alabama congressional delegation to send a 3 December 2009 letter to Secretary of the Navy Ray Mabus:

> It would be a shame for the Department of Defense to make the same mistakes with the LCS as it has made with the [US Air Force

airborne refuelling] tanker competition. For an acquisition project as important as LCS, the best approach is to determine which vessel represents the best value to taxpayers and the Navy. As the Department begins to draft its solicitation for this competition, it's important that this distinction is made clear at the outset. Advanced capabilities that could improve the performance of the ship and save American lives should not be discredited. A low-price shootout will most likely result in the purchase of a less-capable ship.'

The Navy did not concur in this assessment and the competition went ahead. 'I just don't think enough people are looking at the whole way we have reconceived LCS,' Under Secretary of the Navy Robert Work noted in February 2010.[8] 'I think it provides us with a lot of flexibility.'

During the Surface Navy Association's January 2010 symposium, Rear Admiral Murdoch, LCS programme manager said, 'I like them both…

An early computer-generated image of General Dynamics Team's LCS design. Austal USA has now taken over the prime contractor role in the 2010 competition to select just one LCS variant. *(Austal Ships)*

They're like my two kids completely different.' He said both variants met the USN's operational requirements but that the service simply could not afford to buy but one design.

For the down-select, the LCS-2/LCS-4 prime contractor General Dynamics/BIW stepped aside, allowing Austal USA to be prime contractor for the revamped programme. (BIW was not included in the Austal USA-led down-select team. This strategy therefore preserves the ability of BIW to compete for the second-source shipyard, even if Austal USA were successful in the 2010 down-select.) Other General Dynamics' divisions remained subcontractors to Austal USA, viz. Armament and Technical Products Division; Electric Boat Division; Advanced Information Systems; and General Dynamics Canada. Other 2010 Austal USA teammates included:

- Boeing.
- BAE Systems.
- Ericsson.
- General Electric.
- L3 Communications Marine Systems.
- Maritime Applied Physics Corporation.
- Northrop Grumman Electronic Systems.
- MTU.
- Saab.
- Wärtsilä.

The Navy's FY2011 budget request estimates the cost of future sea frames at approximately US$600m. Even then, however, the LCS is less expensive than any other USN surface warship. The upgraded *Arleigh Burke* (DDG-51) Aegis destroyers, for example, are expected to cost approximately US$1.8bn each in the FY2011 programme.

A March 2010 image of *Freedom* (LCS-1) in company with the FFG-7 type frigate *McInerney* (FFG-8) during her maiden deployment. Although the two LCS variants are very different in design, the USN considers that both meet their operational requirements. *(US Navy)*

The most striking feature of *Independence* is her hull design, which is based on the form of the commercial high-speed trimaran *Benchijigua Express*. It comprises a slender, stabilised monohull and two outriggers for both rock-solid stability and high-speed fuel efficiency. *(US Navy)*

LCS-2 CHARACTERISTICS AND CAPABILITIES

Independence's general design characteristics are listed in Table 3.4.1. More specific details include:

A 'Striking' Hull Form: What is most striking about *Independence* is the hull design. According to Austal USA's President and Chief Operating Officer, Joseph J Rella, 'The trimaran hull form has been proven in many years of commercial operations. It allows for rock-solid stability, high speeds and significant fuel-efficiencies. Even at top speeds greater than 45 knots, the ship's range is greater than 1,000 nautical miles [1,850km]. And, at an economical 18 knots, the ship is capable of travelling in excess of 4,300 nautical miles [7,955km].'

The ship is powered by two diesel engines (for low and moderate speeds) and two 28,000hp gas turbines (for speeds in excess of 22 knots). This propulsion plant powers four steerable waterjets that can be reversed to stop the ship quickly. For very slow speeds or manoeuvring in confined waters, LCS-2 is also equipped with a retractable bow-mounted, 360-degree azimuth thruster, powered by a dedicated 600KW electric generator. Another four electrical generators round off the propulsion plant. Power can be switched from one side of the plant to another, a redundancy enhancement. 'And, if the ship lost all primary propulsion,' Rella noted, 'her crew could still make about five knots on the thruster, alone.'

The trimaran design, with its slender stabilised monohull, uses two outriggers – 'amahs' – that allow for weight to be located higher in the ship. The shaping of the hull also provides for enhanced signature reduction – i.e., 'stealth' – a vital factor for safe, near-shore littoral operations. The outriggers are voids and thus contribute to the ship's passive survivability. 'Multi-hulls are more efficient,' Rella explained, 'that is, less power is needed for a given speed than conventional monohull ships. The trimaran, with its long slender centre hull and shorter, shallower-draft outer hulls, is also more conducive to improvements in sea-keeping. This results in less wear and tear on crew members and

Another image of *Independence* (LCS-2) during her April 2008 roll out. The full extent of the two outriggers – 'amahs' – that allow weight to be located higher in the ship is evident. *(Austal Ships)*

allows them to perform their tasks more efficiently and with less fatigue from the ship movements in the sea.'

Sea-keeping and the effects of weather were singled out in the USN's 2009 LCS ConOps as a concern for both variants. Because of the LCS' relatively small size, 'weather is an important consideration when making operational decisions, and sea-keeping and sustainability are important factors that must be considered', the document said, adding that operational limitations need to be delineated for both LCS designs.

Coupled with other design features, LCS-2 has excellent manoeuvrability and stability, which has tactical/operational and 'hotel' benefits. With 36ft (10.9m) of freeboard aft, for example, the design allows for safe operations even in adverse seas and aviation operations in Sea State 5 – winds up to 27 knots and average wave heights of 9.6ft (2.9m). This is something unheard-of in traditional single-hull concepts, according to James Baskerville, GD BIW vice president for surface combatant technology. 'We

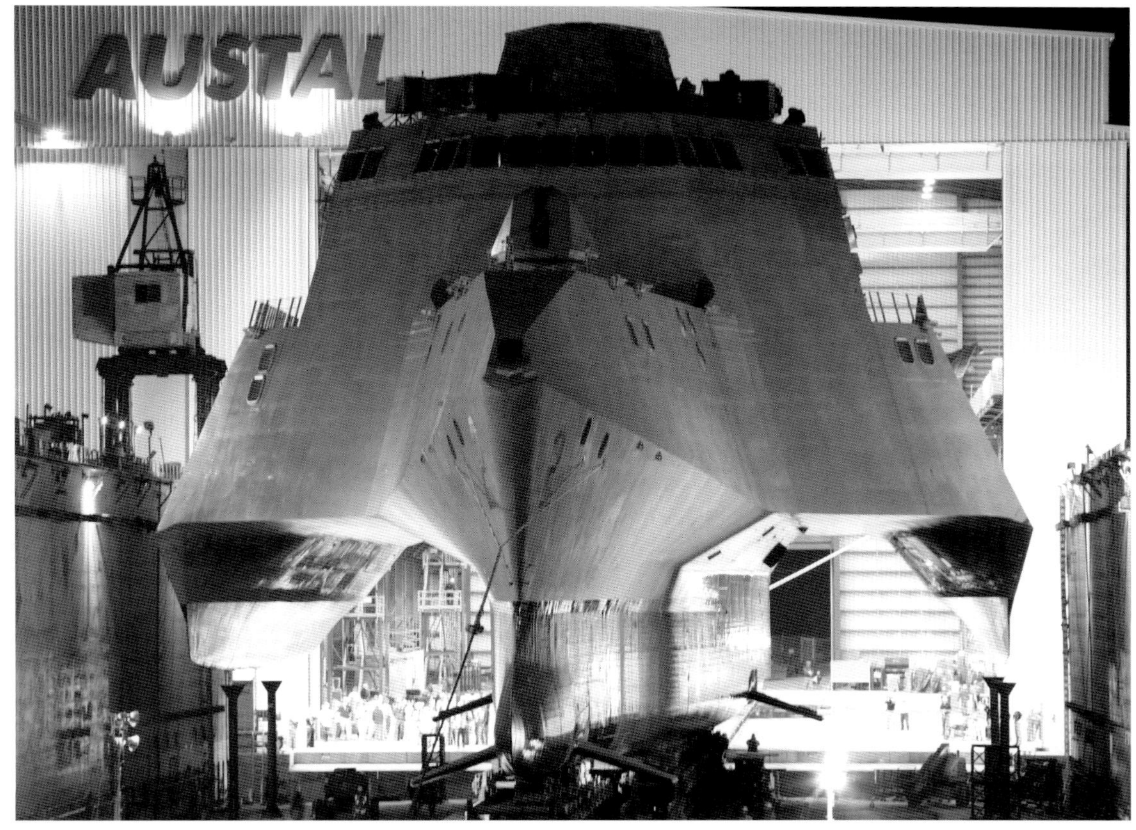

A key benefit of the LCS-2 design is the significant 36ft (10.9m) freeboad aft, allowing aviation operations in adverse weather conditions. This feature is apparent in this view of *Independence* (LCS-2) fitting out at Austal's Modular Manufacturing Facility (MMF) at Mobile, Alabama. *(Austal Ships)*

An image of the stern of *Independence* (LCS-2) whilst under maintenance at BAE Systems Ship Repair facility at Norfolk Virginia. The stern launch door can be seen high up in the ship's stern above the four reversible and steerable waterjets. *(BAE Systems Ship Repair)*

can also launch and recover watercraft, for example, launching 40-foot high-speed boats, within fifteen minutes in conditions of Sea State 4 – waves up to 5 feet and winds up to 21 knots.'

The enhanced stability translates into greater crew endurance and comfort, even at top speeds, underscored by last year's sea trials and first-year operation. There is remarkably little slamming at high speeds and high seas, as the 'stiletto-like' design knifes through the water. Crew endurance is critical in such a minimally manned ship, with just seventy-five people in the core and mission-module crews. Traditionally-manned destroyers and cruisers, for example, have crews in excess of 300. 'The ship handles like a very large jet ski,' Baskerville noted. 'Even at high speeds and tight turns, *Independence* doesn't heel over to any great extent – she glides through the turns. At just 2,800 tons full load displacement, LCS-2 stability supports flight ops in Sea State 5. And the ship's 13-foot draft allows it to transit shallow-water regions that would stop dead much of the rest of the USN's warships.'

Volume and Space Not an Issue: With 11,000m³ of internal payload volume, *Independence* can handle all current mission packages as well as future payloads. For example, if employed in an intra-theatre lift role, in addition to cargo or container-sized mission modules, the LCS-2 design can carry four lanes of multiple Stryker armoured vehicles, armoured Humvees and their associated troops. Access is also important to facilitate operation of the various modules and organic systems. As noted, the LCS-2 is capable of stern launch and recovery of mission package watercraft up to Sea State 4. The stern door opens high above the water and features an extendable twin-boom crane.

'We went with our approach because the Navy's requirements were expansive,' Austal's Rella said. The LCS mission packages include several types of watercraft, including surface and sub-surface MCM vehi-

An aerial view of *Independence* (LCS-2) alongside at Austal USA gives a good impression of the size and volume provided by the trimaran design. *(Austal Ships)*

cles, towed-array sonars, rigid-hull inflatable boats, and swimmer delivery vehicles. 'So, rather than hamstring ourselves with a constrained concept, we designed our launch-and-recovery systems to be able to operate any watercraft that was in the Navy's current specifications and that might be developed in the future.'

The main deck starboard roll-on/roll-off ramp is capable of meeting intra-theatre lift needs in addition to accommodating mission modules and associated equipment. An elevator allows air transport/vertical replenishment of packages up to a 20ft (6m) long shipping container that can then be moved into the mission bay from the flight deck while at sea. A side access ramp allows for wheeled vehicle roll-on/roll-of to a loading dock in port. LCS-2 uses a cargo container mobile transport system to move containers and watercraft around the 90ft (27.4m) wide/15ft (4.6m) high mission bay. A hydraulic system powers the stern doors, side ramp, mission bay crane and a crane in the hangar.

'The ship is required to carry only one mission package, but the mission bay can handle two packages without any stacking,' Rella said. 'We have sufficient volume to double the mission package and not have an issue in our mission bay.' Indeed, growth for unforeseen future applications was a key aspect of the LCS-2 design. 'Our growth margin allows the ship to be tailorable to future missions, whatever the Navy may find it needs,' Baskerville noted. 'We've designed the ship for 30 years' growth.'

Crew Comfort: Habitability and crew comfort are also critical for such a minimally manned ship. LCS-2 is configured for seventy-six crewmembers to have their own bunks and is 'women-at-sea' compatible. All staterooms have their own head and shower, and there are many heads throughout, particularly near work stations. There is ship-wide Internet access, particularly important to the younger members of the crew. The galley has been designed to facilitate round-the-clock operations and handle as many people as can be embarked. 'During builder's trials last year,' Baskerville said, 'we had 150 people on board and the galley had no problems serving all.'

Human systems integration was important in the design process, and great care seems to have been taken to address the human element in system design and arrangements. 'We didn't just "throw" advanced

Two further views of *Independence* (LCS-2) on sea trials, which proved the ship's stability and general 'crew friendliness'. There is remarkably little slamming at high speeds and in high seas, as the 'stiletto-like' design knifes through the water. *(Courtesy of General Dynamics Bath Iron Works)*

Independence's (LCS-2) bridge and integrated command centre (ICC) are co-located to allow seamless connectivity between fighting and driving the ship. However, the two can be divided by a curtain should the circumstances require. *(Courtesy of General Dynamics Bath Iron Works)*

technologies and automation at a problem,' Baskerville noted. 'We thought it through to make sure the human was part of the solution.'

'Open' Core Mission System: LCS-2 features an open-architecture computing environment that is not bound by proprietary systems, hardware or software, Carlo Zaffanella, vice president for open combat solutions, GD Advanced Information Systems, explained. 'The computing "backbone" is flexible and based on industry standards, allowing the USN to take advantage of the rapidly changing advancements in the commercial arena. This supports and enables affordable technology "refresh" and quick upgrades to respond to changing mission requirements and threats.' As an example, the open-architecture design allows the crew to reconfigure electronically the entire bridge area to meet new requirements

LCS-2's core mission system is built on OPEN CI, a flexible information technology spine that provides an adaptable command and control infrastructure capable of hosting a wide array of available weapons, sensors, and combat system applications. 'Importantly,' Zaffanella underscored, 'the technical architecture is not limited by proprietary systems. Any current or future system applications that comply with open architecture tenets can be seamlessly integrated into the ship. This feature makes it possible to take advantage of rapid technology advances, deploy upgrades, and adapt to new and more complex missions – faster and at lower cost than a "business as usual" approach.'

'Our open architecture solution gives the Navy several vital attributes,' Zaffanella enumerated, viz:

- Flexible and scalable systems to adapt to new and more complex missions.
- The ability to incorporate the latest technology with low cost and low risk.
- Fast upgrades to satisfy emerging requirements quickly without having to make the costly investment of rewriting software.
- Interoperability within and outside the LCS-2's lifelines via extensive commonalities and links

among all systems across the fleet, fully compliant with established Navy open-architecture requirements.

Command and Control: LCS-2's bridge and integrated command centre (ICC) are co-located, with the ICC directly behind the bridge. GD's Baskerville explained, 'We combined the two to have a seamless connectivity between fighting and driving the ship.'

The Ship-Wide Area Network (SWAN) allows LCS-2 to be 'fought' from any display or terminal throughout the ship, not just from the integrated command centre and the bridge or the mission package integrated command centre two decks below. Northrop Grumman Electronic Systems provided the integrated combat management system (ICMS), BAE Systems Electronic Systems provided the radio communications system and CAE Marine Systems supplied the automated ship control system.

Design of the bridge took good advantage of the Naval Surface Warfare Center/Dahlgren Division's Integrated Command Environment (ICE) efforts to ensure effective and correct communications among all watch-standers. Visibility is excellent and access to displays, which can be reconfigured almost on the 'fly' to meet changes in the tactical environment, is easy.

Organic Warfare Capabilities: In addition to the organic weapon systems and sensors, *Independence*'s design features three weapon zones that accommodate tailored mission modules. One zone is located on the bow just aft of the gun, and there are also port and starboard zones. The forward superstructure and mast includes the Sea Giraffe air- and surface-search radar and navigational radars, in addition to various UHF, VHF and SATCOM communications antennae providing Link 11 and Link 16 capabilities.

Both the General Dynamics and Lockheed Martin LCS variants are armed with a BAE Systems Land and Armaments (formerly United Defense) Mk 110 57mm naval gun system (the Mk 110 is also the gun installed in the US Coast Guard's national security cutter class). The Mk 110 fires Mk 295 ammunition at a rate of up to 220 rounds a minute to a range of 14km (9nm) and is capable against aerial, surface or ground targets. LCS-2 also carries four .50 calibre (12.7mm) machine guns, primarily for engaging surface targets. They are also effective against low-flying, slow aircraft. Two machine gun mounts are

An unusual forward view of *Independence*'s (LCS-2) 'stiletto-like' forward bow, incorporating the 57mm gun. There is space behind for the non-line-of-sight missile launch system (NLOS-LS) that has suffered development problems and might not be completed. *(US Navy)*

installed port and starboard on the walkway on either side of the hangar and at the stern just below the level of the helicopter deck.

Instead of the baseline Rolling Airframe Missile (RAM) incorporated into the LCS-1 design, GD opted to go with an anti-air warfare (AAW) suite focused on the RIM-116 SeaRAM. The eleven-missile SeaRAM launcher is integrated into an upgraded version of the Mk 15 Close-In Weapon System (CIWS) radar and infrared systems, modified to detect and engage low-elevation, low-radar cross-section threats at greater ranges than the CIWS gun. It will accept the RAM Block 2 missile, a kinematic upgrade for countering advanced manoeuvring threats and regaining battlespace through even greater range.

The LCS-2's AAW suite also includes four Super RBOCs (rapid-bloom off-board countermeasures) and provision for Nulka active radar decoys. The active countermeasures suite includes the ES 3601 tactical radar electronic support measures (ESM) system.

The 2009 LCS ConOps outlined the AAW reality of the LCS operations. 'Although the ship can detect, identify, track and defend itself against many anti-ship cruise missiles and threat aircraft, it is not designed or intended to operate in a high-intensity air defense environment unless these operations are being conducted under the air defense coverage of a carrier strike group or amphibious ready group.'

Aviation Features: The expansive, 7,300ft² (678.1m²) flight deck is larger than that of any other small combatant warship in any navy and is 36ft (10.9m) above the water, which minimises equipment exposure to sea spray and enhances aviation operations. 'That's a tremendous advantage', Baskerville noted. 'It gives our aviators a significant margin to operate helicopters and UAVs safely.'

'Roger that,' retired USN Captain George Galdorisi remarked. The test director of the SH-60 LAMPS (Light Airborne Multi-Purpose System) Mk III Seahawk and the first executive officer and then commanding officer of HSL 43, Galdorisi has extensive operational experience flying helicopters from a variety of surface and amphibious warships. 'A stable flight deck is critical to safe and effective flight operations', he explained. 'In the 1970s and

Independence's (LCS-2) expansive, 7,300ft^2 (678.1m^2) flight deck is larger than that of any other small combatant warship in any navy. It can support operations by MH-60R/S Sea Hawk Helicopters and MQ-8B Fire Scout unmanned aerial vehicles. *(US Navy)*

1980s, the LAMPS Mk I aircraft had relatively constrained deck pitch and roll limitations. While the LAMPS MK III RAST system improved matters, this didn't make flight operations possible in higher sea states. Ship designs that facilitate landing in higher sea states simply mean more effective and safer operations.'

The *Independence* class aviation features include:

- A 3,500ft^2 (325.1m^2) hangar capable of supporting two SH-60R/S medium-lift multi-mission helicopters.
- A flight deck capable of supporting one CH-53E heavy-lift helicopter for logistics support.
- Facilities for up to eight embarked MQ-8B Fire Scout Vertical Takeoff and landing tactical UAVs (VTUAVs), depending on other aviation load-outs. The ship can operate four VTUAVs – two on station and two in transit to/from station – simultaneously.
- A platform elevator that can transport equipment from the mission bay to the flight deck.

A notional aviation complement would be a single H-60 and three VTUAVs.

The MH-60R and MH-60S multi-mission combat helicopters are the twin 'pillars' of the CNO's Naval Helicopter ConOps for the twenty-first century. The MH-60R provides surface and undersea warfare support with a suite of sensors and weapons that include dipping sonar, electronic support measures, advanced forward looking infrared, and precision air-to-surface missiles. The MH-60S will provide mine warfare support and will partner with the MH-60R for surface warfare missions carrying the same forward looking infrared air-to-ground sensors and weapons. The MH-60S will also be reconfigurable to provide Combat Search and Rescue and Naval Special Warfare support to joint theatre operations. Airborne mine countermea-

The LCS-2 design offers significant flexibility for future development. This is a concept image of a heavily-armed Multi-Mission Combatant designed for international markets. *(Courtesy of General Dynamics Bath Iron Works)*

An aerial view of the competing *Freedom* (LCS-1) Littoral Combat Ship design. It is this ship that the *Independence*'s (LCS-2) designers have to beat if their claim that they have built their ship to win is to come true. *(Lockheed Martin)*

sures operations will be accomplished using advanced sensor and weapons packages to provide detection, localisation, and neutralisation to anti-access threats.[9]

The MQ-8B Fire Scout supports warfighting requirements as a part of the LCS' MCM, SUW and ASW mission modules. Fire Scout provides day/night real-time ISR; target acquisition; voice communications relay; and battlefield management capabilities. It is operated and maintained by members of a composite VTUAV/MH-60R or VTUAV/MH-60S aviation detachment. It is a critical 'node' in the LCS 'net' with other USN and joint forces.

THE COURSE AHEAD

'Delivering *Independence* is a significant accomplishment for our team,' GD's Baskerville noted at the LCS-2 ceremony in December 2009. 'Today, we provide the Navy with a new and highly capable warship equipped with extraordinary aviation features, large payload capacity and an open architecture computing environment for future missions – all contained within an extremely fast, stable and efficient trimaran hull form to support the Navy's needs today and tomorrow. We've designed *Independence* to fight – and we've built it to win.'

The deliberations of the Navy's LCS-source selection team that continued into the second half of 2010 will determine whether his statement – '…built it to win.' – was prescient … or not.

Notes

1. This overview of the LCS-2/LCS-4 programme is based on interviews conducted with officials from General Dynamics and Austal on 4 May 2010. For further reading see Ronald O'Rourke, *Navy Littoral Combat Ship (LCS) Program: Background, Issues, and Options for Congress* (Washington DC, Congressional Research Service, 7-5800/RL33741, 4 May 2010); Christopher P Cavas, 'LCS1 Vs. 2: Both Meet Requirements, But Similarities End There', *Defense News* – 3 May 2010 (Springfield VA, Army Times Publishing, 2010); Grace V Jean, 'Builders of the Navy's Littoral Combat Ship Pull Out All the Stops', *National Defense* – March 2010 (Arlington VA, National Defense Industrial Association, 2010).

2. See the author's 'USS *Freedom* Littoral Combat Ship: "Seaframe" for the Future US Fleet', *Seaforth World Naval Review 2010* (London, Seaforth Publishing, 2009), pp 150-66.

3. Please see *Navy Program Guide, 2010* (Washington DC, Office of the Chief of Naval Operations, 2010), pp 53-4. This annual publication, which can be found by searching at www.navy.mil has synoptic information about the LCS and its related programmes, as well as all of the USN's (and some USMC) primary acquisition programmes.

4. This is discussed by Christopher P Cavas in 'Concept-Of-Operations Document Sheds Light on LCS Mission, Needs', *Navy Times* – 24 May 2010 (Springfield VA, Army Times Publishing, 2010). See also: Martin Murphy, *Littoral Combat Ship: An Examination of its Possible Concepts of Operation* (Washington DC, Center for Strategic and Budgetary Assessments, 2010).

5. Please see *Littoral Combat Ship: Actions Needed to Improve Operating Cost Estimates and Mitigate Risks in Implementing New Concepts* (Washington DC, Government Accountability Office, GAO-10-257, February 2010).

6. Certain costs are excluded from the US$480 million cap, which also includes provisions for adjusting the figure over time to take inflation and other events into account. The Secretary of the Navy is permitted to waive the cost cap under certain conditions.

7. O'Rourke, *op.cit.*, summary page.

8. Geoff Fein, 'Navy OK with Either LCS, New Plan Adds Flexibility in Out Years', *Defense Daily* – 18 February 2010 (Springfield VA, Army Times Publishing, 2010).

9. Please refer to Chapter 4.2 for a more detailed overview of the MH-60R Sea Hawk helicopter.

NAVAL MULTIFUNCTION RADARS

An Overview of their Development

Author:
Norman Friedman

Warships are compromises between all sorts of competing claims; their designers juggle weights and volumes and electric power and much more. One other thing they juggle is shipboard real estate. There is a reason why guns and, usually, missile launchers should be on the ship's centreline. Similarly, there is only one best place to put a shipboard radar: the highest point on board the ship. Unfortunately a ship needs radars for multiple purposes, and in the past they have simply competed for the best and next-best places. Often one radar antenna blocks the path to another, or the presence of multiple radars makes for other arrangement problems. With the rise of vital satellite communications, which often use radar-like dish antennas (operating at radar frequencies), topside arrangement has become even more difficult. Radar developers now offer a way out of the mess (or at least a way to a reduced mess) in the form of multifunction sets. These radars, in turn, are possible because of the ongoing revolution in electronic components, which has dramatically reduced their cost and size while making them very reliable. Powerful computers can control radar functions in ways barely imagined a few decades ago.

RADAR SCANNING AND TRACKING

The problem is obvious if we look back to a pre-digital era. Early naval radars could either scan for targets or they could track single targets. A scanning radar swung its beam around periodically, picking up targets. It generally did not revisit any one target until it had completed its full scan. This type of operation was associated with the standard radar display, the map-like Plan Position Indicator (PPI), which creates, in effect, a chart of what the radar sees on a single scan. At least in Western radars, target tracking generally meant that a single dish or electronic lens generated multiple beams, which it tried to place around the moving target. As the target moved out of the centre of the beam pattern, the radar's analogue electronics could sense its direction and command the radar dish to follow.[1]

However, a scanning radar can be given a memory; it can remember that the same target is in different places on scan after scan. Connecting up these 'dots' in effect creates a track, on the basis of which target position can be predicted (for example, for fire control). Such a radar/memory combination is called a track while scan (TWS) device. In effect it was the first approach to the multi-function use of radar. The first memories were radar plots, and one of the first lessons of radar development was that a radar plus a plot was a great deal more than a radar by itself. This kind of tracking was the basis of the very successful Second World War Combat Information Centre (US Navy) and Action Information Organisation (Royal Navy).

Obviously a great deal depends both on how much the target moves between scans and on how precise tracking has to be. Search radars feeding Combat Information Centres made possible effective fighter control during the Second World War, which was a kind of fire control in which the weapon (the fighter) had its own onboard terminal sensor, in the form of its pilot. As aircraft speeds increased dramatically after the War, the factors determining how well the combination worked became more obvious. Much depended on how much the target moved between radar scans (detections) and also on the delays involved in translating radar data to the plot from which target tracks were deduced. Perhaps surprisingly, given the immense amount of operational research conducted to support anti-submarine operations during the Second World War, there seems to have been no effort either in the United Kingdom or in the United States to work out the limitations of the radar/plot combination. After the War it became obvious that human delays in transmitting data from radar to plot could be devastating, and that insight led to the first naval applications of digital computers.

Once computers became reasonably plentiful, in the 1960s, they were applied to all sorts of naval radar systems. For example, in the 1960s the US Navy developed a Mk 86 gun fire-control radar containing a fast-scanning (full scan every second) TWS radar employing a computer. It seemed, at least at the time, that a surface target moved slowly enough for the TWS feature to track it precisely enough for fire control. Aircraft were clearly a very different proposition, and Mk 86 incorporated a separate dish to track them.

Quite aside from the real-estate issue, the split between tracking and searching set the number of fast targets, such as aircraft, a ship could track and, thus, engage in short succession. How many surface ships Mk 86 could handle depended on how much computer horsepower was connected to it (and also on how quickly and precisely targets were entered into that memory). However, how many aircraft the system could track depended on how many dishes it had – a real estate issue, since dishes competed with guns or missile launchers for valuable centreline space.

It might seem that making scanners even faster would have solved the problem: what if Mk 86 had spun, inside a carefully-fitted radome, ten or twenty times per second? Unfortunately, matters were more complicated. To detect a given target, a radar has to pour sufficient energy over it while the target is in its beam. For a set radar output, the faster the scan, the less energy goes out in any one direction. Since the energy goes out as a spreading beam, the further out the target is, the less energy strikes it. Energy output is inherently limited by factors such as waveguide breakdown (if too much energy goes up to the antenna, the waveguide carrying it can short out). That is why longer-range radars typically scan much more slowly than short-range ones. It can be argued, too, that a broader beam offers better range, because a target remains in that beam for longer, hence is washed by more energy. However, a broad beam makes the target's position more difficult to measure, particularly if the radar is rotating.

TARGET INDICATION RADAR

A Second World War example makes the trade-off obvious. Early Royal Navy search (air warning) radars produced extremely broad beams because they operated at what, by later standards, were very low frequencies (multi-metric wavelengths). These radars were not worth connecting to PPIs, but they poured so much of their energy onto any target that they enjoyed good range, even with limited power output. The broad beam left target position so uncertain that any tracking (gun control) radar following up to deal with the target the long-range radar saw would have to spend considerable time scanning its narrow (for precision tracking) beam over the width of the warning beam. The wartime Royal Navy solved the problem by adding an intermediate, narrow-beam scanning radar, which it called a target indicator. To create a narrow beam within reasonable antenna dimensions, the target indication radar had to operate at a much higher frequency.[2] An operator at this radar's PPI could generate a strobe pointing to a selected target, transmitting its bearing and range to

The US Navy's Aegis-equipped cruiser *Vicksburg* (CG-69). The four distinctive octagonal SPY-1 arrays that provide 360-degree radar coverage for Aegis ships were essentially the first successful multifunction radars to be deployed at sea. They were the product of an ongoing revolution in electronic components that permits the use of radars in ways that were barely imagined a few decades ago. *(Conrad Waters)*

The Russian destroyer *Admiral Levchenko* departing Portsmouth in 2006. Her cluttered topsides illustrate the difficulties inherent in finding suitable 'real estate' for weapons, radars and communications systems onboard a crowded warship. *(Conrad Waters)*

US Navy F-14 Tomcat fighters onboard the carrier *Enterprise* (CVN-65) in November 2001. The AWG-9 fire control system designed for this aircraft was built around the first radar with multiple operating modes. *(US Navy)*

Table 4.1.1: RADAR FREQUENCY DESIGNATIONS

FREQUENCY - MHZ	WAVELENGTH	NATO BAND	US DESIGNATION	RADARS REFERRED TO IN CHAPTER
0-30 (HF and lower)	>10m	–	–	–
30-300 (VHF)	10m to 1m	–	–	–
30-250	–	A	–	–
100-150	–	–	I Band	–
150-225	–	–	G Band (WWII IFF)	–
225-390	[c. 1.5m]	–	P Band	Many long-range Second World War radars
250-500	–	B	–	–
300-3,000 (UHF)	1m to 10cm	–	–	–
390-1,550	[c. 20cm]	–	L Band	SMART-L/S-1850M (Netherlands)
500-1,000	–	C	–	–
1,000-2,000	–	D	–	–
1,550-3,900	[c. 10cm]	–	S Band (E/F)	Herakles (France); Sampson (UK); SPY-1 (USA)
2,000-3,000	–	E	–	–
3,000-33,000 (SHF)	10cm to 1cm	–	–	–
3,000-4,000	–	F	–	–
3,900-6,200	[c. 5cm]	–	C Band (G/H)	Type 346 (China)
4,000-5,000	–	G	–	EMPAR (Italy)
5,000-8,000	–	H	–	–
6,200-10,900	[c. 3cm]	–	X Band (I/J)	APAR (Netherlands)
8,000-10,000	–	I	–	–
10,000-20,000	–	J	–	–

Note: The NATO banding system was originally developed for ECM systems designation but its more logical approach has become more generally used. In general terms, higher frequency radars produce a sharper beam for a given size of antenna but have a shorter range.

a director. When the director slued to the indicated bearing, it generated its own strobe on the screen, so that the operator could see whether he had pointed the director properly. This was not quite TWS, because it was a way of dealing with targets generally headed directly for the ship. The less they were headed for the ship (the higher their bearing rates), the less effective the device was. The next step, which the Royal Navy took after the War, was to connect a much longer-range target indication radar to a memory, and thus to create a TWS system. The result was the analogue Comprehensive Display System, which proved an excellent means of controlling a carrier's fighters.[3]

OTHER CONSIDERATIONS

There are other factors, too. Lower-frequency radars enjoy longer range, but their beams break up near the surface of the sea. A higher-frequency (shorter wavelength) radar offers superior surface-search performance. Similarly, the waveform created by the radar also determines what it does best. For example, a pulse Doppler radar, which creates pulses at a very high rate, can detect fast targets effectively and measure their speed (at least in the direction of the radar), but it measures range poorly at best; it is said to have a short unambiguous range. Such a radar has additional advantages when faced with clutter, and its very frequent pulses have a better chance of picking up a stealthy target. Because it measures the speed of an object, it can pick up a small fast target against the massive, but static, clutter of the sea, hence may be particularly useful against a low-flying anti-ship missile. A radar intended to detect targets at long ranges, and to measure their ranges unambiguously, spaces its pulses more widely. Ships therefore typically have multiple radars, operating at different frequencies – which compete for real estate.

AIRCRAFT AND MULTI-MODE RADAR

Aircraft, of course, have the worst real-estate problem. A fighter or attack aircraft cannot easily accommodate more than one radar.[4] For that reason aircraft were the first to employ multi-role radars, and the aircraft experience pointed to shipboard solutions. For aircraft the great split was between conventional ranging, with a relatively slow pulse rate, and air-to-air detection and tracking, for which the rapid pulses of a pulse Doppler radar were better. The difference determined which aircraft could usefully strike ground targets and which were better at air-to-air combat. That might be satisfactory for a land air force with thousands of aircraft, but it was hardly acceptable on board a carrier.

What could be done? The split had nothing to do with the externals of a radar, such as its antenna, and everything to do with the tube at its heart, which created the radar signal in the first place. Through the 1950s, radars were built around tubes with more or less fixed signal characteristics. Thus one of the great post-war radar success stories was the Swedish spin-tuned magnetron, whose signal could be adjusted, albeit over a relatively small range. This degree of adjustment, however, could not change a conventional pulse radar into a pulse-Doppler radar, or vice versa.

By about 1960 computers had matured to the point where it seemed there was a way out. To a great extent the machines of that time represented a false dawn, in that they could not really do very much, and they were typically both heavy and unreliable while not doing so. Even so, some American engineers realised that a computer could create a radar wave form based not on the internal shape of some tube, but on its software. The result would have very little energy, but a new kind of amplifying tube, the Travelling Wave Tube (TWT), could solve that problem. Depending on how the computer was instructed, the radar fed by a TWT could shift from one role to another, in a way previously impossible. It was a true multi-role radar. The first such radar to enter service was the core of the AWG-9 fire-control system carried by the US Navy's F-14 Tomcat. The Tomcat also had a powerful computer memory, to provide TWS performance, and most descriptions emphasised that. However, it was the first radar with multiple operating modes.[5] By the time the Tomcat entered service (1975) computers were shrinking rapidly, so that it was soon possible to put much the same radar capability on board the much smaller Hornet – which was why that aircraft was designated F/A-18, rather than F-18 or A-18. The Hornet demonstrated what multi-purpose meant during the 1991 Gulf War. Two Hornets on a bombing mission were jumped by Iraqi MiGs. The pilots switched radar modes, shot down the Iraqis, then switched back and completed their missions (using radar-based fire control). No earlier fighter, other than a Tomcat, could have done that.

COMPUTERISED DECISION-MAKING

Computers offered another important possibility. A radar-computer combination could decide for itself that it had detected a target. The radar picks up electronic noise mixed with echoes of real targets. A radar operator looking at a display of that input, in whatever form, decides that something is or is not a real target: he detects the target. Radars now typically translate the mix or noise and echoes into digital form, and the most basic kind of automatic detector is set to decide that anything more than a given amount is a real echo. That level is usually set to hold the rate of false alarms to an acceptable level. Stealthy aircraft hope to avoid detection by producing echoes difficult to distinguish from noise. A good radar operator can often do better than a simple computer detector, because he looks at the apparent behaviour of the specks of light on his display; but the computer maintains its alertness forever (the operator cannot), and it can automatically pass what it detects into a tracking computer. Also, as computers become more powerful they, too, can begin to decide based on apparent target behaviour.[6]

Once a radar can decide whether what it has picked up is a real target, it can be programmed to react to that detection. For example, it can pay particular attention to the last known target position on its next scan, or it can be set to change mode to measure target speed on its next scan.

PHASED ARRAYS

The other great fruit of the computer electronics revolution was a new kind of radar antenna. The familiar antennas of the Second World War and later years are all reflectors fed by a single beam (or a very few).[7] The alternative to a reflector is a collection of individual beams so related in timing (phase) that they add up to form a powerful beam pointing in a particular direction. Hence the name phased array for the flat array of radiators. Computers come into the story because it takes one to set (and quickly re-set) the phase relationships between hundreds of beams to point the large beam in the desired direction. The flat antenna covers hundreds of computer-controlled phase shifters.

The effect of the computer is to make it possible to swing the beam rapidly, as quickly as the computer can order the phase shifters to change their settings. In a physical radar, it takes mechanical motion to do that, and the antenna has considerable inertia which resists changes in its motion. For example, it is difficult to imagine suddenly reversing the movement of a large rotating antenna. Electronic beam movement, on the other hand, involves no inertia at all; the beam can point in one direction, then suddenly point in a very different one. The faster the targets, the more attractive (or necessary) it is to move the radar beam at will, and rapidly. The radar antenna, if it has surfaces in enough directions (as in the SPY-1 radar associated with the US Aegis system) need not move physically at all. Alternatively, the radar beam can move relative to a single rotating radar face. Note, however, there was still only one source of radar power feeding all those phase shifters – the first (and still most) phased arrays were passive arrays, the arrays shaping and pointing the beam, but always with just a single radar signal passing through them.

SPY-1 AND AEGIS

The first radar to exploit this technology effectively was the US SPY-1 of the Aegis system.[8] It was conceived in 1965, after a big electronically-scanned

The US destroyer *Halsey* (DDG-97) conducting a refuelling at sea. The SPY-1 arrays are arranged around the forward bridge structure to provide 360-degree coverage. *(US Navy)*

radar (SPG-59) and its associated Typhon missile system were cancelled. In effect SPY-1 appeared just as solid-state electronic technology matured enough to make such a radar both reliable and affordable. It was successfully tested in the 1970s and it entered service in the early 1980s – just as computers became so affordable and reliable that they could be sold, eventually by the million, to individual users.

SPY-1 was the first major multifunction shipboard radar. It searches for targets like a big rotating search radar, and it tracks them like a fire-control radar (it was conceived as a short-range tracker and fire-control radar). Although USN CG-47 type Aegis cruisers also had a longer-range search radar (SPS-49), it turned out that SPY-1 range was good enough for all practical purposes; USN DDG-51 type Aegis destroyers have only the single SPY-1 radar system.

SPY-1 only creates a single radar beam at any one moment: as a passive array it is fed by only a single source of power (in Aegis cruisers, the forward and after pairs of arrays have their own power tubes, but in Aegis destroyers there is only a single tube). However, that single beam can be redirected near instantaneously and it can also be shaped as required. Deep inside the radar, a TWT creates the desired waveform, the amplified beam from which is fed to each of the phase-shifters via microwave plumbing (which is visible in photographs of the back of the array). Because the wave form is created by software, and because the beam is computer-controlled, the radar can be set to change its operation depending on circumstances. Thus the radar can perform volume search, and then suddenly also track a target or a missile that the ship is controlling. Even so, the time it spends on any one task is not available for any other: all functions are time shared. The Aegis system includes a 'command and decision' computer into which the ship's individual combat doctrine is inserted (some Aegis literature calls this the first naval example of artificial intelligence, since the computer makes rule-based decisions). Radar operation takes this doctrine (which, obviously, can be changed as desired) into account. For example, the radar can measure the speeds of the targets it detects. It can be instructed not to insert targets moving too slowly (e.g., seabirds) into its track file.[9]

The beam can thus move both quickly and in any desired direction. Normally it scans the sky to detect targets. If it finds anything, however, its computer can decide to pull the beam back and look around the previously known target position. In this way the

The US Navy deployed the SPS-32/33 combination of electronically-scanned radars on board the prototype nuclear warships *Enterprise* (CVN-65) and *Long Beach* (CGN-9) in the 1960s. The radars were considered failures because of the high level of maintenance required for their computers and the arrays had therefore been removed by the time this picture of *Long Beach* was taken in the 1980s. However, SPS-32 featured the same phase-shifting technology later used successfully in SPY-1/Aegis. *(US Navy)*

radar can set up a target track on a far more precise basis than the track while scan radars of the past. Its track is so good that it can control anti-aircraft missiles; indeed, precision is how Aegis can engage so many targets at more or less the same time. Unlike any earlier naval fire-control system, it is not much limited by shipboard real-estate constraints on the number of tracking dishes.[10]

This radar still has its limitations. Not only can it create just one beam at a time because it has only one radar power tube but this of itself, it can be argued, also creates a single point of failure. The power tube itself has limitations; when US Aegis ships were reconfigured for satellite or missile interception, their power tubes had to be replaced with ones better suited to the low pulse rates and high pulse power involved. There is also a subtler limitation. The radar operates over a set frequency band; for SPY-1, E/F

The Aegis system, shown on board the missile destroyer *Donald Cook* (DDG-75), was the first multi-function system in widespread use. The dishes on the centreline are slaved illuminators which guide the ship's Standard series missiles in their terminal phase; the illuminators are, in turn, pointed by the Aegis computer on the basis of what the SPY-1 sees. Note that destroyers, unlike Aegis cruisers, have no main radar other than the multi-role SPY-1. *(US Navy)*

bands (USN S-band). The designers of SPY-1 chose S-band (10cm wavelength) as a compromise. A shorter wavelength would have given a sharper beam, but it would not have performed as well in rain. A longer wavelength would have given longer range, but worse performance near the surface of the sea.

SPY-1 has four faces, but even a single-faced phased array offers some interesting possibilities. Remember the difference between long-range air search and short-range search of the horizon, for example to pick up sea-skimming anti-ship missiles. Only one antenna can be in the best place for each, at the highest point on board a ship. For long-range air search, the beam should be fairly broad and it should scan relatively slowly. For horizon search, it should scan quickly, because every second after a missile pops over the horizon counts. For precision, the beam should be as narrow as possible; the objective should be to obtain fire control information instantly. In fact, once the target is detected, why wait for a full 360-degree scan before looking again so as to estimate target course? The US SPQ-9B exploits this possibility, producing three beams so that it can re-examine anything it detects.

EMPAR

The first naval radar to exploit these possibilities was apparently the Italian-developed EMPAR (European Multifunction Phased-array radar) subsequently used in the 'Horizon' frigates. Like SPY-1, it combines search and tracking functions. However, it operates at high frequency G-band (C-band), shorter wavelength than the E/F bands of the SPY-1, to hold down its size. On the 'Horizon' class it is therefore backed by the longer range S-1850M three-dimensional search radar. S-1850M – derived from the Thales Nederland SMART L – is a conventional stacked-beam set which scans by rotating.

The EMPAR designers wanted a precision search radar that could undertake two very different roles: volume and horizon search. Volume search meant looking for air targets at relatively long ranges, which (as pointed out) required a relatively broad slow-scanning beam. For horizon search, particularly against sea-skimming missiles, the designers needed a rapid scan. An antenna could have been designed with two motor speeds for two alternative kinds of search, but the designers came up with something much more elegant. They provided a motor with one speed, for rapid horizon search. For that role the radar produces a single beam fixed to the antenna (at most, stabilised with respect to it). No computation is needed to decide where the target is relative to the radar, hence to the ship; this is a quick-reaction mode. For volume search, the beam is swung backwards along the face of the antenna, so that it turns more slowly than the antenna does. There is some distortion as the beam moves back towards the face of the antenna, so that there will be some imprecision, although this does not matter so much for a distant target. The radar also has the capacity to swing its beam back (as long as the antenna is facing in approximately the right direction)

Because switching between the two radar modes is electronic, it can be done instantly, and as often as an operator likes. For example, an operator can interleave a few volume searches with mainly horizon searches. EMPAR is also, in effect, partly a target indication radar, whose function is to provide a

The French 'Horizon' class escort *Forbin* pictured arriving at Portsmouth in April 2010. The ship's single-faced EMPAR multifunction radar rotates in the dome atop the forward mast. Operating at a relatively high frequency, it is backed by the longer range S-1850M three-dimensional search radar derived from Thales' SMART-L. This is located on the mast aft. *(Conrad Waters)*

target track precise enough to bring associated active-homing Aster missiles to within the effective acquisition range of their on-board active radar. However, in the horizon search mode it is also the initial acquisition radar of the system, because the longer range SMART-L/S-1850M does not enjoy any range advantage in this role. The rapid horizon scan of an EMPAR is intended to pick up sea skimmers as soon as possible and with enough precision to direct defending Aster missiles on target.

ACTIVE PHASED ARRAYS

It turned out that miniature transmit-receive (Tx/Rx) modules – in effect miniature radars – could be mass-produced, much as other kinds of electronics can be. The 1975 technology of inexpensive reliable computer-controlled phase-shifters became the 1990s technology of increasingly inexpensive T/R modules, first at higher and then at progressively lower frequencies (shorter, then longer, wavelengths). Instead of controlling the relative phases of the

phase-shifters, a computer could provide each module with both the desired waveform and with the desired phase. A radar whose antenna consists of such modules is called an active array, in contrast to the passive array of a phase-shifter radar like SPY-1. In effect the radar mechanism, apart from the computer which commands it, has been moved above decks.

Active operation has all sorts of potential advantages, although it does carry some problems. Instead of generating a lot of heat below decks, where it can be carried away by water cooling, an active array generates its heat in its antenna. When the Japanese deployed a single-face rotating active array, they had to provide it with a radiator along one edge. Presumably the radiator would make an excellent target for a heat-seeking missile. The situation for fixed-face radars would be better, because a water-cooling pipe could easily be led up behind the array, and the heat bled away below decks. Thus when the Chinese began to test their current active array on

The German frigate *Hessen* displays her active-array system on her forward superstructure; each of four arrays is covered by a shallow circular radome. The big mechanically-scanned radar aft is a SMART-L. *(US Navy)*

board a ship, the give-away that the array was active was the visible cooling pipe leading up into it. Also, an active array is also potentially heavier than a passive one, because more of the radar is concentrated in the antenna. That does not mean much for an aircraft (the centre of gravity might shift a bit forward), but in a ship it means added topweight. Finally, the Tx/Rx technology is only beginning to reach the E/F bands (S-band), so most active arrays in the world operate at I/J bands (X-band) or G/H bands (C-band), hence enjoying shorter ranges than passive arrays like SPY-1.

That having been said, the most interesting thing about the active array is that it can form multiple beams, both for transmission and for reception. Using multiple beams means that, unlike EMPAR, the radar can scan volume *and* the horizon simultaneously, at different rates, with beams of different shapes. It can create fire control (individual target tracking) beams while it scans, without having to compromise (although it will have to split up its total power). It can also manipulate the beams it uses for reception. Faced with jamming, for example, it can null out reception in chosen directions. To what extent these potentials can be reached depends on how many Tx/Rx modules can fit into the limited dimensions of the antenna, and also on how much computer power is available. Since Tx/Rx technology and computer technology seem to be advancing fairly rapidly, what is difficult right now is likely to be fairly easy in the future. From a stealth perspective, which has been advertised for fighters, the active array is interesting because it uses no reflector. Each element of the array receives whatever signals strike the radar, and it does not radiate them back. Another point is that the radar, or part of it, can be used as a receiver, perhaps for radar interception. How well that can work depends on how broadband the Rx part of the Tx/Rx

The UK's Sampson radar system, pictured onboard the destroyer *Daring*, comprises two back-to-back active arrays that rotate within a spherical radome. It can undertake volume and horizon search simultaneously, whilst also carrying out fire-control functions for the active-homing Aster missiles housed in the Sylver VLS cells fitted aft of the main gun. *(Conrad Waters)*

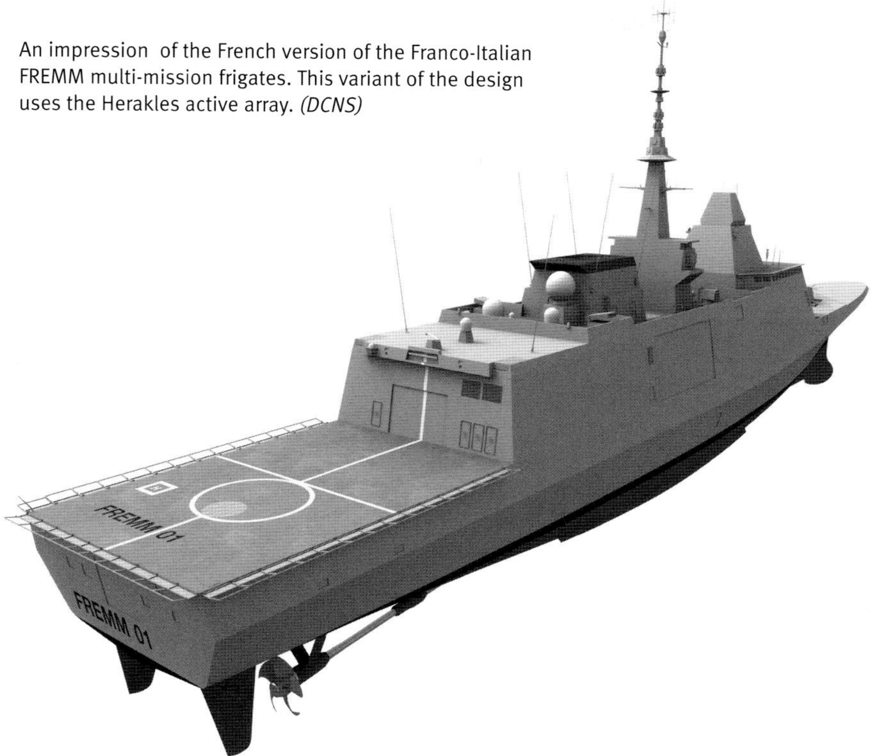

An impression of the French version of the Franco-Italian FREMM multi-mission frigates. This variant of the design uses the Herakles active array. *(DCNS)*

The Chinese Type 346 four-faced radar fitted to the Type 052C *Lanzhou* class destroyers is believed to be a Ukrainian-developed active array. *(Norman Friedman collection)*

is; but a radar designer will want it to be broadband in order to provide greater flexibility as a radar.

Further, if the radar operates at a satellite frequency, it is difficult to see why it (or, rather, part of it) cannot also function as a satellite communications device. In that case an active array would dramatically reduce the congestion atop most ships – if it can see the satellite high in the sky, which may not be easy. Early drawings of the US Navy's *Zumwalt* (DDG-1000) class destroyer suggested that it would use flat (i.e, electronically-scanned) satellite communications antennas atop its superstructure, pointed up.

MODERN ACTIVE PHASED ARRAYS

Probably the first major naval application of this technology was the multi-function APAR (Advanced Phased-array radar) found aboard the Dutch *De Zeven Provinciën* and German *Sachsen* class missile frigates. This uses four faces and controls the ships' Standard missiles – in effect it operates as an I/J-band (X-band) Aegis radar. The ships also have long-range search radars because I/J-band sets lack sufficient range; however, the fact that the radar is sufficiently precise to avoid the need for separate illuminators provides some compensation. Thales Nederland,

which built the four-face radar, has also advertised a rotating single-face version, which is to equip the new Dutch *Holland* class offshore patrol vessels.

The Chinese Type 346 four-face radar on board Type 052C *Lanzhou* class destroyers is apparently a G/H-band (C-band) – i.e., a radar with a longer wavelength than an I/J-band (X-band) – system active array developed by a Ukrainian firm; its designation fits it within the Chinese naval fire-control series. This radar is backed by a long-wave search radar, which may be effective against stealthy targets but lacks definition. There is no intermediate radar like the old British target-indication sets. In the absence of such a set, Type 346 must perform short-range air search as well as target and, presumably, missile tracking, so it must be a multi-function radar.

The next step up in size and range is the E/F bands (S-band). As in other electronic technology, at present E/F-band (S-band) Tx/Rx modules are relatively large, so it is difficult to mount a full four-faced array high in a ship. British and French engineers have approached the problem by using one or two flat faces in a rotating array. The British Sampson, which equips the new *Daring* (Type 45) destroyers, has two flat faces fitted back-to-back that

rotate rapidly within a spherical radome. It enjoys the advantages of EMPAR but does not have to compromise by time-sharing its two main search modes. Using two faces also makes it possible to maintain the same data rate – the rate at which the radar revisits any place – while spinning the heavy array more slowly.

The French Herakles, which equips Singapore's *Formidable* class frigates as well as the French version of the new FREMM Franco-Italian multi-role frigates, takes a very different approach. It uses an electronic lens to bend the beam produced by an array of Tx/Rx modules. The entire assembly rotates within a pyramid-like assembly which is tuned to pass only the radar's frequency (for stealth). The advantage is relatively simple control. The disadvantage is that the electronic lens can form only one beam at a time; in effect this is a superior kind of passive array radar. It may be, however, that by using multiple Tx/Rx modules the designers achieve a kind of monopulse tracking capability.

The US Navy at one time planned an active version of the E/F-band (S-band) SPY-1. This radar would have been combined with an I/J-band (X-band) active array on board the *Zumwalt* class, but as

The Singapore Navy's *Formidable* class frigates were the first to use the French Herakles active-array radar, covered by the pyramid atop the ship's bridge. Final class member *Supreme* is shown arriving at Pearl Harbor in June 2010 before the RIMPAC 2010 exercise. *(US Navy)*

of 2010, the E/F-band (S-band) element of that dual-band radar had been eliminated to reduce the ship's cost. It may still be used on the carrier *Gerald R Ford* (CVN-78). Both ships involved are so large that the top weight associated with E/F-band (S-band) arrays would not be a major consideration.

These radars are only examples of a developing trend. Probably Tx/Rx module development is now being driven mainly by large-scale application to new fighters, which use I/J-band (X-band) and higher-frequency radars. The main obstruction to naval development at and below E/F-band (S-band) is the apparent lack of any other large-scale application in the military or civilian world.

Notes

1. The Soviets developed a very different technique in which the beam was scanned across the radar antenna in a television-like raster pattern. The radar tracked by keeping the target within a box defined by that pattern. The same technique was used in the West to keep television-guided missiles (whose optical sensor raster-scanned) on target, but no Western tracking radar seems to have used this technique. Standard Western techniques were lobe-switching (typical of Second World War fire-control sets), conical scan (one beam spins around the axis of the radar), and monopulse (the radar generates one transmitted beam, but it has multiple receiving beams).

2. Radars are generally primarily described by their frequency, which is inversely proportional to wavelength. In general terms, higher frequency radars produce a sharper beam for a given size of antenna but have a shorter range. Radar frequency bands are subject to two main coding systems derived from US and NATO practice, this book uses the NATO system but gives the US equivalent in brackets. Table 4.1.1 provides further detail.

3. By 1945 the long-wave warning radar was Type 281 and the target indicator was Type 293; the strobed radar display was the core of a target-indication unit within a gunnery-direction system.

4. The most important exception of the 1960s was probably the US A-6 Prowler, which had multiple radars in its massive nose – an attack radar to track ground targets and a terrain-avoidance radar.

5. The fact that the Tomcat radar could handle surface as well as air targets was obscured by the larger fact that, at least at first, bombs it dropped tended to be sucked up into the well between its engines.

6. The successful Iraqi attack on *Stark* (FFG-31) in 1987 illustrated, in effect, the flip side of this development. When *Stark* detected the radar emissions of the approaching Iraqi fighter, her ECM operator thought he was detecting one of the operating modes of an Iranian F-14, because he was primed to expect Iranian rather than Iraqi attention. More generally, the advent of software-controlled radars enormously complicates the task of identifying an approaching radar. It used to be enough to know the standard operating mode of each radar, set out in terms of pulse width (duration) and the typical interval between pulses. If both can easily be changed, identification will depend on far subtler – and far more difficult – measurements.

7. Multiple (stacked) beams have been used for height-finding. Examples include the big French radar inside the radome of the *Suffren* class missile ships and, in very much evolved form, the individually elevating stacked beams of the US SPS-48. Stacked beams are an alternative to a single height-finding beam sweeping up and down over the sky, either mechanically or electronically. Necessarily narrow, the beam spends far too little time looking in any one direction.

8. The US Navy deployed the SPS-32/33 combination of electronically scanned radars on board the prototype nuclear warships *Enterprise* (CVN-65) and *Long Beach* (CGN-9); SPS-32 used the same phase-shifting technology as SPY-1. These radars were considered failures because the computers controlling them were difficult to maintain – as the computers of about 1960 were.

9. This is not an unalloyed advantage. Filtering was necessary because track memory capacity was limited. Unfortunately the criteria used were not always the right ones. On one occasion off Lebanon, for example, an Aegis cruiser was working with a pre-Aegis cruiser. The pre-Aegis ship repeatedly picked up a slow air target, which the Aegis ship did not see on her (filtered) computer screen. SPY-1 was so clearly the better radar of those on board the two ships that the senior officer on board the Aegis ship dismissed the existence of the slow target. Finally the commanding officer of the pre-Aegis ship demanded that he go out on the bridge wing – to see an approaching Cessna. In an age of irregular warfare, the Cessna might be a real threat, loaded with explosives (or, as in this case, a harmless sightseer).

10. Aegis does employ dishes, but they are not trackers, only slaved illuminators. In the last stage of flight, the missile homes on energy reflected by the target. That kind of operation limits the degree of precision the TWS radar needs. The roughly parallel European PAAMS-E (British PAAMS-S Sea Viper with Sampson rather than EMPAR) system avoids using illuminators at all; instead its Aster missile has an active seeker. Proponents of Aegis and its relatives argue that illumination is a better way to overcome stealth, since the ship can pour on power to make up for the reduced amount the target reflects back. Proponents of Aster argue that it is more flexible and that the precision radar can direct the missile so close to the target that there is not much chance of a miss.

4.2 TECHNOLOGICAL REVIEW

Author:
David Hobbs

WORLD NAVAL AVIATION

An Overview of Recent Developments

Despite the global recession focusing attention on the cost of new weapons, 2010 saw steady progress in the construction of new air-capable warships and orders for new aircraft. However, continued delays and cost-growth in the F-35 project have caused a re-assessment of future plans in the United States Navy (USN) and could impact Royal Navy numbers. This year's chapter on World Naval Aviation looks at overall events over the past twelve months whilst describing significant naval aircraft in detail.

A GLOBAL OVERVIEW OF CURRENT DEVELOPMENTS

CARRIER AVIATION

The last of the USN's *Nimitz* class aircraft carriers, *George H W Bush* (CVN-77), had her air-wing spaces and combat systems suite completed in early 2010, together with alterations and additions carried out to bring her into line with the class maintenance plan. Operational deployment followed a work-up cycle based on Norfolk, Virginia. The formal keel-laying ceremony for the first CVN-21 class carrier, *Gerald R Ford* (CVN-78), took place in November 2009, with completion scheduled for 2015. More ships of the class are expected to be ordered at roughly five-year intervals.

The F-35C carrier variant of the Lightning II Joint Strike Fighter commenced its delayed development flying on 7 June 2010. The USN had hoped for initial operational capability (IOC) in 2014, although the extent of delays with the trials

The F-35B STOVL version of the Lockheed Martin Lightning II carrying out its first vertical landing at NAS Patuxent River, MD on 18 March 2010. The F-35 is likely to represent the future of fixed-wing naval aviation for many countries in spite of project delays and cost-growth. *(Lockheed Martin)*

programme makes this seem unlikely. The delay will result in a shortfall of at least 125 fighters as older F/A-18A to D versions of the Hornet reach the end of their service lives. The USN is therefore negotiating a new multi-year procurement plan with

Boeing for continued production of the current F/A-18E/F and EA-18G versions. The last such deal expired in 2009 but the Navy elected to purchase forty aircraft in 2010 and is likely to seek Congressional approval to roll these into an enlarged

The tenth and final USN *Nimitz* class aircraft carrier *George H W Bush* (CVN-77) pictured during her work-up cycle in February 2010. *(US Navy)*

An artist's conception of the X-47B unmanned aerial vehicle (UAV) on the deck of an aircraft carrier. Flight trials of this revolutionary aircraft are scheduled for late 2010. *(Northrop Grumman via US Navy)*

multi-year deal to 2014. The EA-18G now equips several operational squadrons at sea and extra aircraft ordered in 2010 are to equip shore-based squadrons that currently operate the EA-6B in Afghanistan. These were not part of the original plan but there is no other replacement for the vital role they fulfil since the USAF has no tactical jammer and the USMC has no plans to operate the EA-18G. The USN's 2011 budget submission also includes funding for a batch of four low-rate initial production E-2D Hawkeye battle management aircraft.

The first Northrop Grumman X-47B unmanned, long-endurance, strike and surveillance technology demonstration and development aircraft is due to begin flight trials in late 2010. It is to demonstrate its ability to operate from a carrier deck in 2012, slightly later than originally planned. In March 2010 the USN announced a requirement for up to six aircraft similar to the X-47B which could be deployed to a carrier for 'irregular and hybrid' warfare operations as an 'Unmanned Carrier-Launched Air Surveillance and Strike system' (UCLASS). Each aircraft is to be capable of remaining airborne for up to fourteen hours without refuelling, carrying sensors and weapons on sorties that could be flown with no outside input. However, weapon release will only be initiated by human mission controllers and not by the aircraft's systems.

In the UK, work on the infrastructure at Rosyth needed to construct the Royal Navy's new aircraft carriers has been completed and hull sections are beginning to arrive, starting with the bow section of *Queen Elizabeth* in early April 2010. Meanwhile, the existing *Ark Royal* and *Illustrious* have embarked Harriers from the Naval Strike Wing in deployments that have restored embarked fixed-wing operations to an acceptable standard. The Harrier GR9 strike aircraft of Joint Force Harrier (JFH) remain the only British aircraft capable of carrier operations. However, long-term plans for the force had to be changed at short notice after the British Government's December 2009 announcement that one of its squadrons was to be disbanded and the joint base at RAF Cottesmore, which is partially manned by the RN, closed for flying operations to generate funds for the purchase of twenty-two new Chinook helicopters. The RN element of JFH comprises 800 and 801 Naval Air Squadrons (NAS) but the latter has lacked the pilots to fill certain specialised complement billets required by Air Command and has not been recognised as a sepa-

The US Navy's oldest carrier *Enterprise* (CVN-65) returned to the fleet in April 2010 following completion of a two-year maintenance period at Northrop Grumman's Newport News shipyard. A series of trials, including tests of the flight deck sprinkler system (top right), were completed before preparations commenced for the ship's twenty-first deployment. Current plans envisage the *Enterprise* being decommissioned in 2013 on conclusion of her twenty second deployment. By then she will have served for over fifty years from first commissioning in November 1961.

rately deployable unit. In consequence the two have operated together as the Naval Strike Wing. As a result of the cuts, however, one of the two RAF operational units, 4 Squadron, was disbanded on 31 March 2010 and the remainder of the Joint Force is to move to RAF Wittering by 31 March 2011.[1] A later MOD announcement stated that 800 NAS would be the only RN unit in the Force and that the 801 NAS identity will be allocated to the first RN F-35 unit in due course. The Force is to be re-named as the Joint Combat Wing before it moves to Wittering and will comprise only 800 NAS, 1 Squadron RAF and a joint training unit. The Joint Force, seen only a year ago as having reached a 'stable' state, has thus been reduced by two of its original four operational units. More positively, the British Government has ordered three F-35B aircraft to allow British participation in the US initial operational test and evaluation phase of development from 2012. Orders for operational aircraft should follow the conclusion of

trials but there has been no announcement about the number. It is believed that only sixty-six airframe numbers from a previously planned purchase of over 130 aircraft have been allocated for the first batch.

French naval aviation continues to develop its capability and to work closely with the USN. The latest F3 version of the Rafale M has shown itself to be an impressive strike-fighter, making the *Charles de Gaulle* the most effective aircraft carrier outside the USA. Meanwhile, India seems to have resolved its argument with Russia over the cost and delivery timescale for *Vikramaditya* (ex *Admiral Gorshkov*). It has signed a contract for twenty-nine further MiG-29K fighters and agreed a 'final' price tag of US$ 2.3bn for the ship which is to arrive in India no earlier than 2012.[2] A number of Indian Navy pilots have qualified on the type and carried out deck-landing training on the

Russian carrier *Admiral Kuznetsov*; others have undergone deck-landing training in the USA. 303 Naval Air Squadron, the 'Black Panthers', has been formed at INAS Hansa near Dabolim with the first aircraft to arrive in India. The IN still hopes to complement the MiG-29 with a naval variant of the Tejas Light Combat Aircraft (LCA), and has ordered six but the choice of engine for this variant has yet to be decided. Elsewhere, both Spain and Italy are committed to waiting for the F-35B to replace the ageing AV-8B Harriers in their carrier air groups but there is, as yet, no firm date for the type to enter service.

Operationally, aircraft carriers have continued to show their versatility during 2010. In addition to strikes over land-locked Afghanistan from US carriers, the *Carl Vinson* (CVN-70) and the Italian *Cavour* played major roles in the Haitian earthquake disaster. *Vinson* acted as a command centre, air traffic control facility and refuelling base for helicopters, Ospreys and Greyhound carrier on-board delivery (COD) aircraft ferrying supplies ashore. *Cavour* ferried large amounts of humanitarian aid from Europe, including mobile hospitals, in its hangar and on its flight deck. Together with *Nassau* (LHA-4) and *Bataan* (LHD-5) the carriers were able to support helicopter operations which could access inland areas without clogging up the island's only airport.

The British Royal Navy aircraft carrier *Ark Royal* – seen here departing Portsmouth in October 2009 during post-refit trials – has subsequently embarked Harriers from Naval Strike Wing as part of a series of operations intended to restore RN fixed-wing air operations to an acceptable standard. *(Conrad Waters)*

The first British AW159 Lynx Wildcat helicopter flew on 12 November 2009. Although pictured in British Army colours, twenty-eight are also on order for the Royal Navy. *(AgustaWestland)*

SEA CONTROL HELICOPTERS

The US Navy continues to fund MH-60R and S versions of the Sea Hawk, with twenty-four and eighteen respectively sought in the FY2011 appropriations. In the UK, the RN formed 700W NAS in 2009 to act as the development team focal point for the new AW159 Wildcat sea-control helicopter. It will have responsibility for both RN and Army variants and will work in concert with the Rotary-Wing Test Squadron at Boscombe Down, QinetiQ and AgustaWestland. The first Wildcat flew on 12 November 2009; twenty-eight are on order for the RN with IOC anticipated in 2015. The contract with AgustaWestland includes a thirty-year training and support package.

The Australian Government has published a defence white paper confirming the urgent requirement for twenty-four new sea-control helicopters to replace the existing sixteen Sikorsky S-70B-2 'legacy' Sea Hawks and the failed Kaman Sea Sprite Programme under project Air 9000 Phase 8. Following the difficulties with the Sea Sprite, the Government has specified a Military Off-The-Shelf (MOTS) solution with no modification to the aircraft, its sensors or weapons systems prior to purchase in order to minimise risk and hold down costs. Two contenders are being considered: the Sikorsky MH-60R 'second-generation' Sea Hawk and the NH-Industries NH90. A decision is due in late 2010 or early 2011. Both have positive and negative features. The MH-60R is a proven, effective design in service with the USN, giving commonality with Australia's most significant ally. Sikorsky is offering an A$1bn industrial offset package if its helicopter is selected and the unit cost would be lower. The NH90 offers 80 per cent commonality with the MRH90 tactical transport helicopters ordered by the Australian Army and, as a Sea King replacement, by the RAN. These are being built in Brisbane under licence by Australian Aerospace but the sea-control version cannot yet be considered a mature system. Other navies are having to accept aircraft at an 'interim capability standard' because of weight problems and delays in developing the sensor-fusion aspects of software design. Once these shortcomings are overcome, however, the NH90 could offer better long-term

An Australian MRH90 tactical transport helicopter undertaking trials from the amphibious transport *Manoora*. The 'sister' sea control variant of EADS' NH90 helicopter is in competition with the Sikorsky MH-60R to replace Australia's aging 'legacy' Sea Hawks. *(Royal Australian Navy)*

A Netherlands Navy NH90 helicopter. These are being delivered to an interim standard whilst weight and software issues are addressed. *(Royal Netherlands Navy via EADS)*

A Northrop Grumman MQ-8B Fire Scout UAV has been operating successful from the USN frigate *McInerney* (FFG-8). *(US Navy)*

potential but after the failure of the Sea Sprite project, buying a mature weapons system must seem an attractive option and the choice is not an easy one to make. Whichever type is selected, the RAN hopes to achieve IOC by 2016 at the latest. The RAN was the first operator to clear the MRH90 for operation at sea after a trial embarkation in *Manoora* which saw the development aircraft carry out normal and rough-weather take-offs and landings; ammunition transfers and load-lifting to and from the deck. The RAN is to receive six and the Army forty; many of the latter will eventually operate from the two Australian LHDs.

Deliveries of the NH90 to several navies have been delayed because of the issues outlined above. The Dutch Government has agreed a 'meaningful operational configuration' for seven NH90s that allowed them to replace shore-based Lynx helicopters during 2010. Dutch Lynx will continue to serve at sea until 2012, when the weight and software problems with the NH90 are expected to be resolved. The Italian Navy has agreed to accept a batch of four NH90s to a similar standard which it refers to as 'Step A' aircraft that are intended to hasten the type's entry into service. They will be used by the 5th Helicopter Group at NAS Luni near La Spezia to train air and ground crews. The Italian Navy is one of the biggest customers for the new type with forty-six on order plus a further ten navalised versions of the similar MRH90 tactical transport helicopter. France and Norway have also agreed to accept naval NH90s to this interim standard.

The most innovative naval helicopter under development is the Northrop Grumman MQ-8B Fire Scout unmanned air vehicle, which has completed a successful second period of sea trials in the USN's *McInerney* (FFG-08). The helicopter can operate autonomously for up to eight hours from any warship flight deck, spending up to six hours on station at 110nm (203km). It can climb to 20,000ft to act as a communications relay for 'line-of-sight' transmissions between widely separated ships and has electro-optical and IR sensors which give precision targeting for other platforms' weapons. Potential payloads under development include tactical synthetic aperture radar, sonobuoy dispensers and mine countermeasures equipment. Obvious roles for the MQ-8, other than communications relay, are reconnaissance and battle-damage assessment and others will surely follow. Around 23ft (7m) long and with a maximum all-up weight of only 3,150lb (1,429kg), several MQ-8Bs can be carried with, or instead of, conventional

The Spanish Navy's new amphibious assault ship *Juan Carlos I* carried out initial sea trials in September 2009. *(Navantia)*

Russia is in negotiation with France's DCNS for supply of a *Mistral* class *Bâtiment de Projection et Command* (BPC) type amphibious assault ship. *(DCNS)*

helicopters, even in frigates, greatly extending their reconnaissance capability and giving them more 'eyes' with no worries about crew fatigue among the limited number of aircrew available.

AMPHIBIOUS WARFARE

An increasing number of USMC squadrons are re-equipping with the MV-22B tilt-rotor and the type acquitted itself well in operation from *Nassau* during relief operations off Haiti in 2010. *Makin Island* (LHD-8), last of the *Wasp* class amphibious assault ships, commissioned in late 2009. She differs from the earlier ships in having gas turbine engines and electric drive making her the link with the improved LHA-6 class, which will have similar propulsion but feature significant modifications. During her delivery voyage from Pascagoula to San Diego she burned 900,000 gallons less fuel than her steam-powered sisters would have done on the same passage, saving US$2m. The Spanish LHD *Juan Carlos I* carried out initial sea trials in September 2009 and construction work was started on the first Australian LHD, *Canberra*, at Navantia's Ferrol yard in the same month. She is due to be launched in March 2011 and arrive at BAE Systems Australia's Williamstown Dockyard in 2012 for the fitting of the island structure, installation of the

combat system and communications outfits. Metal for the second ship, *Adelaide*, was cut in February 2010, two months ahead of schedule; she is due in Williamstown in 2014. The French Navy laid the keel of a third *Mistral* class *Bâtiment de Projection et Command* (BPC) at St Nazaire on 20 January 2010; she is to be named *Dixmude*. After several months of rumour, media reports claim that Russia is negotiating a deal to purchase a *Mistral* class BPC from France and licence-build at least three more in Russia. The deal has not been confirmed by Moscow, whilst the Head of French International Arms Sales has said that the deal is being examined 'on a technical level' and must be 'vetted at a political level'. The point at issue seems to be the transfer of sensitive electronics fitted in the French ships, as the Russians insist on buying the complete package.

The British Government's December 2009 cuts to fund Chinook procurement contained changes that impact on the RN's Commando Helicopter Force (CHF). Plans to replace the Sea King HC4 with a new joint tactical helicopter appear to have been quietly dropped and, instead, the twenty-eight Merlin HC3 helicopters operated by the RAF are to be transferred to the RN to replace the thirty-seven Sea King HC4s.[3] Five HAS 6Cs, which were added

to the CHF while the HC 4s were cycled through work to upgrade them, were withdrawn from service in April 2010. Whilst the new plan is good to the extent that it will centralise all Merlins in the RN, the HC3 was, unfortunately, not designed to fold or operate at sea. No mention has been made about funding for a replacement folding main rotor head and tail pylon or even the necessary lashing points for the aircraft to be secured on a flight deck. Work needed to identify and provide a minimum 'marinisation package' could be expensive and time-consuming. With the aircraft heavily committed to Afghan operations, it is unlikely to be undertaken soon. France, Spain and Italy seem to be doing things better with a more rational, longer-term plan.

CURRENT NAVAL AIRCRAFT IN DETAIL
FIGHTERS: F-35 LIGHTNING II; F/A-18E/F SUPER HORNET; RAFALE M; MIG-29K

Lockheed Martin F-35 Lightning II: Only the United States, Russia and France currently manufacture fighters capable of carrier operation. The most advanced is arguably the F-35 Lightning II, formerly known as the Joint Strike Fighter. This had its origins in a number of US and collaborative projects in the

The F-35 Lightning II JSF prototype AA-1. Current US estimates suggest more than 2,400 of these aircraft will be purchased for the American armed forces, of which around three-quarters will be 'A' variants for the USAF. *(Lockheed Martin)*

Table 4.2.1: MODERN NAVAL FIGHTER COMPARISONS

AIRCRAFT[1]	F-35B	F-35C	F/A-18F	RAFALE M (F3)	MIG-29K
Length	15.6m	15.7m	18.5m	15.3m	17.3m
Wingspan	10.7m	13.1m	13.7m	10.8m	12.0m
Wing area	42.7m^2	57.6m^2	46.5m^2	45.7m^2	43.0m^2
Height	4.6m	4.7m	4.9m	5.3m	4.4m
Take-off weight – max	27,250kg	31,750kg	30,000kg	24,500kg	24,500kg
Engines	1 x F135	1 x F135	2 x F414-GE-400	2 x M88-2E4	2 x RD-33MK
Thrust – max	19,000kgf (43,000lbs)	19,500kgf (43,000lbs)	20,000kgf (44,000lbs)	15,500kgf (34,000lbs)	18,000 kgf (40,000lbs)
Speed – max[2]	2,000km/h	2,000km/h	1,900km/h	2,400km/h	2,200 km/h
Service Ceiling	c. 18,000m	c. 18,000m	15,200m	16,800m	17,500m
Maximum G-load	7.5G	7.5G	7.6G	+9G	8G
Weapons Stations	11	11	11	13	9
Radar	NG AN/APG-81	NG AN/APG-81	Raytheon AN/APG-79	Thales RBE2	Phazotron Zhuk-ME

Notes:

1 Data has been compiled from manufacturers' documentation, supplemented by publicly-available information as necessary. Due to considerable variations in published information, data should be regarded as indicative only.

2 Speed refers to maximum speed at altitude. Low-level speed is considerably less.

1980s and has evolved into a single-engined strike aircraft to be manufactured in three variants with as much commonality as possible. Current US estimates suggest production of more than 2,400 aircraft for domestic requirements – with more slated for export. The largest customer will be the USAF, which hopes to buy over 1,700 'A' variants; next are the US Navy and Marine Corps, which plan for over 600 of the 'B' STOVL and 'C' carrier variants. These long-term estimates have already shrunk since the programme was first launched and there is much speculation whether these numbers are achievable. A number of other nations have joined the programme but the UK is the only Level 1 partner and has been with the JSF project since it absorbed the previous joint US/UK Advanced STOVL project.

The F-35 was designed from the outset to incorporate stealth technology and is considered to be the only 'fifth-generation' fighter under development; other current naval fighters represent the 'fourth generation', albeit with enhanced stealth characteristics. All F-35s are powered by a single Pratt & Whitney F135 engine with 43,000lb of thrust in full reheat but in the 'B' the engine is modified with a swivelling nozzle aft and a power drive, through a clutch, to a horizontal high-performance lift fan fitted aft of the cockpit. Doors above and below the fuselage open to allow airflow through the fan when it is engaged. Piping from the engine runs to roll-control 'puffer jets' in the wings to control the aircraft when it is not in wing-borne flight. BF-1, the first F-35B prototype carried out the type's first hover landing at NAS Patuxent River, Maryland on 18 March 2010. The aircraft's thrust to weight ratio is not impressive and – with its small wings – it would not perform well in a turning combat but – with its stealth design – it should not need to. An alternative engine, the GE/Rolls Royce F 136, is being developed but has become a political issue and might be terminated to save cost. There is no intention of developing or producing a two-seat version, either for training or operational use.

There are inevitable compromises to deliver the specific performance required of each variant. The baseline 'A' variant has c. 18,000lb (8,163kg) of internal fuel and two internal weapons bays, each capable of containing a BRU-68 2,000lb (907kg) Joint Direct Attack Munition (JDAM) or equivalent and an AIM-120 missile, the latter mounted on the inside of the inner weapon-bay door. In this configuration the 'A' has a radius of action of c. 600nm

(1,110km) but its small wing means high landing speeds and long runways. The 'B' sacrifices internal fuel tanks for the lift fan and its gearing, giving less than 14,000lb (6,349kg) of internal fuel. It also has smaller weapons bays, each only capable of containing a BRU-67 1,000lb (454kg) JDAM or equivalent and the AIM-120. It has a radius of action of c. 500nm (925km). The 'C' version has a larger wing with 43ft (13.1m) span, compared with 35ft (10.6m) for the other variants and an area of 620ft^2 (57.6m^2) compared with 460ft^2 (42.7m^2). The tailplane also has to be larger and the airframe is slightly longer. It has folding wings for carrier stowage and a tail-hook. The enlarged wing gives lower landing speeds compatible with *Nimitz* class carriers and also allows considerably more internal fuel tankage at c. 20,000lb (9,070kg) giving the 'C' a radius of action of over 600nm (1,110km) with two 2,000lb (907kg) JDAM and AIM-120s. Alternative weapons that can be carried internally include the Joint Stand-Off Weapon (JSOW) and Small-Diameter Bombs (SDB) – up to four in each bay in the 'A' and 'C' but only three in the 'B'. The 'A' has an internal 25mm cannon with 180 rounds; the 'B' and 'C' have the option to carry the same type of gun in an external pod with 220 rounds. The gun-

pod has stealth features but might compromise the aircraft's overall stealth 'signature'.[4]

The defining role of the F-35 is long-range strike, using stealth to penetrate and suppress enemy air defences in the opening phase of a full-scale 'theatre-entry' assault against sophisticated opposition. For this it would only operate with internal fuel and weapons to minimise its radar reflective area. In addition to the stealthy design, careful construction to extremely fine tolerances of panels and doors helps to reduce the type's radar-reflective properties. It has a radar-absorbent coating which is said to be superior to the fragile examples used on the USAF's B-2 bombers and F-22 fighters, both of which have had a major negative impact on their availability.

Once enemy air defences have been suppressed, all three variants can be fitted with three weapon carrying pylons under each wing and one under the fuselage centreline giving a total – including the internal bays – of eleven hardpoints. The inner wing stations have 'plumbing' to take 426-US gallon drop tanks, which would dramatically extend the aircraft's radius of action. Once external weapons and fuel are fitted, however, the radar cross-section of the aircraft is markedly increased and, in effect, the F-35 ceases to be stealthy. The aircraft can carry the full range of

US tactical air weapons on the pylons except for the outermost wing stations. The maximum launch weight is 70,000lb (31,741kg) for the F-35C and 60,000lb (27,211kg) for the other variants.

All the F-35 versions will be equipped with a powerful, advanced-technology sensor suite. This flew for the first time in the fourth F-35B development aircraft on 7 April 2010, a year later than initially planned. The main sensor is the Northrop Grumman AN/APG-81 Active Electronically Scanned Array (AESA) radar, which provides active long-range target detection and acquisition against land, sea and air targets. It is augmented by the passive Electro-Optical Targeting System (EOTS) fitted under the nose. This gives results comparable to the external Lockheed Martin Sniper XR targeting pod on other aircraft but does not compromise the F-35's stealth. A unique feature is the Distributed Aperture System (DAS), which functions as a missile warning system, reports missile launch locations, and detects and tracks approaching aircraft spherically around the F-35. It replaces night vision goggles for the pilot. The AN/ASQ-239 Barracuda Electronic Warfare System (EWS) is designed by BAE Systems.

All sensor information is combined through a computerised 'sensor fusion' process to provide radio frequency, optical and IR tracking information on 'head-down' screens, the 'head-up' display or into the pilot's Helmet-Mounted Display System (HMDS). This allows the pilot to 'see' targets continually – even those below the aircraft or off the centreline – and target weapons without having to 'point' the aircraft at them. Information from other platforms can be received and displayed via a Multifunction Advanced Data Link (MADL) and the F-35 can transmit its own sensor information, including moving pictures, using compatible network-centric systems such as NATO Link 16. After landing, F-35s will be able to down-load information – including synthetic aperture maps of the terrain they have over-flown and all detected radio and radar transmissions – for analysis by specialists to detect targets the pilot might not have been aware of in flight. This important capability is already used by some current strike fighters on a daily basis in Afghanistan.

The original F-35 Mission Statement described the F-35 as being 'affordable and effective' but the need to reduce fuselage weight to allow the 'B' to land vertically with unused weapons and a number of other development issues have increased costs and delayed progress. In asymmetric warfare, aircraft may

A Lockheed Martin F-35B Lightning II in STOVL mode. Outlets for the lift fan fitted behind the cockpit and for the swivelling nozzle aft can be seen clearly. *(Lockheed Martin)*

An F-35C variant of the Lightning II undergoes drop testing to simulate an aircraft carrier landing at Vought Aircraft's Dallas facility. The F-35C has a markedly larger wing-span than other versions of the F-35. *(Vought Aircraft)*

fly several anti-insurgency missions without releasing a weapon; precision-guided weapons are expensive and not usually available in large numbers so having to ditch them to land is not a viable option. It has not yet proved possible to forecast accurately what the price of each variant will be but 2010 data from the US Government Accountability Office suggest total unit costs creeping steadily towards US$150m. The latest standard Block II F/A-18 E/F is considerably less expensive.[5] Figures prepared by the USN in 2010 also show that the F-35 will be more costly to operate.

Against this, the F-35 has undeniable potential, particularly as part of a balanced air group. By 2020 the USN plans to operate carrier air groups with twenty-four F/A-18E/F; twenty-four F-35C; four to six EA-18G electronic attack aircraft and four E-2 D battle-space management aircraft together with two helicopter squadrons, each of twelve aircraft. Meanwhile, the USMC still hopes to achieve IOC for the F-35 in 2012 but admits that it will have to redefine what that means in order to achieve it. Many commentators have described the F-35 as, potentially, the last manned fighter and the rapid growth in the numbers of Unmanned Combat Air Vehicles (UCAV) is tending to support that view. The 'window of opportunity' in which the F-35 is perceived as the best platform for suppressing enemy air defences at the start of a conflict may be a short one. The USN is already exploring the possibility of replacing the F/A-18E/F with a UCAV system from about 2030 and X-47B derivatives may be in service before that. The F-35 can carry a considerable amount of ordnance externally but so can less expensive aircraft and it is a question whether the expense of its stealth design will be justified by a service life that may be shortened by the introduction of even more stealthy UCAVs that provide a better option.

Overseas customers, such as the UK, have further problems. The purchase deal may not allow access to the aircraft's software codes giving rise to concerns over the 'sovereignty' of its operation. The F-35 is supported in US service by a Global Sustainment System (GSS) run by Lockheed Martin. The UK has yet to decide to what extent to buy into this. Buying in might affect sovereignty but failure to do so could limit operations until satisfactory arrangements are in place. The aircraft is so complex that the UK development squadron and the first two operational squadrons will have to form up and train in the USA, not being able to embark in an RN carrier or land at an air station ashore until a sustainment system is in place. The development unit will remain in the USA to benefit from the better facilities.

Boeing F/A-18E/F Super Hornet: The F/A-18E/F is the operational result of a 'model' project that has, to date, delivered aircraft on-cost and, in most cases, early. At first the Super Hornet was seen as 'insurance' for advanced projects such as the A-12, Navy Advanced Tactical Fighter and A/F-X. However, as these expensive, stealthy projects were cancelled in the 1990s it became central to the USN's future plans. The aircraft was undoubtedly aided by the experience generated in the earlier 'legacy' Hornet programme but – in the Block II version of the Super Hornet now in production – the USN has what is arguably the best strike fighter in service anywhere in the world. Like other modern aircraft the F/A-18E/F is made of a variety of advanced, lightweight but strong materials, including carbon epoxy (19 per cent); titanium (21 per cent) and steel (15 per cent). The airframe is covered in a signature-reducing coating which lowers the possibility of detection, although not as much as a 'clean' F-35. The two General Electric F414-GE-400 engines each develop 22,000lb (9,977kg) of thrust in full reheat and are modular, with 2,000 flying hours between overhauls for the hot section and 4,000 hours for the cold. They have full-authority digital engine control (FADEC) and use of reheat is unrestricted. In 2010 Boeing noted that the aircraft had suffered no losses in seven years of combat operations and no losses due to system failure or design deficiency in half a million flying hours. Some 420 F/A-18E/Fs out of a planned purchase of over 500 units had been delivered as of April 2010.

The F/A-18E/F was the first aircraft in operational service with AESA radar, the AN/APG-79. Introduced with the Block II variant of the aircraft deployed from 2006, the radar may not need to be removed for maintenance through the life of the aircraft. Sensor information is fused into head-down screens, a head-up display and Joint Helmet-Mounted Cuing System (JHMCS). An electro-optical targeting pod known as the Shared Reconnaissance Pod (SHARP) can be mounted externally and so can an Advanced Tactical Forward-Looking Infra-Red system (ATFLIR). The integrated defensive electronic countermeasures system includes an ALR-67(V)3 radar warning receiver; an ALQ-214 on-board jammer; ALE-47 countermeasures dispenser; and an ALE-50 towed decoy. The open-architecture computer system allows the incorporation of new or up-dated systems or weapons and integrates sensor information with communications, including Link 16, secure V/UHF, and navigation.

Both 'E' and 'F' versions are fully capable of operations in the fighter, strike and reconnaissance roles in a single sortie although the single-seat 'E' tends to specialise in strike and the 'F' in fighter operations. The two-seat 'F' is not a trainer but has facilities for a naval flight officer (NFO) in addition to the pilot to make better use of the available data and information. In Block II aircraft sensor information can be de-coupled to allow the two aircrew to fight different battles. For instance the pilot could use the radar and ATFLIR to engage a small moving target on land while the NFO uses off-board data from another platform such as an E-2 C and the radar to engage an airborne target. Both have JHMCS enabling them to aim at targets off the bore-sight without having to 'aim' the aircraft. This flexibility has led the type's first export customer, Australia, to procure only the 'F' version.

The Super Hornet has eleven weapons stations, all of them external, increasing the radar cross-section. Weapons that can be deployed include JDAM, JSOW, Harpoon, Maverick, HARM, any bomb in US service, AIM-120 and the AIM-9 IR-guided missile. External fuel can be carried in up to five 480-gallon external tanks fitted to positions on the centreline and inboard wing pylons giving c. 30,000lb (13,605kg) of fuel on start-up in both versions but slightly less in the 'F' because the second cockpit reduces internal fuel tankage by 942lb (427kg). External dimensions are identical; both have folding wings and a maximum all-up weight on launch of 66,000lb (29,932kg). Both versions can be fitted with 'buddy' refuelling pods to act as tankers extending the radius of action of strike aircraft and to orbit the carrier during recoveries to give a margin of safety for returning aircraft that are low on fuel. With four AIM-120 and two AIM-9 missiles and a centreline fuel tank the F/A-18 F can maintain a Combat Air Patrol, CAP, 200nm (370km) from the carrier for two-and-a-half hours with three potential combats in the time on task. With four JDAM or laser-guided bombs, two AIM-120 and two AIM-9 and a single tank the Super Hornet can strike targets out to

An F/A-18F Super Hornet on operational duty over Afghanistan in 2009. The image shows the significant ordnance and fuel capacity provided by the eleven external weapons stations. *(US Navy)*

F/A-18F Super Hornets of Strike Fighter Squadron (VFA) 41 demonstrate the type's 'buddy' refuelling capability. *(Boeing)*

A *Marine National* Rafale M fighter practices touch and go landings on the USN carrier *Dwight D Eisenhower* (CVN-69). *(US Navy)*

A Rafale M fighter is launched from the French aircraft carrier *Charles de Gaulle*. *(Dassault Aviation – V Almansa)*

400nm (740km) acting as its own escort but with three tanks it has a radius of action out to 800nm (1,480km); in-flight refuelling could extend this to beyond 1,000nm (1,850km). As mentioned above, the cost associated with a Super Hornet is much less than that potentially arising from a Block I F-35. Whilst, therefore, it may not have the stealth characteristics of the F-35, the F/A-18E/F and its EA-18 G 'cousin' pose searching questions about the need for, and cost of, stealth.

Dassault Rafale M: Other 'enhanced fourth-generation' naval fighters entering service include the latest F3 version of the French Navy's Rafale M and the Russian-designed MiG-29K and KUB fighters of the Indian Navy. The former has a Thales RBE2 radar which gives multi-track air-to-air, ship track, terrain-following and synthetic aperture navigation modes. From 2012 the present radar will be replaced by a developed AESA derivative that will need very little maintenance. The Spectra electronic-countermeasures system is fully internal and includes a radar warning receiver; active jamming, infrared missile approach warning, laser detection and chaff & flare dispensers. A front-sector optronics (FSO) device is mounted in a ball-type housing on the nose and contains a high-magnification TV sensor and infrared search and track sensor. A Damocles target designation pod and NG/Areos reconnaissance pod can be carried externally both of which can data-link information to ground stations via Link 16. The data from all the sensors is fused to be viewed by the pilot either in cockpit displays or his helmet-mounted sight.

The Rafale has thirteen hardpoints capable of carrying up to 20,000lb (9,070kg) of weapons. The centre five can carry 330-gallon fuel tanks; the centre three tanks can carry 539-gallon tanks but, if carried, these limit the aircraft to subsonic speeds and reduce the 'G' limit until they are empty. The Rafale can act as a 'Buddy' pod-equipped tanker. Weapons include the Mica IR or radar-homing air-to-air missile, a 30mm cannon, ASMP-A and SCALP-EG stand-off missiles, Exocet anti-ship missiles and the French AASM precision bomb. Earlier versions of the Rafale have been in successful service with the French Navy and Air Force for several years, demonstrating the wisdom of the French Ministry of Defence in specifying a type that could fulfil both roles, unlike the rival Typhoon which could have been even better but remains firmly land-bound. Rafale is powered by two

Two images of a two-seat MiG 29KUB fighter in Indian Navy colours on the deck of the Russian aircraft carrier *Admiral Kuznetsov*. The Russian Navy is also reportedly interested in the design. *(RAC MiG)*

Snecma M88-2E4 engines each delivering 17,000lb (7,710kg) of thrust in full afterburner and a maximum all-up weight of 54,000lb (24,490kg). The aircraft has a lively turning performance and is capable of Mach 2 at altitude, slightly faster than the two American aircraft.

According to the latest French official reports, the unit cost of a Rafale M is significantly in excess of €100m (US$135m). Its relatively high cost is probably explained by considerably lower production runs than for its US rivals, with 180 out of a planned total purchase of 294 for the French Air Force (234) and Navy (60) ordered as of mid-2010.

Russian Aircraft Corporation MiG-29K: The Mig-29K has a maximum take off weight of c. 54,000lb (24,490kg). It is powered by two Klimov/Sarkisov RD-33MK engines. These each give c. 20,000lb (9,070kg) of thrust in full afterburner giving the aircraft a thrust/weight ratio of near one-to-one even at take-off. The KUB version has two seats but less internal fuel; the second cockpit has both dual controls and operational equipment and can be used either as a conversion trainer or an operational aircraft. It will operate from the deck of the INS *Vikramaditya* using a Russian-developed STOBAR technique in which the aircraft carries out a free take off from a 'ski-jump' but lands into arrester wires

with a tail hook. The MiG-29K is coated with a radar-absorbent material which the manufacturer claims reduces its signature by a factor of four to five, compared with earlier versions of the type.

Sensors include an electronic intelligence system; electronic countermeasures; IR countermeasures; navigation system and a Phazotron Zhuk-ME radar which has a detection range of 80nm (148km) against a $5m^2$ target and a track-while-scan capability to engage four targets simultaneously. In addition to an electrifying turning performance, The Mig-29K can carry no less than eight alternative types of air-to-air missile and twenty-five alternative air-to-surface missiles on eight under-wing hardpoints, with another on the centreline. The two inboard pylons under each can be fitted with tandem bomb racks which effectively increase the number of hardpoints to thirteen. Radius of action on internal fuel is 450nm (833km) with a small strike load and 700nm (1,295km) with external tanks.

The MiG 29K has only been delivered to the Indian Navy to date, with a total of forty-five 'K' and 'KUB' versions being ordered in two batches as of mid-2010. It has been reported that the Russian Navy is also considering an order in replacement for the existing Sukhoi Su-33. The contract price for the more recent Indian order suggests a unit acquisition cost of c. US$55m.[5]

'BATTLE MANAGEMENT' AIRCRAFT: E-2D 'ADVANCED' HAWKEYE, SEA KING ASAC7

Northrop Grumman E-2D Hawkeye: The USN is developing a new version of the long-established Hawkeye, which it describes as a 'battle management' rather than an airborne early warning platform. Development aircraft flew throughout 2010 and IOC is intended in early 2015; seventy-five production airframes are planned with construction continuing until 2021. The type typifies the USN approach of matching affordable, tried and trusted airframe designs with new, cutting-edge avionic equipment and open-architecture computer systems. The key element of the new system is the Lockheed Martin AN/APY-9 radar. This operates in the C-Band (US L-Band) like the E-2C's AN/APS-145 but is a completely new and unique combination of mechanical and electronic scanning, in which 360-degree coverage is achieved using the rotodome which rotates once every ten seconds; sector scanning or investigation of a particular target is achieved by stopping the antenna and scanning electronically. The opportunity has been taken to install improved ESM, defensive aids and communications. The 'D' will be able to transmit its radar picture using Links 4, 11, 16 and the USN's Co-operative Engagement Capability (CEC) network. Like the 'C', the 'D' will

Two prototype E-2D Hawkeye battle management aircraft pictured in formation in March 2010. *(Northrop Grumman)*

A Royal Navy Sea King airborne surveillance helicopter. This is an image of an earlier AEW2 variant which has subsequently been upgraded to the ASaC7 standard. *(US Navy)*

have a crew of five; two pilots and three naval flight officers/observers. The screens in the new 'glass' cockpit will be able to display tactical information, allowing the non-flying pilot to act as part of the search or as a controller if necessary. Another major improvement will be the installation of an in-flight refuelling capability that will enable the Hawkeye to stay airborne for over seven hours. It is to be fitted to 'D's on the production line and retrofitted to the majority of 'legacy' E-2Cs in service. Initial clearance will be for naval tankers such as the F/A-18 E and C-130 but eventually clearance for all Allied tankers is anticipated. The E-2D is powered by two Rolls-Royce T-56-A-427A turboprops driving eight-bladed NP 2000 propellers, each developing 5,100shp. The engines have FADEC and a propulsion control monitoring unit reduces vibration significantly from that in the 'C'. The maximum all-up weight is slightly heavier than the 'C' at c.56,500lb (25,624kg).

AgustaWestland Sea King ASaC7: The Royal Navy has had considerable success with an even more cost-conscious and pragmatic approach to airborne battle management with the Sea King ASaC7 – airborne surveillance and area control – helicopter, which equips 849, 854 and 857 NAS. The Sea King was adopted as an airborne early-warning radar platform in the early 1980s because no other aircraft capable of carrying a suitable radar could operate from the small *Invincible* class carriers. None of the aircraft were new: in fact most are now about forty years old, all were converted from their original anti-submarine role and all have now been upgraded from AEW2 to ASaC7 standard with the Thales Searchwater 2000 Radar. Maximum take-off weight is c. 21,500lb (9,750kg).

The Searchwater antenna gives 360-degree coverage by rotating inside an inflatable dome on the starboard side of the aircraft which is inflated and lowered after take-off, giving the aircrews their nickname of 'baggers'. Control is exercised through the Cerberus Mission System which uses touch-screen displays to control the radar beam; RN observers were closely involved in its development and the result is an intuitive system that allows the two observers to call up anything they want from the radar in three key presses. Unusually for a wide-area surveillance task, the Searchwater operates in I-Band (US X-Band) which gives less range but a very narrow, precise beam which enables targets to be pinpointed accurately. The radar is frequency-agile and has both pulse and pulse-doppler modes; the latter displaying objects that have motion with no 'clutter' or 'sea-returns'. The speed of the sweep and angle of the antenna can be altered to give the optimum for the search in progress and each observer can make changes although these will affect what both observers see on their screens.

The basic ASaC mission was to act as part of a task force controlling strike aircraft and CAP fighters; giving early warning of approaching hostile aircraft, especially at low-level; surface search and direction of anti-surface vessel missiles. A new dimension was added after the type's first operational deployment during the 2003 Gulf War, however, when ASaC7s patrolling the littoral waters off the Al Faw Peninsula found that they could detect moving vehicles and even smaller objects including people on land. This capability has been refined and, from 2009 onwards, a permanent detachment of ASaC7s has been deployed in support of NATO forces in Afghanistan with 854 and 857 Squadrons rotating personnel. Three Sea Kings have been modified with Gnome 1400-1T engines, new Carson rotor blades and a new five-bladed tail rotor to give better 'hot and high' performance. They are used to provide wide-area ground surveillance to give understanding of the pattern of life in Helmand, Nimruz and Kandahar Provinces. This means familiarity with what is normal, the ability to see the absence of normality and recognition of the abnormal. The observers can use their radar to control Allied aircraft either through Link 16 or by voice to achieve a variety of effects and ground forces can be kept clear of people on the ground or guided to intercept them. The 'picture' is built up continuously to inform interaction by the troops with the local population's pattern of life. Other modifications to the basic Sea King include the fitting of an AN/AAR-57 missile warning system, ALQ-157 IR jammer and M 147 chaff & flare dispenser (only flares are loaded as there is deemed to be no radar threat). A 'rifle-rack' is fitted for three long-barrelled SA-80 assault rifles which the crew can use to defend themselves if the helicopter is forced to land in a 'hostile' area; the pilot and two observers also have pistols and body armour as part of their individual aircrew survival assemblies.

The Sea King ASaC7 is an undoubted success and has a vital part to play in the Royal Navy's expeditionary warfare capability. Under present plans it is to remain in service until 2022 by which time the airframes will be over fifty years old. No firm replacement has been identified but the costing assumption is that a number of Merlins will be converted from the anti-submarine role and fitted with the Cerberus system. Within that cost 'ceiling', other ideas are being considered to operate from the *Queen Elizabeth* class carriers and maintain this essential role for the foreseeable future.

SEA CONTROL HELICOPTERS: MH-60R SEA HAWK; MERLIN HM2; NH90

Sikorsky/Lockheed Martin MH-60R Sea Hawk: The MH-60R is not simply an upgrade of the earlier 'B' Seahawk model but a new system evolved by the USN to meet its anti-submarine and anti-surface ship helicopter needs for the next thirty years. It will be embarked alongside its 'utility' partner, the MH-60S. Powered by two General Electric T700-GE-701C engines it has a maximum take-off weight of c. 23,000lb (10,431kg). It can be armed with up to eight AGM-114A Hellfire missiles, two Mark 54 torpedoes or a missile and torpedo mix, with a 7.62mm or 0.5in (12.7mm) machine gun mounted in the cargo door. The Hellfire missiles can be fitted with a variety of warheads and are intended as a counter to small, fast vessels operated by terrorists or pirates in littoral waters. Larger targets would be taken out by fast jets in the USN battle plan but the open-architecture computer programme allows other weapons to be programmed on export versions.

Sensors include the AN/AQS-22 Folding Lightweight Acoustic System for Helicopters (FLASH) designed by Thales and an AN/UYS-2A enhanced modular signal processor that interprets information from both the FLASH dipping sonar and sonobuoys. The AN/APS-147 multi-mode radar fitted under the nose gives 360-degree coverage and the aircraft has effective ESM and defensive aids packages. The 'R' entered operational service in December 2005 and in common with its policy of implementing continuous, spiral, improvement, the USN has fitted Link 16 and CEC broadband data transfer systems; improved ESM; up-graded acoustic processing; digitised sonobuoys and an enhanced mode in the radar to improve periscope detection. More spiral improvements are planned to keep the aircraft effective until at least 2040. The 'R' is in production through a series of multi-year contracts with over 300 units planned. Its partner the MH-60S more closely resembles the US Army Blackhawk and is used in the battle group for a variety of embarked tasks including light strike, vertical replenishment and, potentially, mine clearance.

A US Navy MHR-60R Sea Hawk helicopter firing an AGM-114A Hellfire missile. The Hellfire is particularly potent against small, high-speed vessels, such as those used by terrorists. *(US Navy)*

Table 4.2.2: MODERN SEA CONTROL HELICOPTER COMPARISONS

AIRCRAFT[1]	MH-60R SEA HAWK	MERLIN HM2	NH90
Length	15.3m (19.7m rotors)	19.5m (22.8m rotors)	16.1m (19.6m rotors)
Width	3.0m (16.4m rotors)	4.5m (18.6m rotors)	3.6m (16.3m rotors)
Height	3.8m (5.1m rotors)	4.7m (6.6m rotors)	4.2m (5.3m rotors)
Internal volume[2]	11m^3	28m^3	15m^3
Take-off weight – max	10,500kg	15,000kg	11,000kg
Engines	2 x T700-GE-701C	3 x RTM 322	2 x RTM 322/2 x GE T700-T-6E
Speed – max cruising	270km/h	310km/h	300km/h
Hover Ceiling IGE	4,500m	3,400m	3,200m
Endurance – max	3.5 hours	6 hours	5 hours
Crew	3	3	3

Notes:

1 Data has been compiled from manufacturers' documentation, supplemented by publicly-available information as necessary. Due to considerable variations in published information, data should be regarded as indicative only.

2 Internal volumes are without equipment and are significantly less in practice for the sea control versions of the helicopters described. For example, Sikorsky states that the usable cabin volume of a MH-60R is 8.5m^3

AgustaWestland Merlin HM2: The Royal Navy's Merlin is a larger helicopter and has a much greater maximum all-up weight of more than 32,000lb (14,512kg). Much of the airframe is made from carbon fibre, making it resistant to corrosion. It is powered by three Rolls-Royce/Turbomeca RTM322 engines, each developing well over 2,000shp. It is fitted with the same FLASH sonar as the SH-60R, designated the Type 2089 by the RN; this is believed to be capable of detecting submarines down to their maximum diving depth and has range-scales from 1nm to 26nm (1.85km to 48km) using high-resolution doppler processing and shaped pulses to allow detection of targets as slow as one knot. Extended duration frequency-modulated (FM) pulses even enable the detection of near-zero doppler targets. Operational modes include active continuous wave (CW) in pulses of up to ten seconds; FM in up to five-second pulses and passive listening. It also has an underwater telephone mode for communication with submarines. Like other sea-control helicopters, the Merlin uses active and passive sonobuoys and has an AQS-903A acoustic processor to analyse their inputs. The Blue Kestrel radar gives 360-degree coverage and, since 2005, its software has included the capability to read the Automatic Identification System (AIS) carried by most of the world's merchant ships. This gives ship name, radio callsign, position, course and speed, cargo and destination and is an invaluable help in anti-piracy and anti-drug smuggling missions. For its first ten years in service the RN Merlin has lacked an optical surface-search capability but this shortcoming has been partially redressed by RN procurement of six Wescam MX-15 electro-optical systems, which can be fitted to aircraft weapon stations for specific missions. Since 2007 a detachment of three Merlins has operated out of Seeb in Oman in support of coalition operations in the Gulf of Oman. Two are fitted with Wescam MX-15s and the third aircraft is an 'in-theatre spare' to support the others.

Merlin armament has, to date, been limited to anti-submarine weapons comprising up to four Stingray lightweight torpedoes and up to four Mark 11 depth-charges or a mixture of these. Approval has been given to fit a door-mounted 0.5in (12.7mm) M3M machine gun to stop attacks by small boats in anti-piracy or anti-narcotic smuggling operations.

In 2006 the RN awarded a contract to Lockheed Martin to upgrade thirty of its forty-two Merlins to HM2 standard. This will involve replacing the HM1's dated computers with an open architecture system with much greater processing capacity. The Wescam MX-15 will be fitted as standard, radar will be modified to give synthetic-aperture and inverse synthetic-aperture images to improve surface search capability and the modernised helicopter will be able to carry the future air-to-surface missile, giving a vastly improved operational capability. The cockpit will be made night vision device (NVD) compatible.

The first Merlin HM2 is due to fly in late 2010

A Royal Navy AgustaWestland Merlin HM1 helicopter. The modernised HM2 version is expected to fly towards the end of 2010. (*AgustaWestland*)

and the RN hopes to have all thirty back in service by the end of 2014. The current plan is to retain the HM2 in service until at least 2030, although no incremental upgrades are funded beyond the present work. Of the remaining twelve Merlin HM1 airframes, four are used for development work and will not be upgraded. The remaining eight could be converted for either the ASaC or commando role but no firm decision about their future has been made.

Eurocopter/EADS NH90: The NFH (NATO Frigate Helicopter) version of the NH90 has the same FLASH sonar as the others, can deploy sonobuoys and is fitted with a TMS2000 acoustic processor and 360-degree radar. It has similar external dimensions to the MH-60R but has a 60 per cent greater floor area and 35 per cent greater internal volume. Other positives include large door openings on either side and a rear loading ramp which, taken with the large cabin, allow a six-man boarding party to be deployed without having to remove any of the internal role equipment. Machine guns can be fitted in the doorways on each side of the aircraft. It is smaller than a Merlin and, with only two engines, is more economical to operate. Engines can be either RTM 322s or GE T700-T-6Es, as specified by the customer; both have similar performance. Designed maximum weight is c. 24,000lb (10,884km).

Weapon options include two torpedoes (Eurotorp MU90 or equivalent) or two Marte Mark 2S air-to-surface radar-guided sea-skimming missiles. These have 150lb (68kg) warheads and offer a genuine ship-killing capability. They have a range of 20nm (37km) and can thus be fired outside the radius of

An Italian NH90 sea control helicopter undergoing sea trials on a wet, pitching deck. *(NH-Industries)*

many ships' defences. The NH-90 is the newest of the three designs compared and has an airframe made largely of carbon fibre which is extremely corrosion resistant. It is designed to float for at least fifteen minutes after a ditching in rough seas and has been selected by the navies of Belgium, Finland, France, Germany, Holland, Italy, Norway, Portugal and Sweden.[6]

Notes

1. The RAF 4 Squadron identity will be retained in a new 4 (Reserve) Squadron, which will take over the training duties that were previously carried out by 20 (Reserve) Squadron.

2. The twenty-nine additional MiG-29K fighters are reported to cost a total of US$1.6bn as compared with the original US$1.5bn price of the package for *Gorshkov* and sixteen jets first contracted in 2004. Some reports in the Indian press suggest it will not be until 2013 that *Vikramaditya* enters service.

3. These numbers were accurate as at the end of 2009.

4. It should be noted that information on fuel capacity, range and other technical characteristics of the aircraft described vary significantly, even on 'official' websites. The information set out in this chapter should therefore be regarded as being only an approximation.

5. Aircraft procurement costs seem as difficult to estimate and compare as those for warship acquisition. The defense-aerospace website – www.defense-aerospace.com – has attempted to use the Pentagon's Selected Acquisition Report data on the total cost of major programmes (actual or estimated) to provide meaningful calculations of Programme Acquisition Unit Costs (PAUC), including research and development charges, for major US aircraft. These suggested a PAUC of US$133.6m for the F-35 and US$93.4m for the F/A-18E/F in terms of FY2010 US$ as of 31 December 2009. Whilst the Super Hornet's PAUC has been stable over this period in real terms, the Lightning II's cost has been rising markedly. Similar calculations from figures published by the French *Cour des Comptes* (Court of Audit) suggest a PAUC of as much as €142m (US$180m) for the Rafale.

6. This chapter has been compiled from a wide range of periodicals, of which *Air International*, *Flight*, *Jane's Defence Weekly*, *Warship World* and *The Navy* (the journal of the Navy League of Australia) provide particularly good sources of further reading. Reference should also be made to the following publications, as well as to the websites of relevant aircraft manufacturers and navies:

Gunter Endres and Michael J Gething, *Jane's Aircraft Recognition Guide – Fifth Edition* (London, Collins-Jane's, 2007).

Norman Friedman, *The Naval Institute Guide to World Naval Weapon Systems* – Fifth Edition (Annapolis, MD, Naval Institute Press, 2006).

Jane's Fighting Ships – Various Editions (Coulsdon, Surrey, Jane's Information Group).

The Type 42 destroyer *Edinburgh* pictured on 1 April 2010 during the middle of her final upkeep period in Portsmouth Naval Dockyard's 'D' Lock. At this stage, flooding-out of the dock was only two weeks away. *(Conrad Waters)*

Author:
Conrad Waters

4.3 TECHNOLOGICAL REVIEW

UK WARSHIP SUPPORT

Last Type 42 Destroyer Refit Completed Against a Background of Change

2010 saw the end of an era at the British Royal Navy's Portsmouth Dockyard as the refit of the Type 42 destroyer *Edinburgh* progressed towards its conclusion. Representing the final scheduled deep maintenance and docking period for a class that first entered service with the commissioning of the ill-fated *Sheffield* in February 1975, the refit will allow *Edinburgh* to remain operational until the class' planned out-of-service date in 2013. Around that time the last of the new Type 45 destroyers, *Duncan*, will be commissioned and the handover to the new generation of air-defence vessels will be completed. The refit itself also takes place against a backdrop of significant changes to the way in which British warship maintenance is managed. This includes a much greater emphasis on supplier-customer co-operation under the evolving Surface Ship Support Alliance, as well as a more subtle softening in the traditional distinction between lengthy dockyard refurbishments and operational support through increased reliance on routine upgrades during 'fleet time' support.[1]

WARSHIP SUPPORT IN TRANSITION

Major refurbishment and modernisation work on British warships following privatisation of the formerly state-owned Royal Dockyards in the last years of the twentieth century was initially based around an allocated programme of major refits. Under this arrangement, the major dockyard management companies – Devonport Management Ltd at Plymouth, Fleet Support Ltd at Portsmouth and the Babcock Thorn consortium at Rosyth – were contractually entitled to an agreed forward

Liverpool departing Portsmouth in October 2009. *Liverpool*'s £6m refit preceded the work carried out on her sister. *(Conrad Waters)*

The installation of a transom flap to increase fuel efficiency was just one of a number of modifications specified in the work package for *Edinburgh*'s refit. *(BAE Systems)*

workload. This approach provided considerable certainty for the dockyards. However, it was also potentially inefficient for the Ministry of Defence (MOD), as the companies would still be entitled to payment if operational requirements resulted in the postponement or cancellation of a refit without provision of compensating alternative work. The introduction of revised arrangements saw refits allocated by competition. This process drove short-term cost savings for the MOD but hindered the achievement of longer-term efficiencies. The competitive environment made it difficult for industry to share information and, by its nature, dictated that specifications and prices were fixed early in the tender process, often before the scope of work was completely understood. It also did little to encourage future investment. The situation was compounded by considerable over-capacity as overall workload reduced through tightening budgets and an overall fall in warship numbers. The result was – what one industry executive described as '…a torrid time for all concerned'.

The sustainability of these arrangements was considered in a Surface Ship Support Study initiated in August 2004. Its conclusions formed one of the strands of the maritime component of the *Defence Industrial Strategy* (DIS) that was published in December 2005.[2] The study determined that an alliance between the MOD and industry was the only option that would ensure the key objectives of achieving sustainable support and the ability to react flexibly to future changes in workload. To some extent, this conclusion reflected the partnering arrangements that were already working well with respect to day-to-day fleet time maintenance under the Warship Support Modernisation Initiative, as well as the desirability of adopting a common approach given the previous distinction between this support work and lengthier refits had become increasingly blurred.

Whilst the precise details of the resultant Surface Ship Support Alliance (SSSA) were in the course of development as of June 2010, the overall conclusions of this and other maritime elements of the DIS are already having a significant impact on the UK's shipyards and support infrastructure under the Maritime Change Programme. At a strategic level, there has been consolidation down to just two major shipbuilding and refitting groups for complex warships with BAE Systems' purchase of the former VT Group's maritime interests – including its stake in Fleet Support Ltd – and Babcock International's acquisition of Devonport Management Ltd. The longer-term sustainability of these operations has been assured by the MOD's signature of fifteen-year terms of business agreements (TOBAs) with BAE Systems and Babcock in return for commitments by industry to deliver substantial savings to the MOD. At a more operational level, change can be seen in much greater collaboration in determining where and when refits will be allocated, as well as in a shared approach between industry and the MOD as to how the scope of specific work packages are drawn up and managed. This approach is evident in the advance preparation carried out for *Edinburgh*'s final refit.

REFIT PREPARATION AND SCOPE

The final refit carried out on *Edinburgh* is one of a series of major upkeeps on Type 42 destroyers carried out by BAE Systems and its predecessors at Portsmouth in recent years. The yard completed an upgrade for *Liverpool* – the last operational Batch II variant of the class – under a contract with a reported value of £6m (US$9m) in 2009. A more extensive, £17m (US$26m) refit of *York* was undertaken previously. The scope and timing of all these programmes is ultimately the responsibility of the Capital Ships Team within the MOD's Defence Equipment and Support function. The Capital Ships Team directs through life engineering support, upkeep and capability upgrades for all the remaining Type 42 destroyers, as well as for the *Invincible* class carriers and major amphibious ships. As such, it is effectively BAE Systems' customer for the *Edinburgh* refit and the counterparty which ultimately determines the extent of the overall work package.

Under the new era of collaborative working, however, drafting of the initial refit requirement is

An early task during the refit is the removal of equipment for repair or replacement onshore, no easy task given cramped nature of many onboard areas such as aft auxiliary machinery room (a). The process is assisted by access trunks (b) that form part of the ship's design and provide an entry/exit passage from the principal machinery spaces to deck level (c). *(Conrad Waters)*

Work under way on *Edinburgh*. With over 100 workers of various trades sometimes onboard – often occupied in confined spaces – attention to health and safety is paramount. (BAE Systems)

now typically carried out under the guidance of a joint planning team. This comprises representatives from the MOD, BAE Systems Surface Ships (in the case of *Edinburgh*'s refit at Portsmouth) and, frequently, major suppliers such as Rolls Royce, Thales and BAE Systems' Insyte division. The aim is to devise a work package that trades the often competing factors of capability, affordability and time in an as effective and realistic a fashion as possible. The openness involved in the process is aimed at facilitating the creation of a certain and practical refit specification which, in turn, should drive delivery to time and budget. The final package is a detailed document sub-divided into a number of constituent sections covering areas such as required electrical, mechanical and structural work.

The work specification prepared for *Edinburgh* was relatively substantial compared with recent Type 42 refits, as evidenced by its reported £17.5m (US$27m) cost. Its overall scope encompassed the replacement or refurbishment of all four gas turbines, modernisation of weapons and communications systems and the installation of a transom flap to increase fuel efficiency.[3] Together with the application of a hull coating of new Sigma 990 paint, this is claimed to reduce overall fuel consumption by up to 15 per cent. Crew habitability was also an area of focus, with improvements including modernisation of mess decks and cabins, as well as the renewal of fresh water systems and of galley and laundry equipment. Another significant element of all refits relates to structural work, largely the replacement of corroded steel. Much of this is only identified when a ship has been docked down and the refit underway. The overall costing of the work package therefore included a provision for additional jobs identified, largely determined on the basis of past experience. Whilst specific information for *Edinburgh* has not been released, an allowance

An added complication with *Edinburgh*'s refit is the ship's age. The analogue-era machinery control room pictured here certainly betrays a core design dating back to the 1960s. Decommissioned members of the class can be a source of replacement equipment that is no longer in production. *(Conrad Waters)*

for emerging work costing around 25 per cent of the basic package is typical for a major warship refit.

Although subject to collaborative working, the content of works packages drafted by joint planning teams are still reviewed by the MOD's Capital Ships Team for content and affordability. Once this process was completed for *Edinburgh*, the final requirement was then forwarded to BAE Systems in Portsmouth for detailed costing prior to the submission of a formal bid. Following completion of any outstanding negotiations, this ultimately resulted in signature of a refit contract. *Edinburgh* subsequently left the operational Royal Navy fleet at the end of June 2009 prior to commencing the upkeep period on 17 July. This saw the majority of the usual 250-strong ship's company depart their vessel to leave a small residue of Royal Navy engineering and logistics personnel working alongside but accommodated elsewhere to support refit requirements. Docking down was carried out on at Portsmouth's 'D' Lock on 7 September 2009.

REFIT IMPLEMENTATION

Implementing the refit of a major warship is clearly a complex task, involving a wide range of engineering and other disciplines. Much of the work is carried out by the shipyard's own workforce, albeit refurbishment of specialised equipment such as propulsion machinery and weaponry is often carried out off-site by the relevant supplier. In addition, specialist sub-contractors are employed for tasks such as cleaning, sanitation, painting and flooring. This can involve over 100 different workers of various trades onboard ship at any particular time. Ensuring the security of these personnel requires close attention to health and safety, an approach typified by rigorous controls on entry and exit to the ship. Onboard, clearly defined 'green' exit routes are established before work commences to facilitate rapid evacuation in case of emergency.

The removal of equipment for repair or replacement is an early task and can involve considerable challenges. Each of *Edinburgh*'s four main machinery spaces – two engine rooms and two auxiliary machine rooms – is equipped with an

Repairs underway on *Edinburgh*'s forward masts and superstructure. The emergence of structural work that was not identified in the initial work package is generally one of the more significant hurdles to be overcome. *(Conrad Waters)*

A major step in *Edinburgh*'s last refit was reached on 15 April 2010 with the flooding-out of the dock in which the refit took place in line with the agreed schedule. The overall flooding-out process is quite an intricate process and took several hours to complete. *(BAE Systems)*

access trunk to allow major items of equipment to be hoisted out to the upper decks without structural alterations. *Edinburgh*'s refit saw all four gas turbines removed in this fashion, as well as some additional items of auxiliary machinery. However, not all equipment can be accessed in this way and it can be necessary to open up the ship's side once in dock to allow the required access. Even then, the removal of some plant is simply not practical. In such cases, any necessary repair work is carried out *in situ*. It is also worth noting that the previous practice of carrying out the block renewal of equipment to a fixed schedule is now increasingly being replaced by much

The second Type 45 destroyer *Dauntless* seen entering Portsmouth Harbour in December 2009. The class output management plan devised for the maintenance of her and her sisters is likely to provide the model for future warship support arrangements. *(BAE Systems)*

greater use of ongoing monitoring and diagnostics to limit the total amount – and cost – of work undertaken. A degree of common sense is used here. For example, replacement will still be mandated if subsequent equipment failure would require a further docking.

An additional challenge with *Edinburgh*'s refit has been the ship's longevity. She was first commissioned twenty-five years ago in 1985, whilst the basic Type 42 design has its origins in the late 1960s.[4] As such, much of her configuration predates decimalisation and the digital age and some equipment is no longer in production. The steady

withdrawal of older members of the class has eased this problem to an extent and the upgraded *Edinburgh* will incorporate items recycled from her sister-ship *Nottingham* following the latter's decommissioning on 11 February 2010. The dockyard workshops are also capable of fabricating a wide range of items. For example, some of *Edinburgh*'s cabins were constructed to a bespoke design by original shipbuilders' Cammell Laird and BAE Systems were asked if it would be possible to manufacture replacement fixtures and fittings to fit the space available. Such specialised requests can add both to the time and cost of a refit and, therefore, their

impact on the overall progamme has to be considered carefully.

Effective monitoring of the refit's ongoing progress is essential to ensure timely completion. All core elements of the work package are therefore subject to ongoing review against pre-determined timelines by dockyard staff – headed by the project manager – to ensure potential areas of difficulty are identified and remedial steps undertaken. As mentioned previously, emergent structural work is a common hurdle to overcome: *Edinburgh* required extensive work around her sole (starboard) anchor housing – an area particularly vulnerable to corrosion. Changes in specification are initially reviewed by the team of MOD surveyors, who are also responsible for checking that overall refit standards meet required specifications. The number of these overseers is quite small – just five in *Edinburgh*'s case. Detailed changes to the refit specification can be agreed at local level. Reference back to the Capital Ships Team's management is only required if the overall budget is exceeded.

BAE Systems' Portsmouth facilities have already established a good track record of ensuring timely delivery of refits under the developing alliance arrangements. These include the carrier *Ark Royal* during 2009, as well as the Type 42 destroyer projects already referenced. At the time of writing, the support programme for *Edinburgh* also looks set to be a success following flooding-out of the dock on schedule on 15 April 2010. Thereafter, work has continued on completing outstanding tasks at a non-tidal berth in readiness for crew's return at the end of June. Commencement of the setting to work process will follow shortly afterwards. The current plan is for sea trials to commence in September 2010, with return to fleet scheduled towards the end of October. The overall programme will therefore have taken around sixteen months from start to finish.

THE FUTURE

Looking to the future, warship maintenance will increasingly be driven by the evolving collaborative arrangements envisaged by the SSSA. Ensuring the most cost-effective allocation of work through an intelligent examination of total load (including fleet time maintenance, upkeep packages and non-MOD commercial contracts) is obviously a key part of this process. However, an even more fundamental change is the development of the Class Output Management

(COM) concept. Under COM, the maintenance programme for specific classes of warship is based on delivering a defined level of overall availability to the MOD. Pilot COM arrangements within the overall scope of the SSSA have already been set up for the 'Hunt' class mine-countermeasures vessels (lead by BAE Systems) and the four Batch III Type 22 frigates (headed by Babcock). The resulting pilot COM teams are already achieving significant success in improving the availability/cost balance of the relevant warships. Subject to MOD approval, it is therefore likely that the concept will be extended to the rest of the fleet.

A key factor in the apparent early success of the COM process is a significant improvement in the shipyards' understanding of the material state of the ships under their overall care. So far as the 'Hunt' class are concerned, this has allowed a material reduction to be achieved in the extent of the maintenance packages needed to meet the level of availability required. The overall collaborative ethos behind the SSSA is another driver for improvement. Incentives offered to industry to drive down costs encourage the sharing of best practice and industry-wide benchmarking. COM also reflects the increasing integration between fleet time support and upkeep periods, as maintenance is organised and programmed to best match overall availability targets. In overall terms, early experience with the pilot COM projects suggests that savings of of around 10-15 per cent compared with previous maintenance arrangements are achievable.

The development of the output management process has been taken to its furthest extent to date with the COM arrangements for the new Type 45 *Daring* class destroyers, which are steadily replacing *Edinburgh* and her sisters in the air-defence role.

Established outside of the SSSA through a direct agreement with BAE Systems, this £309m, availability-driven support contract takes industry accountability to another level, not least through the delegation of design authority responsibilities to the COM team. Derived in part from availability concepts introduced with the 'River' class offshore patrol vessels but which have never been used previously for a capital ship, the agreement is based around key performance indicators (KPIs) in six principal areas, viz:

- Availability.
- Material State.
- Safety Performance.
- Maintenance Clearance Rates.
- Responsiveness.
- Continuous Improvement Processes.

An important part of the agreement is the flexibility it provides to the customer, as availability and cost can be flexed according to developing Royal Navy requirements. The contract also provides for the initial establishment of overall maintenance arrangements for the class, including the provision of spare parts and the creation of an overall support infrastructure. Given that BAE Systems has 'turnkey' type responsibilities for sustaining class sub-systems supplied by sub-contractors such as Thales, Converteam and Ultra Electronics, around 80 per cent of which are new to service, the deal is not without its risks. However, the contract offers the MOD significant savings in overall annual running costs compared with those for 'legacy' vessels such as the Type 42 and is likely to prove a model for future warship support provision in an increasingly cost-conscious era.[5]

Notes

1. The maintenance of Royal Navy warships has traditionally been divided between (i) the provision of ongoing operational support whilst a ship remains with the fleet and (ii) the repair and upgrading of capabilities as part of more complex refit periods, during which time the ship passes into dockyard control. Whilst this distinction remains good to a certain extent, there has been a steady move towards a more integrated model under which many routine upgrades and modifications are now programmed as part of 'fleet time' support.

2. Driven by former industrialist Lord Drayson, the *Defence Industrial Strategy* (London, UK Ministry of Defence, 2005 – cm 6697) was widely praised as an intelligent attempt to

set out the indigenous manufacturing and support capabilities required for Britain's future defence needs and establish a road map for their sustainment. Although its wider promise was curtailed by Lord Drayson's departure from the MOD, it has had a major impact on many elements of UK defence procurement.

3. The first Type 42 destroyer to be fitted with a transom flap was *Manchester* in 2006. Payback on the cost of installation is less than one year, justifying fitting to even relatively elderly ships. A good review of the technology can be found in David K Brown's 'Half a Century of Transom Flaps', *Warship 2009* (London, Anova Books, 2009), pp 175-6.

4. The best description of the Type 42 destroyer class is

contained in Leo Marriott's *Modern Combat Ships 3: Type 42* (Shepperton, Surrey, Ian Allan Ltd, 1985). Reference can also be made to Norman Friedman's *British Destroyers & Frigates – the Second World War and After* (London, Chatham Publishing, 2006), Chapter 14 for a broader background to the class's design.

5. The assistance of the following BAE Systems Surface Ships' personnel in the preparation of this chapter is acknowledged with gratitude.

Paul Bowsher, Type 45 Through Life Support Director
Malcolm Fudge, Project Manager of Edinburgh's refit
Andy Gimpel, Director UK Ship Support Programmes
Mal Lewis, Director Naval Base Support

Contributors

Richard Beedall: Richard is a Senior Manager at Mazars Consulting in Ireland. Born in England, he served for fourteen years in the Royal Naval Reserve as a rating and later as an officer, often working with USN and local naval forces around the world. He has a long-standing interest in the Royal Navy and naval affairs in general, and is the founder of the *Navy Matters* website. He has written extensively on naval developments for many organisations and publications, including *AMI International*, *Naval Forces* and *Warships IFR*. He is married with two young daughters.

Leon Engelbrecht: Leon Engelbrecht is editor of defenceWeb – www.defenceweb.co.za – an online news resource established in September 2008 for defence and security professionals with an African interest. He has been writing on matters military since 1996 and has been published in the *US Armed Forces Journal* and the *African Armed Forces Journal* as well as in the South African and international press. He has lectured at the SA National Defence College and the SA National War College on media studies. Mr Engelbrecht was commissioned in the South African Infantry Corps and for five years served in various posts and units in the SA Army.

Norman Friedman: Norman Friedman is one of the best-known naval analysts and historians in the US and the author of over thirty books. He has written on broad issues of modern military interest, including an award-winning history of the Cold War, whilst in the field of warship development his greatest sustained achievement is probably an eight-volume series on the design of different US warship types. A specialist in the intersection of technology and national strategy, his acclaimed *Network-Centric Warfare* was published last year by the US Naval Institute Press. The holder of a PhD in theoretical physics from Columbia, Dr Friedman is a regular guest commentator on television and lectures widely on professional defence issues. He is a resident of New York.

David Hobbs: David Hobbs is a well-known author and naval historian. He has written eight books and co-authored eight more. He writes for several journals and magazines and in 2005 won the Aerospace Journalist of the Year, Best Defence Submission. He lectures on naval subjects world-wide and has been on radio and TV in several countries. He served in the Royal Navy from 1964 until 1997 and retired with the rank of Commander. He qualified as both a fixed and rotary wing pilot and his log book contains 2,300 hours with over 800 carrier landings, 150 of which were at night.

Mrityunjoy Mazumdar: Mr Mazumdar, whose father served in the Indian Navy, has been writing on naval matters since 1999. His words and pictures have appeared in many naval and aircraft magazines around the world. He is a regular contributor to *Jane's Fighting Ships*, *Flotes des Combat*, *Combat Fleets of the World* and *Weyers Flotten Taschenbuch*. He also maintains a comprehensive website on the Indian Navy at www.bharat-rakshak.com. Mr Mazumdar lives with his wife in Alameda, California.

Scott Truver: Dr Scott C Truver is Director, National Security Programs, at Gryphon Technologies LC, specialising in national and homeland security, and naval and maritime strategies, programmes and operations. Since 1972, Dr Truver has participated in many studies and assessments – most notably supporting the inter-agency task force drafting the US *National Strategy for Maritime Security* (2005) – and has also written extensively for US and foreign publications. He has lectured at the US Naval Academy, Naval War College and Naval Postgraduate School, among other venues. His further qualifications include a Doctor of Philosophy degree in Marine Policy Studies – the first PhD in this field ever awarded by an institution of higher education – and an MA in Political Science/International Relations from the University of Delaware.

Conrad Waters: A lawyer by training but a banker by profession, Conrad Waters was educated at Liverpool University prior to being called to the bar at Gray's Inn in 1989. His interest in maritime affairs was first stimulated by a long family history of officers in Merchant Navy service and he has been writing articles on historical and current naval affairs for the last twenty years. This has included six years producing the 'World Navies in Review' chapter of the influential annual *Warship*. When not combating the aftermath of the global credit crunch in his role as Head of Credit Analysis at the European arm of one of the world's largest banks, Conrad lives with wife Susan and children Emma, Alexander and Imogen in Haslemere, Surrey.

Devrim Yaylalı: Cem Devrim Yaylalı was born in Paris and raised in Istanbul, where he currently lives. He has a degree in economics from the University of Istanbul. His interest in naval issues began by taking photos of warships visiting Istanbul. His first photos were published in *Jane's Fighting Ships* in 1991. Since then his photos and articles have been published in various naval publications both Turkish and foreign such as *Combat Fleets of the World* and *Warships International Fleet Review*. He is the author of webpage: www.turkishnavy.org and blogs in: turkishnavy.blogspot.com. He is married with one son.

Jacket picture credits
Front:
Main: *Astute*, UK *(Crown Copyright courtesy BAE Systems)*; top, left to right: *Independence*, USA *(US Navy)*; *Helge Ingstad*, Norway *(Conrad Waters)*; *Guaicamacuto*, Venezuela *(Navantia)*; NH-90 helicopter, Italy *(NH-Industries)*; *Casma* and *Angamos*, Chile *(US Navy)*
Back:
Top left: *Dauntless*, UK *(BAE Systems)*; top right: *Jason Dunham*, USA *(US Navy)*; lower left: *Carvajal*, Peru *(US Navy)*; lower right: *Edinburgh*, UK *(BAE Systems)*.

INDEX

Page references in *italics* indicate illustrations.